LORDS OF
THE RING

LORDS OF THE RING

The Triumph and Tragedy of College Boxing's Greatest Team

DOUG MOE

THE UNIVERSITY OF WISCONSIN PRESS
TERRACE BOOKS

The University of Wisconsin Press
1930 Monroe Street, 3rd Floor
Madison, Wisconsin 53711-2059
uwpress.wisc.edu

3 Henrietta Street
London WC2E 8LU, England
eurospanbookstore.com

Printed in the United States of America

Library of Congress Cataloging-in-Publication Data
Moe, Doug.
Lords of the ring : the triumph and tragedy of
college boxing's greatest team / Doug Moe.
p. cm.
ISBN 0-299-20420-0 (cloth : alk. paper)
1. Boxing—Wisconsin—Madison—History—20th century.
2. University of Wisconsin—Sports—History—20th century.
3. College sports—Wisconsin—Madison—History—20th century.
I. Title.
GV1125.M64   2004
796.83'0977'583—dc22   2004005363

ISBN 0-299-20424-3 (pbk.)

Terrace Books, a division of the University of Wisconsin Press, takes its name
from the Memorial Union Terrace, located at the University of Wisconsin–Madison.
Since its inception in 1907, the Wisconsin Union has provided a venue for students,
faculty, staff, and alumni to debate art, music, politics, and the issues of the day.
It is a place where theater, music, drama, dance, outdoor activities, and major
speakers are made available to the campus and the community.
To learn more about the Union, visit www.union.wisc.edu.

ISBN 978-0-299-20424-2 (pbk.: alk. paper)
ISBN 978-0-299-20423-5 (e-book)

For Quinn and Olivia

CONTENTS

ILLUSTRATIONS

LORDS OF
THE RING

1. The Field House in Madison, packed for a 1938 match. By putting chairs on the basketball floor, the UW boxers drew crowds of up to 15,000, by far the largest in all of college boxing.

APRIL 9, 1960

In remembering those days many of them would say that waiting was the worst.

Bob Morgan, who was sitting in the bleachers that night, knew all about waiting. In a college career that included a national championship, he had endured the wait twenty-seven times.

Always, there was a voice in his ear, telling him that the fight would go on as scheduled. There would be no tornado or earthquake to stop it. His opponent would not get sick or flee the country. He would be there.

"You'd meet him at the weigh-in that morning," Morgan said. "I never knew my opponents. I didn't want to. But you would meet them, and then later, the self-doubt would start creeping in. Am I really any good?"

So he'd try to kill time. Take a nap, read a book, go for a walk. It wasn't an easy thing to explain, Morgan felt. Telling someone who had never been in a boxing ring what it felt like to climb into that ring was almost impossible. Sometimes Morgan would compare it to having a dream where you find yourself in trouble and start yelling but no one can hear you.

"You'd climb up those steps and your knees would get weak," Morgan said. Once in the ring, he was okay. That's what he was there for. The wait was over.

By 1960 it had been eight years since Morgan had won his National Collegiate Athletic Association (NCAA) boxing championship at 147 pounds. There had been thirteen thousand wildly excited fans in the University of Wisconsin Field House that night and now, eight years later,

Morgan was one of them, sitting among the people in the bleachers in Madison.

Morgan had come up from Rockford, Illinois, a drive of a little more than an hour. His hope was that this night, April 9, 1960, would see his old team, the University of Wisconsin Badgers, capture an unprecedented ninth national collegiate boxing championship. Few doubted they could do it. To many across the country, the Wisconsin Badgers *were* college boxing. "I liken boxing at Wisconsin to football at Notre Dame," Cal Vernon would say, a half-century after capturing his national championship with the Badgers in 1948. "We were the Notre Dame of boxing." Since the 1930s, the Badgers had boasted the biggest crowds and best teams. There was an aura surrounding them. Destiny seemed perched in their corner.

On the night of April 9, six Badger fighters had made it to the Saturday night finals of the NCAA tournament. The team had eaten together, a late afternoon meal of steak and potatoes at the Memorial Union. Coming out of the union, on the shore of Lake Mendota, they felt a strong swirling wind across the lake from the north. The temperature was dipping into the twenties, cold for April. Vern Woodward, their coach for the past two seasons, suggested they pair up and take a walk. The Field House was only a couple of miles away. He would see them in the locker room at 7:00 p.m.—an hour before the first bout.

Morgan, years removed from his own moment of glory, knew what the boxers were going through in the locker room.

"I'd get my hands taped," he remembered, "put my robe on, lay on the bench, get up, take a leak, put the towel over my head, get up again, throw warmup punches at the air, at the mirror, at the image of my opponent." Anything, Morgan said, "to get rid of nerves, energy—and time."

Occasionally the locker room door would open and in that instant you sensed the anticipation in the arena. "A babbling sound when the door opened," Morgan remembered. "A muffled, foot-shuffling buzz when the door closed."

Bob Meath, a close friend of Morgan's and himself a national champion with the Badgers in 1954, was sitting ringside the night of April 9. Meath remembered that electric Field House atmosphere and the unique perspective you had of it sitting in the locker room. "Inside the locker room it was very quiet," Meath said. "Then someone would crack the door and you would hear this tremendous roar."

Bobby Hinds knew about waiting, too. He was in the Field House crowd that April night in 1960. Hinds called the wait "the hardest part of boxing."

Hinds had grown up poor in Kenosha, Wisconsin, and been taken in by the family of football legend Alan Ameche. In the early '50s, Ameche came to Madison to play football, and Hinds came to box. Ameche would win the Heisman Memorial Trophy while Hinds would fashion a brilliant boxing career that included an undefeated record in dual matches pitting the Badgers against a single team.

Hinds would stay in Madison and become one of the city's most colorful characters, a hustler and self-promoter who was at the same time charming and without guile, a man who made an unlikely fortune in the jump rope and portable gym business. Traveling celebrities loved the gyms in an era before hotels had health clubs. Hinds sold his gyms to actors and artists, and in the last years of the century he corresponded with the notorious racketeer John Gotti, who by that time had plenty of time for letters as he was residing in the federal prison in Marion, Illinois. Their correspondence began after a night Hinds spent in New York when he demonstrated his portable, rubber hose workout gym in, of all places, the bar at Sardi's, the famous theater hangout. A well-dressed man in a dark suit came up to Hinds and said, "You could use that in a small space, couldn't you?"

Hinds agreed, and the man pulled one hundred dollars out of his money clip and asked Hinds to send one to the man whose address he then wrote on a card. It was Gotti, in federal prison in the Midwest. Hinds dutifully sent the gym, but it came back in the return post with a note from the Dapper Don saying that since they didn't let him have shoelaces in prison, they were unlikely to let him have a portable gym. But he appreciated the gesture and he had, Hinds said, elegant handwriting.

That kind of thing just seemed to happen to Hinds. In his college days friends and fans regarded him as a free spirit. About boxing he was serious. Hinds remembered the wait on fight days. Those afternoons, Hinds recalled, he would lie down in bed. Asked if he slept, he replied, "No."

It was the humiliation factor you never forgot, Hinds said. There was no other sport like it. He had run track and played football, but what was the worst that could happen? You don't make the first down or you finish a sprint five yards behind another guy. In boxing, and it happened to every fighter, even the greats, the first time you got hammered in the ring stayed with you like a scar. You were helpless and your body wouldn't listen to what your mind was telling it and the crowd was buzzing and your legs were like rubber.

Meath said: "With me it started about Wednesday for a Saturday fight. I was a nervous wreck. I wasn't afraid of fighting but I was afraid of losing. I just hated to lose."

One Badger boxer from the 1940s, Dick Miyagawa, had felt the locker room tension closing in during the moments before an NCAA tournament bout. Miyagawa found a unique release. He reached in his locker, pulled out a ukulele, and started playing "On Wisconsin."

Hinds did not miss that endless wait. It was easier in the bleachers, where Hinds was on April 9, 1960. As always in Madison, the packed Field House was quite a sight. Nowhere else in America would there be a crowd like it for college boxing.

The fans—young and old, men and women—would begin to arrive two hours before fight time. There would be folding chairs on the basketball floor, and in the twenty-seven years varsity boxing had been in the Field House as many as fifteen thousand people would eventually fill the chairs and bleachers of the arena known affectionately as the old barn. The University of Wisconsin (UW) band would play rollicking tunes, such as "The Beer Barrel Polka," and necks would crane as people spotted their friends and neighbors in the throng.

In a 1938 *Wisconsin State Journal* column—just five years after NCAA boxing came to Madison—sports editor Henry McCormick couldn't avoid superlatives in describing the crowd for a dual meet: "[It was] an amazing crowd even for Madison. The mammoth Field House was jammed to the roof by 7:40, and that was 20 minutes before the show was to start. Hundreds had to be turned away because there was absolutely no available room."

"There was just nothing like when the lights went down," Tom Butler would recall. Butler became a well-known *Wisconsin State Journal* sportswriter but he couldn't cover boxing. "McCormick was very protective of the beat," Butler said. Still, Butler had loved the fights growing up. He was an east side Madison kid and in the '30s he would ride the bus to the Field House with his brother and buy a ticket for fifty cents. The Butler boys liked the first row of the first balcony. The house lights would dim and a big spot would come up and the Badger team would run down into the ring together. They'd line up and stare down the opposing team lined up on the other side. The national anthem was played, then both teams ran back to the locker room, and the fighters came back out 1 bout at a time. Even as a kid Butler realized he was witnessing not just sport but marvelous theater.

It wasn't only die-hard male sports fans in the seats, either. A March 1940 newspaper story was headlined, "Madison Is Wild About the Fights; Especially Women." The story began: "Whether they are dressed formally and sit in ringside seats or whether they arrive in sports clothes and play bridge for an hour before the match, enthusiastic Madison townswomen and University of Wisconsin coeds make up more than a third of the 14,000 fight fans who religiously attend the university boxing matches in the Field House. Forgetting their customary poise and dignity, women prominent in social, civic and university circles here shout and cheer like the most ardent of the masculine contingent."

The Madison crowds were unique and unprecedented. On March 29, 1940, Joe Louis defended his professional heavyweight title in New York's Madison Square Garden against Johnny Paycheck. A crowd of 11,620 people saw the fight. In Madison that same night, more than fifteen thousand saw the Badgers defeat Washington State in a dual meet. The NCAA and college boxing administrators soon recognized the obvious and began bringing their showcase event, the spring NCAA championship tournament, to Madison as often as possible. Butler said the 1939 tournament in Madison was the first time the NCAA made money on an event and the Field House eventually hosted seven NCAA championship tournaments.

It was more than the festive atmosphere that brought people to the Field House. Who doesn't like a winner? The Badgers were good—better than good. Eight national championships. Thirty-five individual NCAA titles. The UW was widely acknowledged as the greatest college boxing program ever.

The names of the Badger champions were celebrated in Madison lore and around the country where fans knew college boxing. Omar Crocker—the Haymaker. That was one of a number of nicknames given the fiercest of the Badger boxers. In his April 5, 1938, column, sports editor McCormick wrote of him: "This Crocker is dynamite. He hits harder for his size than any fighter I've ever seen."

The night before that column appeared, McCormick had been at the Field House and witnessed a classic Crocker performance. In a dual meet with Washington State—five hundred fans were turned away from a packed Field House—Crocker fought at 135 pounds against the Cougars' captain, Paul Waller. That was the bout many of the fans had come to see. No opponent had gone the distance with Crocker all season, and Waller, no slouch himself, had raised the ante the day before when he told a reporter, "I've heard a lot about Crocker. But there's one thing I haven't heard and I'd like to know. Can he duck?"

Crocker dropped Waller in the second round.

The Cougar fighter got up, and the fight went the distance, but the decision went to Crocker.

They almost all went to Crocker. Crocker's fabled college boxing career at Wisconsin was comprised of 24 bouts—22 wins, 1 tie, and 1 loss. The single loss only added to Crocker's legend because it had been a mistake. It was in the 1940 NCAA championship tournament at Sacramento, California. The final night, Crocker fought a kid from Louisiana State University (LSU) named Snyder Parham. Crocker lost a 2–1 decision but later that night, as the judges gathered their papers and prepared to leave, a judge named Jack Downey looked at his sheet and saw he had marked down Parham for the decision rather than Crocker, who he felt had won the fight. Downey made the NCAA committee aware of his mistake and asked that they make Crocker the champion. The committee called a hurried meeting and got out the rule book. There it was—a decision must be rendered immediately after a bout. The decision stood and Crocker had lost. His legend was undiminished. But the man who many felt was the greatest college boxer ever wasn't in the crowd for the 1960 national tournament in Madison. Crocker had died four years earlier, at forty, of cancer.

Crocker's teammate—and frequent sparring partner in practice sessions—beat an LSU opponent at the 1940 NCAA tournament in Sacramento and won his second individual championship. But when people in Madison remembered Swancutt later, it was usually for heroics outside the ring. Immediately after the 1940 tournament, Swancutt, who had been studying to be a doctor, enlisted in the Army Air Corps. He wound up flying forty-nine combat missions in the Pacific theater including leading the first daylight formation of B-29s over Japan. Swancutt's uniform could barely hold his medals. In Madison he had been known to enter the Field

House ring with a black-and-white checked towel slung over his head. When Swancutt piloted the B-29 that dropped an experimental atomic bomb on Bikini atoll in 1946, the checkered towel hung on the back of his seat in the aircraft.

That night in April 1960, the man most responsible for Crocker, Swancutt—all the legends and the boxing mania in Madison—was in the Field House.

John J. Walsh had stopped coaching the Badgers after the 1958 season. His twenty-five-year run had been so successful that the NCAA named the team championship trophy in his honor. *Esquire* magazine had profiled him in 1954. A decade earlier, *Esquire* had asked Walsh himself to write an article explaining his great success at UW. Walsh had spent a quarter century on top as a coach. Writers would call him the Knute Rockne of boxing. The more astute writers also saw a touch of P. T. Barnum.

Jackie Gibson, a UW fighter in the early 1940s, was in the Field House that April night in 1960. As a kid growing up in Madison, Gibson watched the Badger fighters practice and was adopted as the team's unofficial mascot. Of Walsh, Gibson said, "He was more than a great coach. He knew how to put on a show."

2. Ring Master: UW boxing head coach John Walsh, who became so successful leading the Badgers that the NCAA national championship team trophy was named after him.

Walsh had stepped down mainly because his law practice was demanding so much of his time that he could no longer do justice to his boxers. Besides, Woodward, his longtime assistant, deserved a shot as head coach. Walsh could never let it go entirely, of course. He would help officiate at the April 9 finals.

That night, as Walsh surveyed the Field House crowd, he made it at about ten thousand. Boxing programs nationally, any of them, could only dream of attendance like that, but Walsh would not have been overly pleased. It was easily the smallest final night crowd of any of the seven NCAA tournaments Madison had hosted.

Even for a true believer like Walsh, there was no denying what was happening around the country. His sport was in trouble. By April 1960, college boxing was under attack. Around tournament time the year before, *Sports Illustrated* college boxing writer Martin Kane had produced a lengthy piece on the sport's problems that began: "Less than a dozen years ago, college boxing, which is a beautiful sport to watch, seemed on its way to becoming one of the most popular of minor intercollegiate sports."

By 1959, Kane wrote, many schools had dropped the sport. At the schools that continued it, attendance was down. Professors and administrators were questioning whether academia should sanction hand-to-hand combat as sport. A decade before, in 1948, the UW–Madison faculty had been concerned enough to commission a detailed medical study which included monitoring college boxers with electroencephalograms.

The study was initiated after a UW professor of economics, Walter Morton, made a motion to abolish boxing in a meeting of the UW–Madison faculty senate.

Years later, in an unpublished interview with the Wisconsin Oral History Project on campus, Morton said the idea really wasn't his but rather a member of the medical school faculty, Bill Lorenz.

Morton was a feisty, well-respected, if not always well-liked, economist who later in life became an inveterate writer of letters to newspaper editorial pages. He recalled that Lorenz had approached him at the University Club, sometime in either 1947 or 1948.

"He was adverse to boxing," Morton said of Lorenz. "But having been a member of the athletic board, and very intimately associated with the people on the athletic board and the athletes, and with members of his own faculty who were sympathetic to boxing, he did not want to take

the initiative. He mentioned it to me. I said, 'Well, I'll make the motion
to abolish it.'"

Morton recalled that this did not make him a great many friends in
Madison.

"It aroused tremendous emotion. There were attacks on me in the
paper. Members of the faculty who had boxed in college said I must be
crazy. Didn't I understand it was a gentleman's activity?"

Morton said later that he did get some support, including a letter
from W. J. Wittich, director of health and physical education at the State
Teachers College of La Crosse, Wisconsin, who wrote: "I'm indeed glad to
learn that someone at the University of Wisconsin has the good judgment
and audacity to look into this so-called boxing sport. I'm an alumnus
of Wisconsin and I must honestly say I am somewhat ashamed my alma
mater will tolerate the program of boxing."

The faculty did not vote to abolish boxing in 1948 but rather on April
5 of that year made a request to the athletic board "to furnish the faculty
with the facts pertaining to boxing as a collegiate sport."

Morton said, "The committee that was appointed consisted of medical
people."

That was only partly true. Dr. John Brown from the medical school
was asked to head the study of the medical aspects of boxing in college,
but there were also non-medical professors looking at scholastic aspects
of boxing. Still, the medical issues were the lightning rod, and Morton
said, "They were supposed to do research. I think it was farcical research."

Walsh, the boxing coach, could not have disagreed more. In his 1951
book, *Boxing Simplified*, Walsh called the study "one of the most thorough, authentic, and significant studies of a sports activity ever undertaken on a highly academic plane."

The report was released in stages and finally completed and published
in 1952. Signed by the eight members of the UW athletic board it would
seem to have exonerated college boxing. "These observations suggest that
acute injuries of serious nature do not occur frequently during active
participation in boxing in college, as conducted by member institutions
of the NCAA. . . . In keeping with the principles of the University, it is
believed that intercollegiate boxing is being conducted in an exemplary
manner. It is possible the conduct of intercollegiate boxing at Wisconsin
may lead to general progress in the sport."

The report, widely circulated, may have quieted critics for a time, but opposition rose again. The sport's backers responded in kind. It hinged, as always, on the propriety of a college sanctioning an activity where the primary goal was to inflict physical punishment on your opponent. There were fanciful arguments on both sides but that was what it boiled down to. Boxing was violent. There was a rugged beauty, too, a test of courage and character and athleticism as old as man's history. But not even the most devout fan could deny that what happened between the ropes was violent. College boxers wore padded gloves and headgear and the bouts lasted only three two-minute rounds but if it was fast, it was also furious. By the time of the *Sports Illustrated* story in the spring of 1959 some powerful forces had allied against it. Kane's piece was titled, "You could blame it on the moms."

Of course, there was none of that in the local press that first week of April as Madison welcomed the 1960 NCAA tournament. In his story previewing the championship McCormick noted that tournament officials were ensconced at the Edgewater Hotel, on the shore of Lake Mendota, hammering out the seedings and pairings for the three-day event.

"Included in the field of 60 contestants," McCormick wrote, "slated to begin competition here Thursday afternoon in the 23rd annual National Collegiate Athletic Association boxing tournament are eight who have won individual titles and five others who have been runners-up."

Naturally, McCormick was not the only newspaper writer writing about the tournament. Butler was back on the sports desk at the paper but the *State Journal* had a columnist at the tournament who was a writer like no other, a man who might have been as large a character as any of the boxers he wrote about. Joseph Leo Coughlin began covering boxing for the *Wisconsin State Journal* before Walsh came to Madison and before the UW had a team that competed in matches with other schools. Coughlin covered UW boxing when it was nothing but an intramural sport and would annually bestow an award on the boxer he deemed to be the "fightin'est fighter." He also often served as referee.

Coughlin's nickname was Roundy, and he called his daily sports column "Roundy Says. . . ." From 1924 to 1971, in more than seventeen thousand columns, Coughlin wrote the best-read column in the history of Madison newspapers. It was a nearly indescribable mix of opinion and observation, tossed off with little or no regard for grammar or sentence structure. It was an "items" column that predated the greatest items guy of them all, Herb Caen in San Francisco. For that matter, Coughlin predated Caen's original hero, Walter Winchell.

Coughlin's column on Friday, April 8, 1960, the morning of the second day of the tournament, opened like this: "I seen all the NCAA boxers the other day they got more boxers here than people thought Wisconsin would beat Washington in the Rose Bowl and that's a mob."

That run-on effort was followed by a small line of separation and then another observation: "I'll have some of the bouts in my column Saturday. What more could be fairer?"

Next Coughlin moved off of boxing with the observation: "A man owes it to himself to be successful; after that he owes it to the Bureau of Internal Revenue." Another separating line, and then this: "Housewarming: Last call for wedding presents."

Coughlin, then, did not limit himself to sports. He once covered a visit by Gertrude Stein to Madison and first-hand observers declared the match, in boxing parlance, a draw.

There's no question Coughlin's passion for boxing helped popularize the sport in Madison. The week of the 1960 NCAA tournament boxing was foremost on his mind and in another column Coughlin noted: "Charlie Mohr won his bout he was quick and shifty and boxed more than other times Charlie can throw you off balance and this helps his punching power it was the finest fight I ever saw Mohr put up in the Field House."

Coughlin loved Mohr, but then, everybody did.

Mohr was one of those eight former NCAA champs in the 1960 tournament to whom McCormick had alluded. He'd had a brilliant boxing career at UW, but it was more than that. Mohr was a champion but also a sportsman. The year before, in winning the 1959 NCAA championship at 165 pounds, Mohr had been named recipient of the John S. LaRowe Trophy. Named for a former coach at the University of Virginia, the award went to the NCAA tournament boxer "whose sportsmanship, skill and conduct perpetuate the finest attributes of collegiate boxing."

That, most everyone in Madison felt, was certainly Mohr.

Jim Doherty, a magazine writer who had been on the UW campus with Mohr, remembered the boxer in a piece four decades later: "Back in the days when rebels without a cause were hip, Charlie Mohr, a goody-two-shoes if ever there was one, stuck out like a sore thumb. When you saw

him bopping around the campus at the University of Wisconsin in his
dorky horned-rimmed glasses, long brown overcoat and green Irish-tweed
cap, you never would have guessed he was a celebrated national boxing
champion. Or that he was one of the most indelible characters who ever
turned up in Madison, or, for that matter, in any other college town. He
wasn't just a superb athlete. He was a folk hero, a living legend known as
'the saint with boxing gloves' whose decency touched thousands."

Later in his article, which was published in the *Smithsonian* in April
2000, Doherty pointed out that in the months prior to the 1960 boxing
season Mohr had visited a Madison psychiatrist on at least two occasions
and that he was struggling with his allegiance to boxing. In the public's
perception he might be a much-loved rugged altar boy, but the truth
about Mohr, Doherty wrote, was much more complicated. It usually is.

3. Charlie Mohr, a gifted
boxer and national
champion, was even more
respected out of the ring
for his modest demeanor
and volunteer work in the
Madison community.

Still, Gibson, the '40s-era boxer who was in the Field House the night of April 9, 1960, said Mohr probably came as close to some kind of selfless ideal of humankind as any mortal could, and Gibson was in a position to know, having had Mohr as a boarder in his University Heights home in Madison during the 1959 school year.

Later, when people told stories about Mohr, they were rarely set in the boxing ring. If they wanted, they could have talked about the program for the 1959 Pan American Games that included a piece headlined, "Mohr and Clay Rate as Potential Olympic Champions." Pretty heady company. Clay was an eighteen-year-old Louisville, Kentucky, schoolboy who later changed his name to Muhammad Ali.

But when Woodward, Mohr's coach, was asked for "a Charlie Mohr story" by an interviewer in the mid-1980s, Woodward chose to talk about a road trip the team had taken in 1959 to the West Coast. One night a group of twelve Badger boxers, trainers, and coaches went to a restaurant. When Woodward went to settle up, the restaurant manager said a thirteenth had been at the table. It turned out a panhandler had approached Mohr outside the restaurant, asking for spare change, and instead Mohr smuggled the man inside with the team. "I'll pay for him, Coach," Mohr said, on being found out.

That was Mohr. He came from a strict Catholic family in Merrick, New York. His dad was a butcher and his mom worked at Western Union, and Mohr first began boxing only because he had a paper route to help out at home. Delivering the papers on his bike, he began noticing a lone man padding along the side of the road in running shoes. Dick McNally was an amateur boxer who, when Mohr asked, explained that all boxers needed to do roadwork. A fighter needed wind, endurance. A minute of real boxing could leave a well-conditioned basketball player bent over and sucking wind. Mohr began jogging, too, and eventually McNally took him to a gym in nearby Long Beach, on Long Island, where Mohr first tried on gloves. It wasn't too long a step from there to the aged neighborhood gyms in the Red Hook section of Brooklyn where a tough street kid named Pete Spanakos—who would later join Mohr at the UW—first saw Mohr fight.

Pete Spanakos was one of seven Spanakos kids who grew up in Brooklyn where their parents ran a lunch counter called the Paramount Food Shop. The sign in the window said, "Eat with the elite." He and his twin brother, Nick, became boxers in self-defense. "The Italian kids beat us up one day," Spanakos said, "and the next the Irish beat us up and then we said, 'Well, we're going to learn to fight then.'"

Spanakos would recall seeing Mohr fight in Red Hook. He just showed up one day and a neighborhood regular, a tough kid named Jackie Allen, took a look at him and said, "I want him."

Mohr beat Allen, and Spanakos remembered where he had seen Mohr before. It was at the Madison Square Boys Club in Manhattan and walking in the locker room Spanakos was shocked to see a kid with thick glasses sitting on a bench reading a book. It was the first book Spanakos had seen in a fight gym.

Spanakos came to Madison to box for Walsh in 1957 and Mohr followed. There were a couple of stories about how Mohr had ended up in Madison. One had it that Mohr had been brought to Walsh's attention by a man named Peter Mello, a Catholic Youth Organization (CYO) coach in New York. Walsh and Mohr swapped letters and Mohr ended up in Madison. But Vince Ferguson, who had come to Madison from New York to box in 1956, said he had approached Walsh, at Mohr's request, and that at Ferguson's suggestion Walsh and Mohr began corresponding.

However he came to Madison, Mohr was one of the six Badger fighters still in contention as the final night of the 1960 NCAA approached. If waiting for fight time was hard on all the boxers, it may have been hardest of all on Mohr, who would face a familiar foe, Stu Bartell of San Jose State, in the finals at 165 pounds. Doherty wrote, "before a fight, Charlie fretted endlessly." Walsh, who wasn't coaching Mohr by 1960 but knew him well, called him a worrywart.

The afternoon of April 9, before the team meal at the union, Mohr ran some errands. He stopped by Paisan's restaurant, where he worked, and asked owner Roy McCormick if he had tickets for the night's finals. He did not, and Mohr gave him a pair.

The matches began at 8:00 p.m. with the lightest weight class first. Wisconsin's Jim Mack lost a unanimous decision to Heiji Shimabukuro of the College of Idaho. The next Badger boxer was Brown McGhee at 132 pounds, and McGhee decisioned Joe Bliss of Nevada, 3–0. In between, at 119 and 125 pounds, two San Jose State boxers won. And when San Jose's Steve Kibas decisioned the Badgers' Howard McCaffery at 139 pounds and Nevada's Mills Lane beat Wisconsin's Gary Wilhelm at 147 pounds, it was clear the remaining two UW fighters would have to win or the 1960 championship would go to San Jose State.

The Badgers' Jerry Turner would fight Sacramento State's Terry Smith at 156 pounds, and then the last Badger, Mohr, would fight Bartell at 165 pounds.

As the 156-pound bout was being announced, Mohr, the worrywart, paced outside the locker room. He looked around and smiled at a familiar young face. Coming up to say hello was a nine-year-old boy named Tommy Moen, whom Mohr, with typical kindness, had adopted as a mascot and introduced to all the members of the boxing team. Moen came up and wished Mohr luck before every fight. "In my mind it was important for me to do that," Moen recalled later, "and Charlie was nice enough to make me think it was important to *him* for me to do that."

They had met a year or two before outside Camp Randall Stadium, next to the Field House, before a UW football game. Moen lived with his family in an apartment on Breese Terrace, right across from the stadium, so on game days he and his best buddy, a kid named Suey Wong who had walked across China with his mother before emigrating to the United States, worked the sidewalk hoping for extra tickets. Often kindly strangers would give them extra tickets for no charge. The boys were so appreciative that they would walk down a block before selling the tickets to somebody else, then squeeze through a fence, and see the games anyway for free.

Moen met Mohr on a football Saturday when Moen looked down at the pavement and saw a twenty-dollar bill lying not far from a stand where a young man was selling programs. For some reason he's still not sure of, except perhaps destiny, Moen took the bill up to the program seller and said, "Did you maybe drop this?"

It was Mohr. Mohr said he wouldn't know whether or not the money was his until he balanced his drawer. Moen told him where he lived and that evening Mohr showed up and said, yes, he was twenty dollars short. Moen gave him the money and when Mohr paid him a reward of a few bucks, the young boy asked him inside to meet his dad, Arnie, who was a boxing fan and delighted to meet the young Badger star. Before long Mohr was stopping by the Moen home regularly for spaghetti dinners and conversation. After each home fight, Mohr would walk across Breese Terrace and the Moens would let him use the phone to call home to New York and tell his parents how he did.

The night of April 9 Moen wished Mohr luck and as the band started playing "On, Wisconsin" the youngster climbed back up to the seats he shared with his dad. There was good news: Turner, the Badger fighting at 156 pounds, had won a close decision.

The 1960 NCAA championship now hinged on the 165-pound match between Mohr and Bartell.

Center stage, a ring announcer wearing a dark suit stood in the middle of the white canvas ring. He held a microphone in his right hand and index cards in his left. Mohr, under a white robe with "Wisconsin" printed on the back, was dancing in one corner while Bartell stood almost motionless in the opposite corner. The ring announcer called Mohr's name with a flourish and toss of his left hand as if he meant to throw the boxer the index card. Mohr smiled and walked quickly to Bartell's corner. Mohr whispered into Bartell's left ear and the San Jose fighter nodded. Mohr shuffled back to his corner and the bell sounded.

The first punch of the fight was an overhand right by Bartell that grazed Mohr. The fighters went into a clinch and then Mohr, a lefthander, began jabbing with his right. There were frequent clinches in that first round, as the boxers got into the rhythm of the fight. When they clinched the referee, John O'Donnell, a newspaper sports editor from Davenport, Iowa, would separate them. The pattern was for Bartell to bore in and for Mohr to dance, with the Wisconsin fighter's longer reach allowing him to score points while staying out of harm's way. Most felt Mohr had won the first round, but it had been close.

Back in his corner after the bell, Mohr sat on a stool as Woodward, his coach, offered a few short bursts of advice. Woodward felt Mohr wasn't dancing enough.

"You've got to move, Charlie," Woodward said. "You're standing still out there. Box him like you did last week!"

Mohr nodded. "Okay."

The bell sounded for the second. Later, O'Donnell would remember that Mohr hit the canvas twice in the second round. About half way through the two-minute round, a clinch turned into a slip and both fighters went down.

"The first time Mohr went down, Bartell went down with him," O'Donnell recalled. "They were really wrestling and no strong blows were traded. The second time Mohr went it was from a long blow."

In his *Smithsonian* piece, Doherty, who was sitting in the audience that night with his wife, described that punch as a "terrific sock." Doherty wrote: "Charley came off the ropes and ran into a wild haymaker that landed flush on the left side of his forehead."

O'Donnell, however, wasn't so certain the haymaker had done damage: "It was a long blow, which is usually weaker than a short one."

Mohr was up off the canvas on the count of two. In college boxing, a knockdown necessitated a mandatory nine count. O'Donnell barked out the numbers, dusted Mohr's gloves, and checked the boxer's mouthpiece. On nine he asked Mohr if he was all right.

"I feel fine," Mohr replied.

O'Donnell looked into the Mohr's eyes and later recalled, "I don't think I ever saw a boxer who looked clearer than he did."

There was maybe a half-minute left in the round. Mohr danced and Bartell prowled after him. At the ropes, Mohr leaned back as Bartell bore in and then Mohr reached for him and they went into a semi-clinch on the ropes. "No effective punches can really be made in a clinch," O'Donnell said. He stepped in to break it up as Bartell was half-pushing a left at Mohr's head and the referee caught Bartell's next, a right, in his shoulder.

O'Donnell turned slightly and noticed that Mohr's legs appeared to be buckling beneath him. His hands just hung there. "That's it," O'Donnell said, after a moment, stopping the fight. He had waited that second because he had seen boxers go momentarily slack and then recover, and, too, as he would later recall, he didn't feel the blows Mohr had received were "as hard as the ones scored in 15 or 20 other bouts in the tournament." Nevertheless, Mohr's lethargy was not momentary. "One minute he appeared clear-eyed and alert and the next minute was wobbly and seemed unable to defend himself." In that moment, with eleven seconds remaining in the second round, O'Donnell stopped it. Bartell had won.

Woodward helped Mohr back to his corner and the boxer plunked on the stool. "I let the team down," Mohr said.

"Forget that, Charlie," Woodward said. "It means nothing."

Walsh, who would be referring the next fight in the tournament, leaned in toward Mohr and said, "I'm so sorry about this."

Mohr answered: "I guess I zigged when I should have zagged."

Mohr left the ring under his own power. A number of fans yelled keep-your-chin up encouragement, but back in the locker room, Mohr remained dejected. Woodward, who had followed his fighter in, found him sitting on a bench with his head in his hands. "How do you feel, Charlie?" Woodward asked.

"I let you down," Mohr said.

"I mean physically how do you feel?" Woodward said.

"I've got a little headache," Mohr said. "Nothing much."

Woodward motioned to a mat on the locker room floor. "Why don't you lie down? I'll be back in a minute."

"Okay, Coach," Mohr said.

Nine-year-old Tommy Moen, who came down to the locker room after every fight, found his hero lying on the padded mat on the floor.

"How do you feel, Charlie?" Moen asked.

The boxer replied, "Not too good."

Confused and afraid, Moen went looking for his dad, and found him back in their seats. "Dad, Charlie wants to see you," Moen said. Later, the boy would recall, "Charlie hadn't said that, but I thought maybe my dad could help."

It was then that Moen came face-to-face with Bartell, whom he had met through Mohr. "He's not feeling too good," Moen said. Bartell said gently, "I'm sorry I hurt your friend, Tommy."

Moen searched the stands and let Mohr's sister and girlfriend know that he wasn't feeling well. Then he and his dad headed back toward the locker room.

Woodward, meanwhile, had left the locker room for ringside but before he got there someone tapped his shoulder frantically from behind and said, "Something is wrong with Charlie."

When Woodward got back to the locker room Mohr was stretched out on the mat and John H. Flinn, the director of student health at UW–Madison, was kneeling over him.

"What's wrong, Doc?" Woodward said.

"It doesn't look good at all," Flinn said. Mohr convulsed and Flinn thrust his hand into the fighter's mouth to prevent him from swallowing his tongue. Another convulsion and Flinn's hand began to bleed from being bitten. Finally the doctor got a tongue depressor in place.

Horrified and helpless, Woodward shouted, "What's the matter!"

"We've called an ambulance," Flinn said.

Now Moen and his dad, Arnie, came into the locker room. "The doctor was there and Mohr didn't say anything," Moen recalled. "We went outside and I waited while they put Charlie in the ambulance. Then we went home."

Also at home that night was Dr. Manucher Javid, an associate professor of neurosurgery at UW–Madison. Dr. Javid's phone rang and he was summoned to the University Hospital to operate on Mohr. Dr. Javid would later recall he made it to the hospital in five minutes.

The patient was in the operating room when Dr. Javid arrived. Mohr's head was shaved. Dr. Javid knew at once it was serious. Mohr's pupils were fixed and nonreactive. He was not breathing by himself. He was in a coma. Inside Mohr's head, Dr. Javid found what he later described as "subdural hemotoma secondary to the injury"—in lay terms, Mohr had a very large blood clot in his brain and a tear in a major vein. Dr. Javid

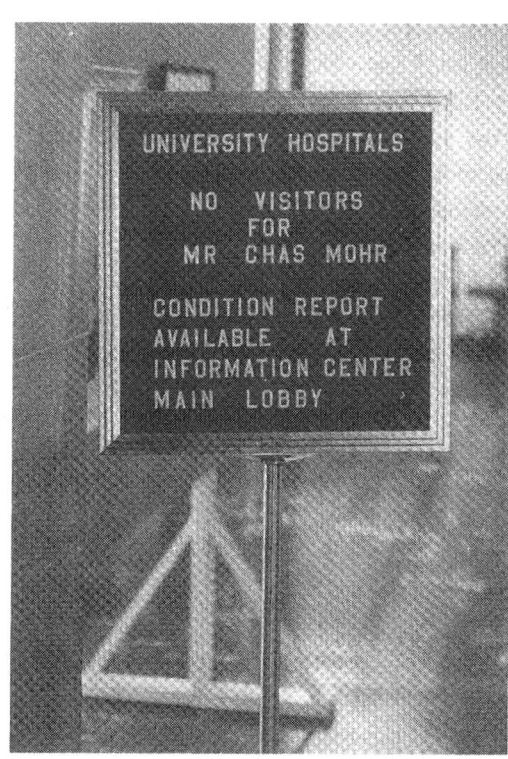

4. Charlie Mohr's life, and the future of college boxing, hung in the balance after Mohr slipped into a coma in the Field House locker room following a bout.

operated for three hours and managed to both stop the bleeding and drain the blood. It was a successful operation, but Dr. Javid knew the damage to Mohr's brain was substantial and, in all probability, irreversible.

Mohr's parents arrived in Madison from New York on Sunday. Their son remained in a coma. At some point shortly after they got to Madison, Mohr's dad had a brief conversation with a reporter and said he and his wife had always approved of their son's participation in college boxing.

"So you don't blame boxing?"

"Absolutely not," Charles Mohr said.

But as the hours passed others weren't so sure. An April 12 newspaper headline in the *Wisconsin State Journal* read, "Regents See Full Review of Boxing."

Woodward, the coach who loved Mohr like a son, said in his grief, "This is ironic, as Charlie was symbolic of all that was fine in college boxing."

As Mohr lay in a coma in a Madison hospital bed, the future of the greatest college boxing team of all time, indeed, the future of college boxing itself, lay with him.

Kane, the *Sports Illustrated* writer, did a story in which he wrote that "the tragedies of sport, whether they occur in football, sports car racing or most other hazardous games, grieve families, sadden fans and stir up resentments against the hazards. When a tragedy occurs in boxing, the resentment is against the sport itself."

Maybe the wonder is that boxing was able to build a tradition at all at America's universities, and of course it did, a storied tradition, nowhere more so than at the UW. A generation later, so many people, even in Madison, could scarcely believe it had ever happened. The Field House was full? For boxing?

It did happen. A door opened. A spotlight shone in a dark arena. Out came the lords of the ring.

chapter 2

WALSH

It was no accident that when Ernest Hemingway wrote about Robert Cohn being a middleweight college boxing champion, the college was Princeton. *The Sun Also Rises* was published in 1926 and up to that point college boxing was an eastern game.

The *Boxing Guide*, first published in 1935 by the NCAA Boxing Rules Committee, includes a brief history of college boxing that notes: "Boxing found its way to the college campus in the same fashion as most of the other collegiate sports—through the medium of intramural competition. As far back as 1880 Harvard University carried boxing on its intramural program."

The *Boxing Guide* notes, "the sport gained much impetus from the world war." A Princeton professor, Joseph E. Raycroft, is generally credited with convincing various academic administrators, in the aftermath of World War I, that boxing in college would be a positive thing. During the war Raycroft had served the war department as head of army training camp activities and found boxing's mix of conditioning, tactics, and sportsmanship to be health enhancing and more.

In his estimable book on college boxing, *The Six-Minute Fraternity*, author E. C. Wallenfeldt noted, "Raycroft drew up a comprehensive set of guidelines governing the conduct of participants and officials."

In the abundant and often-critically applauded literature of boxing, precious little attention is paid to the sport as practiced by the nation's colleges. Simply put, Wallenfeldt's book is about it, and it filled a gaping void when it was published in 1994.

It's not surprising to learn that Wallenfeldt was first turned on to the college sport while growing up in Madison.

In a preface Wallenfeldt noted: "As a youngster growing up in Madison, Wisconsin, in the late 1930s and 1940s and as a student at the University of Wisconsin in the early 1950s, I was fascinated by the sport of boxing because [UW] teams drew crowds of 15,000 for dual meets and national tournaments in the UW Field House."

Wallenfeldt had a keen sense of the neglect the sport had received in posterity. He dedicated his book to "the deceased participants in NCAA boxing who never received the recognition they so well earned and deserved."

Wallenfeldt wrote that the eastern schools, spurred on by Raycroft, took the early initiative. Schools like Penn State, Yale, Princeton, Penn, and Navy developed teams in the early 1920s that boxed matches with other schools, though the sport was not yet sanctioned by the NCAA.

In particular Wallenfeldt credited Penn State and its athletic director, Hugo Bzdek, who in November 1922 hired Leo Houck as his boxing coach. "Houck was a colorful character," Wallenfeldt wrote, "a card-playing, cigar-chewing high school dropout who could dazzle people with his vocabulary." Houck had first boxed as a teenager in 1902 and went on to fight in virtually every weight division, including 2 no-decisions with eventual heavyweight champion Gene Tunney. Houck was revered throughout boxing. For all his flamboyance he was a true sportsman who, Wallenfeldt wrote, felt "the purpose of boxing at Penn State was not to prepare professionals, but to give people a chance to get an education and become better human beings."

If that sounds a lot like Walsh's later credo at the UW, well, Houck would eventually bring his Penn State teams to Madison for some of the most hotly contested matches ever fought at the Field House, and the two coaches formed an immense mutual admiration society.

It may have been Houck's charm and influence that in 1924 got four schools—Penn State, Navy, Penn, and Syracuse—to participate in a tournament that matched fighters in every weight class to determine a champion at every weight and a team champion as well. It looked a lot like a small version of subsequent NCAA tournaments, which were still almost a decade off.

Back in Madison, the sport was just starting to get some notice on campus. The Wisconsin students, returning from the war, who had boxed in Raycroft's training camps, found themselves with the itch to put on the gloves. Their solution, in April 1920, was to organize an "all university" boxing tournament with champions crowned in 6 weight divisions. It was held at the building on Langdon Street called the Armory, though kids and most Madisonians knew the building as the Red Gym. It was not, in spring 1920, yet a big deal in Madison—neither of the city's two daily newspapers had a line about the tournament the next day, while the *Wisconsin State Journal* had a couple of paragraphs about the national amateur boxing championship held simultaneously in Boston. There were 122 "club and college" boxers entered in the Boston event while at UW–Madison's all-university tournament the middleweight division went without a champion because two entrants could not be found.

Yet the tournament survived and grew. By 1924 eight hundred people watched the final matches in the Red Gym. The next year, the tournament—always held in either late March or early April—drew one thousand spectators for the first time. The champion in the heavyweight division was Ray Stipek, nicknamed "Bull," who came to Madison from Montana and excelled at football, where he played guard, wrestling and, of course, boxing—his 1925 campus championship was his fourth in succession.

When the propriety of boxing on campus would be questioned, as it always would, with varying degrees of intensity, throughout the years, Walsh and others who loved the sport would point with pride to the achievements outside the ring made by individuals who had boxed in college. Later in life many were highly accomplished in a wide range of endeavors. Just maybe, there was something about boxing that helped lift them, something inherently beneficial in the sport that stuck with those who stuck with it.

Woody Swancutt, the national champion who went on to become an air force general, was asked by Wallenfeldt to explain the significance of the sport in his life.

Swancutt responded in a letter: "I am certain it had an important impact on shaping my character and influencing decisions under stress over life. There is no question it allowed me to develop confidence in myself and to establish the foundation for the establishment of the disciplines that were essential in my chosen career. It was the first real test in my young life that began to tell me, removed from the subterfuge we sometimes use to fool ourselves, what kind of person I was. Boxing is an individual sport where, if you continue it, you will eventually be faced with a situation that demands the real you to stand up and be counted and you will either pass the test or you will quit."

Doubtless everyone who boxed at UW took something different away from the experience, but it's unfailingly interesting to see what became of the boxers in later life. Even in the pre-Walsh club era of the '20s, some of the UW boxers made impressive names for themselves outside the ring.

The 1928 and 1929 all-university tournament heavyweight champion was Arthur "Dynie" Mansfield. Mansfield won by knockout both times, and his bouts were seen by increasing numbers of people—eighteen hundred came to the Red Gym for the finals in '28 and the next year twenty-five hundred showed up. Boxing was on the cusp of breaking loose in Madison.

Mansfield was a great all-around athlete—he also played varsity football, basketball, and baseball at the UW. He said his unusual nickname—Dynie—came from his days selling newspapers as a boy on a street corner in his native Cleveland, Ohio. That corner, Ninty-eighth Street and Loraine, was evidently a very good place to sell newspapers because Mansfield would recall selling 550 in one night. But prosperity brought jealousy and one night another kid showed up and said it was now his corner.

"I had to fight to protect my rights," Mansfield recalled. "I got in a lucky punch that knocked him down." A ring of people had formed to watch and when Mansfield dropped the interloper one of the bystanders said, "Wow! He's dynamite."

Mansfield entered the UW–Madison in 1925 and stayed in the city until his death in 1985. He coached the UW baseball team for thirty years, from 1940–70, winning two Big Ten championships and 441 games overall. He also served on the Madison School Board and when he retired from coaching the outdoor athletic facility at Madison's new high school, Memorial High School, was named in his honor.

In an interview with Robert Gard for Gard's book on UW–Madison, Mansfield recalled that sometimes the all-university bouts of the 1920s, especially in the preliminary rounds, were not always classic exhibitions of boxing skill.

"One time I was fighting a preliminary match over at the old Red Gym," Mansfield recalled, "in a corner on the third floor, a turret, so there is just a small ring. That is where they fought the pre-lims in the mid-twenties. I was matched with a guy from Chicago and we were both trying to get to the finals of the tournament. We were wearing real big gloves, and it was very hard to hurt anybody with them. My opponent was not hard to hit, and maybe I had a little advantage in arm length. In those days the round ended when you knocked a man down.

"Well," Mansfield continued, "I was hitting and hitting and hitting, and my arms were getting tired. I was using my right hand as hard as I could, but I couldn't put down this Chicago guy. After going and going and going, I finally put him down. The round ended and we came out for the second round. Again I am hitting and hitting, and this guy didn't show any signs of being hurt. He just kept boring in, and finally about the middle of the second round he throws up his hands, both gloves, right up in the air! Right in the ring! I stopped fighting, and the Chicago guy takes a glove and puts it by his mouth, a big boxing glove, and then he got down on his hands and knees and starts looking around. I didn't know what he was looking for, but I got down on my hands and knees too, and there we are down on our hands and knees looking around.

"I said, 'Hey, what are we looking for?' And he said, 'We're looking for my tooth!' He had a peg tooth which I had knocked out."

Mansfield concluded: "The ref stops the fight and gives me a technical knockout, and everybody who is watching is laughing himself crazy. They never saw a fight quite like that one."

Another two-time all-university tournament champion was Tony Curreri. He came to Madison from Long Island, New York, because his high school biology teacher was a UW–Madison grad and talked the school up. Curreri won at 128 pounds in 1927 and 135 pounds in 1930. He went on to become a physician and a pioneer in the battle against cancer. He was the personal physician to Wisconsin governors Lee Dreyfus, Warren Knowles, and Pat Lucey and earned a Distinguished Public Service award from the federal government.

Curreri also taught at UW–Madison and would occasionally be summoned out of Madison to consult when a prominent figure was diagnosed with cancer. In October 1961, Curreri flew to Dallas to treat Sam Rayburn, the Speaker of the House of Representatives, with a drug developed at the UW in the 1950s.

Curreri never lost his love and respect for college boxing, and he served the sport in a number of capacities, including chairing the national rules committee on more than one occasion.

If much of Curreri's later life was lived in the public arena, another champion of the 1927 all-university boxing tournament at UW–Madison spent a lifetime trying to escape the glare of publicity. Nevertheless, the circles in which he moved and the people he knew were such that he might be the most intriguing figure of all the young men who laced on boxing gloves while at the University of Wisconsin. His name was Sidney Korshak.

Korshak came to Madison in 1925 and studied in the UW's College of Letters and Science. He joined the Phi Sigma Delta fraternity and lived in the frat house at 145 Iota Court. He won his all-university title March 26, 1927, before one thousand spectators in the Red Gym.

Korshak had been born in Chicago on June 6, 1907. His father, Harry Korshak, was a Jewish immigrant to Chicago's west side from Kiev, Russia, late in the nineteenth century. Korshak was one of three sons, and he attended Marshall High School in Chicago. On leaving Madison after the spring semester in 1927 he enrolled at DePaul University in Chicago and graduated law school there in 1930.

Over the next six decades, Korshak became, in the words of Chicago writer Eugene Kennedy (writing in the *New York Times Sunday Magazine* in 1996), "one of America's least known but most influential men."

5. Over the years any number of colorful characters boxed at UW–Madison. One of the most intriguing was Sidney Korshak, a student from Chicago who went on to become a lawyer with close ties to Hollywood celebrities and Las Vegas mobsters. Korshak won an intramural title in Madison in the 1920s.

Korshak was dead by the time Kennedy wrote those words—he died in January 1996 and his *Los Angeles Times* obituary was headlined: "Sidney Korshak, Alleged Mafia Liaison to Hollywood, Dies at 88."

Four months after Kennedy's piece was published in the *New York Times Sunday Magazine*, the best and most extensive article ever written about Korshak appeared in the April 1997 issue of *Vanity Fair*.

Titled "The Man Who Kept the Secrets," it was written by acclaimed Dean Martin and Sonny Liston biographer Nick Tosches. One of Tosches best sources was Bill Roemer, who had been a college boxing champion at Notre Dame and then a marine. Out of the service he joined the Federal Bureau of Investigation and in 1958, while investigating allegations of organized crime in Chicago, he called on a Chicago lawyer named Sidney Korshak. Roemer told Tosches that he considered Korshak "the most important contact that the Mob had to legitimate business, labor, Hollywood and Las Vegas."

But the only formal legal trouble Korshak had was with the Internal Revenue Service (IRS), which hounded him in the 1970s, though eventually all fraud charges were dropped and Korshak settled for twenty cents on the dollar. His Hollywood friends included the writer and producer Dominick Dunne and producer Bob Evans; Chicago columnist Irv Kupcinet told Tosches Korshak dated Stella Stevens and Jill St. John. The Robert Duvall character in "The Godfather" was rumored to have been based on Korshak, but that wasn't true—author Mario Puzo had never heard of Korshak when he wrote the book, which was fine with Korshak, who much preferred living in the shadows. Star *New York Times* investigative reporter Seymour Hersh poked a light into those shadows in a 1976 series of articles following Korshak's IRS woes; the articles, however, were long on speculation and short on hard evidence of Korshak's wrongdoing. As Kennedy observed in his *New York Times* piece, Korshak favored the telephone, which left no paper trail.

When Hersh's articles were published in the *New York Times* in June 1976, Madison's *Capital Times* carried a story headlined, "Crime-Linked Attorney Was Student at UW." That story mentioned his all-university boxing championship and concluded with Hersh's assertion that Korshak "was one of the five most powerful members of the underworld."

Korshak died at home in Beverly Hills in 1996. For all his reputed influence, few in Madison—or anywhere else—any longer recognize his name and fewer still know that he was a boxer in the Red Gym. His name recognition may rise if his friend Evans follows through on a plan to make a movie based on Tosches's *Vanity Fair* article, as Vanity reported he might in late 2002. An East Coast investigative reporter, Gus Russo, is also researching a book on Korshak.

Publicity for the all-university tournament, and subsequent fan interest, began to pick up with the arrival of George Downer , a few years after Korshak left, in Madison.

Downer had spent the previous decade in Milwaukee—first as a *Milwaukee Journal* sportswriter, then *Milwaukee Sentinel* sports editor. He wrote a sports column in the *Sentinel,* complete with a mug shot, titled, "Following Through With Downer." The UW recruited him to come to Madison to handle athletic publicity in 1929. His actual title was associate professor of physical education and publicity director. One of Downer's duties, which until his arrival had been handled by an assistant football coach named Leonard "Stub" Allison, was to organize and promote the all-university boxing tournament. Allison was a line coach for the football Badgers and eventually left to become head coach at the University of California.

One of Downer's first initiatives was to move the all-university tournament from the cramped Red Gym to the UW Stock Pavilion, on the far west end of the campus. That move came in 1930. The finals on March 25 drew six thousand fans.

John Hickman arrived in Madison from Milwaukee about the same time as Downer. Hickman would eventually become UW swimming coach. "He was a lot older than me," Hickman recalled some seventy-two years later. "But the position he held would be somewhat comparable to what today is called an associate director of athletics. George was in charge of boxing."

In *Esquire* magazine some time later, Walsh would say, "We bestowed on George the title of 'Father of Midwest Intercollegiate Boxing.'"

Downer's enthusiasm for the sport was infectious. Hickman recalled: "He was a very, very fine person, kind of soft-spoken. I don't know of anyone who didn't like him."

In 1931 the University of Wisconsin Field House at the corner of Breese Terrace and Regent Street opened and Downer immediately secured the facility for that year's all-university boxing tournament.

The sport's growing popularity in Madison was evidenced by the top-line headline on page one—the front page, not the sports section—of the March 24, 1931, *Wisconsin State Journal,* "Expect 8,000 At Boxing Finals."

The official program for the March 24 finals listed 11 bouts. It was the first time that the venue, which would become the most fabled in all the annals of college boxing, was used for the sport. Seven thousand people showed up. One of them was the sports columnist Coughlin, who afterward bestowed his "fightin'est fighter" award on a fellow Irishman, junior lightweight John J. O'Connor, who had come to Madison from Pittsburgh.

Downer looked around at the seven thousand people in the Field House and realized he was on to something. Around that time, Downer had been corresponding with a man named Roy Simmons. Simmons had quarterbacked the football team at Syracuse in the early 1920s and was still a student when he began the boxing program there in 1924, eventually building it into one of the best in the country. He encouraged Downer, who didn't need a lot of prodding. By 1933 Downer had taken the UW boxing program to the next level, beyond the intramural competition of the all-university tournament into real intercollegiate competition.

The first match was scheduled for the Field House on March 21, 1933. The opponent was St. Thomas College of St. Paul, Minnesota, and it brought to Madison the young man who over the next twenty-five years would etch himself into sports history as the greatest college boxing coach of all time. John Walsh was still a student when he brought his St. Thomas team to Madison, but he was already his team's coach. Downer, meeting Walsh and later observing him both in and out of the ring, could not have been more impressed. Downer began to wonder: Was there any chance of bringing Walsh to Madison to coach the Badgers?

It seemed unlikely. His roots were in Minneapolis, Minnesota, where he was born in 1912.

"He had two sisters and a mother who adored him," Audrey Walsh, John's wife of sixty years, said. "About his father, he had mixed feelings. But there were these three women who loved him."

Walsh's parents divorced after he had moved from the house in south Minneapolis where he was raised.

Audrey said he got his start boxing by just showing up at various gyms, one of which was called the Pillsbury House. "It was something to keep him busy," Audrey said.

"I started boxing up there at about 8 years of age in a little exhibition," John said, late in his life.

Another time he said, "I have loved boxing ever since I was old enough to walk."

His mom wasn't thrilled. "Mother is a good fellow about it now," Walsh told a reporter when he was in his late teens. "She objected strenuously at first, but when she discovered that I didn't intend to make it anything but a hobby, her opposition gradually dwindled until now she seldom objects."

Walsh and a boyhood chum named Harold Segal gave exhibitions all over the Twin Cities, at smokers, stag parties, and community centers. Boxing was big in Minneapolis, and Walsh fell under the tutelage of Leo Ryan (to whom Walsh would in part dedicate his book, *Boxing Simplified*). Ryan in turn had been schooled by Twin Cities boxing legends Tommy and Mike Gibbons. Walsh had read a book on the Gibbonses' style—jabbing and weaving and waiting for your opponent to drop his hands, at which point you let fly with a left hook, the centerpiece of the Gibbons method.

"I was fortunate enough to be brought up in Minneapolis where they had very good boxing," Walsh said. "Tommy Gibbons was a heavyweight and his brother, Mike, was one of the best middleweights in history." Ryan got young Walsh in the gym, pointed at the heavy bag, and taught him how to throw a left hook. "The right hand boy's best friend," Ryan said.

"Leo Ryan showed me how to do it," Walsh said. "I learned on a punching bag."

Walsh learned quickly and well.

"Apparently Leo could teach the Gibbons style," Walsh noted later. "One night when I was boxing, with Tommy Gibbons refereeing, he remarked that the style I used was more like his brother Mike's than any he had ever seen before."

In an October 1944 article he wrote for *Esquire* magazine, Walsh elaborated on the Gibbonses' style: "The Gibbons method, as taught to me and passed on, incorporates a fast jabbing left hand, mixed up with a sharp right and followed by left hooks. Just three punches, but used in many variations. The head is always moving side to side, sometimes ducking in, sometimes moving out, and just slipping and rolling the blows by a small fraction—really no intricacies nor anything up the sleeve; however, slipping the blows often creates a hazard. 'Zigging' instead of 'zagging' sometimes causes trouble and this is always the hard point to teach the boys. I'll always remember a remark I heard Mike Gibbons whisper to his son Jack during a bout: 'Don't try to punch hard, Jack, just fast. The speed will take care of the punch.'"

Walsh's schoolboy record was spectacular—98 wins in 100 fights, and multiple Golden Gloves amateur championships. It was late in that schoolboy career that Walsh really began incorporating Ryan's lightning left hook into his arsenal. Young Walsh had the nagging worry that the left hook left you vulnerable to a sharp right return. Ryan, who would later tour vaudeville as a rapid-fire rataplan bag puncher, had convinced him. The left hook was a boy's best friend, something Walsh would often repeat.

In 1932 Walsh was at St. Thomas when the American Legion sponsored the Midwest Intercollegiate tournament in Chicago Stadium. Walsh entered and asked Ryan to go with him. Ryan couldn't make it but he said, "You don't need me. You have my left hook."

In Chicago Walsh and his left hook clicked. He later recalled, "In the very first bout we walked to the center of the ring, I feinted the left jab to the body and then BOOM! The left hook. My opponent fell forward and was counted out. There was no one in the stadium more surprised than I was. Two more bouts followed for me and they also ended the same way in the first round as the result of the 'Ryan Hook.'"

By 1933—the year he first brought St. Thomas to Madison—Walsh was twenty-one years old, planning to go to law school but still fearsome in the boxing ring.

Asked by a Minneapolis reporter if he might turn pro, Walsh replied, "I have been swamped by offers from managers to try the money game. But I'm going to pursue a legal career. I'm getting the fundamentals at St. Thomas now and some day I intend to blossom out as a full fledged member of the bar in this state."

Just a few weeks before the road trip to Madison, Walsh had boxed in the annual Northwest amateur championships in Minneapolis. He had 5 bouts that lasted a total of eight minutes. Here is how a Minneapolis paper described Walsh's 5-fight run to the title:

"His thorough workmanship, ability and all around class made him the outstanding man in a field of more than 200 competitors. Walsh scored a

KO in his opening bout in 24 seconds and came back three hours later to register the second in a round and a half. In his third bout, the lightweight champion [Walsh fought in Madison at 147 pounds later that month] accomplished his purpose in the second round to go into the semi-finals. Johnny took care of his strongest opponent, Emmett Walker of St. Paul, in 30 seconds, landing just two blows. In his final bout Walsh took 38 seconds to decide the championship."

You may want to take a moment to read that paragraph again. In 3 of the fights Walsh had his opponent vanquished in under forty seconds. The other 2 didn't last 2 rounds. He was, let us be certain, a tremendous boxer.

Walsh was also boxing for the St. Thomas team and that year, 1933, he became coach as well. "The original coach had been hired just for intramural and backed out when it became intercollegiate," Walsh recalled later.

The St. Thomas administration came to Walsh with a question and an offer: Could he box and coach? "I was working as a secretary [in the athletic office], short hand and typing and I said, 'Fine, we will just change jobs.' Take that away from me and I will be glad to do the coaching."

The 1933 Madison trip came about almost by accident. A year earlier, a UW assistant football coach, Fred Swan, had been invited to St. Thomas to help coach a clinic that the St. Thomas football coach, Joe Boland, was putting on. During a break in the clinic, Boland and Swan began talking boxing. Swan was a fight fan and happened to mention that the all-university tournament down in Madison was starting to draw thousands of spectators into the just-completed Field House. Boland—who wound up as a radio announcer in South Bend, Indiana—said that he was sure the Wisconsin crowds were great, but if St. Thomas and Wisconsin ever fought a match, St. Thomas would more than hold its own. Boland mentioned Walsh and said he was a better fighter than anyone in Madison.

Well, Swan said, not believing it, maybe there should be a match. You've got it, Boland replied.

By the time of the match a year later, Walsh was not only boxing but also coaching St. Thomas. On March 21 Walsh and St. Thomas came to Madison. It was the first intercollegiate boxing match ever in the Big Ten Conference and 3,500 people showed up at the Field House to watch. The match was a 4–4 draw; at 147 pounds Walsh decisioned the Badgers'

Fausto Rubini. "Some people say the bout was close," *Capital Times* sportswriter Bonnie Ryan observed later, "while others say Walsh toyed with him."

"John absolutely annihilated him," Audrey Walsh, who wasn't there but heard the subsequent stories, said. Rubini wound up as boxing coach at the University of Maryland, eventually bringing his team back to compete against the Badgers.

By the spring of 1933, Swan had left Wisconsin for Temple. If he was responsible for getting Walsh down to Madison from Minneapolis, at least for that first match, it was Downer who managed—just barely—to keep him. Downer, seeing Walsh in the ring against Rubini, could tell he was a highly skilled boxer. But it was everything else that really impressed Downer—the manner in which the twenty-year-old coach acted and carried himself. This, Downer told himself, was a class act.

Walsh recalled that it was the following summer, August 1934, when Downer got back in touch, phoning him in the Twin Cities. Downer asked about the chances of Walsh coming down to Madison to box and coach.

"I said, 'No, I don't want to come down,'" Walsh recalled. "I mean, I would have loved to come down, but I was all set to go to law school at St. Thomas."

Audrey Walsh picks up the story. "They called and offered him the job. He said no, he did not want it. He wanted to be a lawyer. He had just finished his two years of pre-law. The following semester, he was entering the St. Thomas law school. So it was thanks but no thanks."

At which point fate stepped in.

Audrey said, "The very next day he went to St. Thomas and found out they had dropped the law school." Walsh said later it had something to do with an arrangement St. Thomas had with Notre Dame running out, and part of the fallout from that was St. Thomas closing its law school.

On getting the news Walsh called Downer in Madison. "If the job is still open, I'll take it."

"It's good you called," Downer said. "We were just about to call our second choice."

So Walsh came to Madison and entered law school. He was eligible to box himself, and Downer thought perhaps Walsh could do both, as he had on his earlier trip to Madison with St. Thomas.

6. Signed, sealed, delivered. UW athletic director George Downer (right) was
so impressed with young John Walsh when Walsh came to Madison to box
with his St. Thomas, Minn., team in 1933 that he offered Walsh the Badgers
head job the next year. Here they are with the contract.

"They asked me to box and coach," Walsh recalled, "but after that one night at St. Thomas doing both, taking care of seven boys, coaching them, and then going into the ring, I found that I expended more energy coaching in the corner fighting for them than I did for myself."

It was, Walsh decided, a little like an athletic director who tried to be his own football coach. It was one job too many. He would coach boxing and go to law school.

Walsh's first Badger team, in 1934, had only 3 matches for the season, all in March and all at home in the Field House. The first match, Walsh's debut as Badger coach, was won by UW, 6–3. One of the victorious Badgers, at 125 pounds, was Bobby Fadner. Fadner decisioned Haskell's Leslie Oliver. Fadner was left-handed; consequently, the Gibbons' method, appropriated by Walsh, called for him to develop a right-hand hook, "which is seldom seen in a southpaw," as Walsh later observed.

Two years later Fadner would become the Badgers' first national champion. The 1936 NCAA tournament was held in the Memorial Gymnasium of the University of Virginia at Charlottesville on March 27–28. Fadner fought a University of West Virginia boxer named Denver Welsh, who by coincidence was also a lefty. Fadner employed Walsh's strategies to perfection while Welsh swung from the heels. Fadner, who later had a brief try at a pro career—rare for any of Walsh's fighters—won the bout and the national title at 125 pounds. Following his short stint in pro boxing Fadner became a school principal.

Walsh was by all accounts what is called in boxing a terrific "corner." That is, someone who stands just outside the ring and jumps inside the ropes between rounds to give counsel. That was fine for the fight of the moment, but what about later, when the boxer thinks back on the bout and what he might have done differently? Here Walsh was terrific as well.

Walsh credited Harry Stulhdreher, the Wisconsin football coach and athletic director, with suggesting he speak into a tape recorder as he watched the bouts, with the comments to be transcribed later. "Each week," Walsh noted, "the boxer was given a typed copy of his errors and strong points of the previous week."

Madison native Gibson, whose father was a UW professor and had a home near the Field House, became a mascot for the those earliest 1930s Badger teams, and when Gibson became a UW boxer himself, he benefited from Walsh's wisdom from the corner. Six decades later, Gibson unfolded and handed me a single sheet of paper with the following typed at the top: "Wisconsin vs. Miami, March 17, 1941."

It was the typed transcripts of Walsh's comments from ringside as Gibson fought George Lichtfield of Miami in the 120-pound bout before twelve thousand fans in the Field House. The commentary comes in short staccato sentences, resounding with the rat-a-tat-tat of a fighter hitting the heavy bag.

7. Coach Walsh and his boxers at a practice session. So good a teacher was Walsh that his boxers often commented that their toughest bouts were against one another in practice. *Look* photo by Phil Harrington.

ROUND 1:

"Jackie a nice exchange of punches but you were slapping instead of punching."

"Jackie you are standing up against the ropes and letting him take pot shots at
    you."

"You are still not punching Jackie, you're slapping."

"Your left is dropping when you're throwing your right."

"Now you're punching straighter and harder, keep that up."

ROUND 2:

"You started out using a swell left jab keep it up."

"Jackie when you throw that right hand keep that left hand high."

"Keep boxing with this boy."

"Now you're getting against the ropes and you got hit with a sucker right hand."

"You threw two looping right hands without a left jab, that's suicide."

ROUND 3:

"Jackie you had a beautiful right hand shot and you looped it instead of shoot-
    ing it straight."

"Jackie you're looping those rights."

"Jackie when you throw your left hook your right hand is down by your hip."

"Last part of the round Jackie keep that left hand moving and jabbing."

Gibson won the bout, and as many of Walsh's boxers observed of their
own time in the ring, he got stronger as the match went on. There were
two reasons for that: They received Walsh's advice in the breaks between
rounds, so when the bell sounded for the third they were coming out with
a succinct idea of how they were doing and what still needed to be done.
The other reason was they were also in top condition.

As Walsh would often say, peak condition for three two-minute rounds
of college boxing was not the same as conditioning to run a marathon.

Walsh traced his conditioning regimen back to an old Minneapolis fight
gym, Pott's, and a friend he made there named Joey Thomas. Thomas was
a pro fighter. For conditioning the two would go on three and four miles
runs on the slippery Minnesota roads and sidewalks. "It was drudgery,"
Walsh recalled but they kept at it because that's what boxers did.

At least they did until Thomas came back from a trip to New Zealand
and Australia where he met a physical education specialist who suggested
long runs only at the beginning of the season.

"The first part of the year you get your training," Walsh said, "you get your legs in shape, you get your body in shape by the hard arduous running and pounding the pavement." But as the actual boxing season approached, Thomas told Walsh, the more effective method was what Walsh came to call "walk-jog-sprint."

The coach said, "It's the way you do it in boxing your two-minute rounds." On those Minneapolis streets Walsh would walk a block, jog a block, and then sprint full out for a block. Over and over and over. Walk, jog, sprint. Walk, jog, sprint. He brought the training method with him to Madison and used it with his Badger boxers, who rarely tired near the end of a bout.

The '34 team finished with 2 wins and 1 tie, the tie coming in the season's last match with West Virginia. Wisconsin did not send any boxers to that year's national championship tournament—and wouldn't until Fadner went, and won, in 1936—but they were looking forward to an expanded schedule in 1935. Six dual matches were on tap. Walsh was settling in and his 1935 squad would be the first to show that something extraordinary was happening in Madison.

The 1935 Badgers included a fighter at 155 pounds whom Walsh would later call "perhaps the best boxer we ever had." Omar Crocker may have been more fearsome, but Walsh loved the tacticians more, anyway, and Gordy Harman could really box.

Harman came to Madison from Superior, Wisconsin, in the 1930s. Like a lot of the boxers, he had a job at Manchester's on Madison's Capitol Square. Today there are maybe three retail stores on the square. In the middle years of the century there were more than fifty, including big department stores like Manchester's. It had a restaurant too and among its lunch counter customers was architect Frank Lloyd Wright. "I'd catch a bus at Park Street," Harman recalled, "and ride up to the Square to go to work."

McCormick called Harman "as fine a 155 pounder as you could find in college ranks." He earned columnist Coughlin's "fightin'est fighter" award for 1935. Walsh would recall one match in particular. Harman, he said, had been worrying about his left hook. Walsh worked with him on the big bag leading up to a match with Syracuse, who at 155 pounds had Mike Button, team captain and Eastern Intercollegiate champion.

"I prevailed on him to throw his left hook the first punch of the match," Walsh said. The match was March 22, 1935, at the Field House. As the fighters came out of their corners they danced a bit and at first Harman feinted to Button's midsection with a right. He then threw the left hook he'd been practicing for days and sent Button to the canvas, where the referee counted him out.

"Gordy stood in the center of the ring more amazed than anyone in the crowd," Walsh recalled. The fight had lasted thirty-five seconds. It would remain the shortest knockout in UW boxing history.

Harman boxed for three years and actually made news out of the ring by romancing one of the city's most beautiful young women, Edith Jane Walker, a student of speech and drama at UW–Madison. Walker was better known as Dolly Madison, the pen name she used to write a column on fashion for the *Capital Times*. Their wedding in June 1939 received abundant press coverage including a lengthy piece by *Capital Times* society editor Kathryn M. Ruff who spared no detail in describing the festivities that began with nuptials at New York City's Little Church Around the Corner, followed by a reception at Louis and Armand's restaurant, and a dinner party at the Starlight roof of the Waldorf Astoria. The *Cap Times* also published a picture of the couple holding hands at the famed Stork Club. They honeymooned at Niagara Falls.

Over the next half-century the Harmans became fixtures on the city's cultural landscape—a part of Madison society, if such a thing exists in a city not much given to formal dinners or pomp of any sort. Harman became a downtown alderman and Dolly, as she was known, published a glossy magazine called *This Is Madison*. The couple bought one of the city's most storied homes, at 752 E. Gorham, a house originally built in the 1850s.

Harman never won an NCAA championship. The tournament was in its infancy during his boxing career and the strong 1935 Badger team didn't even send a fighter to the tournament that year. The next year was UW's first NCAA appearance. In that tournament, at Charlottesville, Virginia, Harman won his quarterfinal bout but lost in the semifinals.

The previous year, 1935, the Badgers not only did not lose any of their 6 dual meets, they didn't lose more than 2 decisions to any opponent. The scores went like this: Wisconsin over Pittsburgh, 5½–2½; over Michigan State, 6–2; over Haskell, 7–2; over Syracuse, 6–2; over West Virginia, 6–2; and finally North Dakota, 6–2. Wisconsin boxers totaled 15 knockouts in the 6 matches.

Walsh took a particular liking to his '35 boxer at 165 pounds, Charlie Zynda, who had been Coughlin's "fightin'est fighter" the year before. Walsh noted that "at Wisconsin, the real satisfaction for a coach lies in the boys he has seen come in raw and uncertain, and then go out of the game with poise, confidence and manliness." Zynda, Walsh went on, exemplified the kind of athlete who might lack another's athletic gifts but makes up for it with that intangible sometimes called "heart."

Walsh on Zynda: "He caught a couple of tough rights against an Eastern champion, and between rounds, when I wanted to stop the bout, he remarked, 'We've been in tougher ones before, Coach!' He jumped off the stool at the bell, swung a short overhand right and the bout was over."

Another fighter with heart, Walsh recalled, was Gibson, who actually showed up at the Badgers' practices in 1935 as a young teen—his parents lived near the Field House. Once he was old enough and made the varsity squad, Gibson—"our 120-pounder who never weighed over 115," in Walsh's words—faced a tough opponent in Teddy Kara of Idaho.

Kara, according to Walsh, was "a former Olympic champion and one of the best amateurs I have ever seen. I wanted Jackie just to last out the match and told him to keep boxing and moving away. His reply was, 'Coach, you always said you can't win going backwards!'"

His grandfather, Gibson later recalled, had been a German electrician who worshipped pro heavyweight Max Schmeling. Jackie had boxed even as a preteen—"I remember I gave the football coach's son a nosebleed"— and once he hit his teens he began haunting the practice sessions of the new varsity program at the UW. "I sparred with Omar Crocker," Gibson remembered fondly, six decades later. As a teen he became a mascot of sorts for the Badger boxers and may have inspired a program that eventually became known as Little Badger Boxers and brought thousands—a total of over five thousand, by one informed estimate—of young boys in Madison to the sport of boxing and taught them conditioning and self-defense in the bargain.

Walsh began the program not long after he became UW coach. "He needed the cash," author Wallenfeldt wrote, but if so, it was also a labor of love. Walsh invited boys aged six to sixteen to come down to the Badgers' practice facilities inside Camp Randall Stadium next to the Field House. (When Walsh started as UW coach maybe twenty high schools in the state of Wisconsin had either boxing teams or some sort of boxing program; within a decade the Badgers' success had helped spike that number to over two hundred.)

The Little Badger Boxers were pre–high school. Walsh began the program and soon handed it over to a Badger boxer who in 1938 became his assistant coach. When Vern Woodward was called into the navy for World War II, he handed the program over to Nick Lee, a Badger heavyweight from 1939 to 1941 who loved working with the kids.

Capital Times sports editor Hank Casserly wrote about the program in a lengthy 1944 piece that pictured Lee with no less than fifty young boxers. Navy classes in Camp Randall Stadium Saturday mornings had forced Lee to move the boxing classes to afternoon and Casserly noted, "Lee has been besieged by parents wishing to enroll their boys in these Saturday classes. He has been forced to turn down more than 15 boys because of the inability to get the use of the boxing quarters until Saturday afternoon. But Lee has worked overtime in giving those enrolled every bit of instruction possible and the boys and their parents appreciate the fact."

Casserly continued: "The lessons learned and the discipline maintained by Lee and his aides has been amazing to parents. The more the youngsters learn, the less liable they are to pick quarrels. Boys not fortunate to be enrolled in Lee's classes have learned from sad experience that it doesn't pay to tangle with Nick's pupils"—particularly bullies, Casserly wrote.

"These boys come from all walks of life and the melting pot in the boxing quarters has broken down any gang tendencies. Maple Bluff, Shorewood, Nakoma, South Side, East Side, West Side and youngsters living in the central portion of Madison have found that in the ring everyone is on his own and that money, position and other things count not a single iota."

For most of the two decades that the Little Badger Boxers program thrived, it was Woodward who made it work.

If Walsh was the genius behind Badger boxing, Woodward was his less decorated but indispensable second in command, a hard worker with a good heart who came, like Walsh, from the Twin Cities.

As a kid in Minneapolis Woodward boxed what amateur fights he could find and eventually crossed the border into Wisconsin where he won the Golden Gloves light heavyweight title three years running, starting in 1931. He attended River Falls Teachers College and played football, basketball, and baseball before transferring to UW–Madison where he boxed for Walsh in 1936–37.

8. Vern Woodward (right) came to Madison to box for John Walsh and wound up
   spending decades as Walsh's assistant coach. Woodward took over as head coach
   when Walsh retired in 1958.

Hinds, a Badger boxer of the early 1950s, would recall being recruited by Woodward when he was a high school kid in Kenosha and best friends with another Kenosha high schooler by the name of Alan Ameche, later to become a Heisman Memorial Trophy winner as a Badger running back and later a star in the pros with the Baltimore Colts. Woodward came to Kenosha to talk to Hinds, whose family troubles resulted in his spending his senior year living in the Ameche home. Hinds did not have any great interest in attending college, but he was impressed with Woodward—his genuine warmth and honesty. So was Ameche. Even though Notre Dame eventually pulled out all the stops recruiting Ameche for its storied football team, Ameche signed with the Badgers, and Hinds is convinced it was because of the impression made on those early visits by Woodward.

It was a great fit in 1938 when Woodward decided to stay on as Walsh's assistant with the Badger boxing team. The program was beginning to jell and fans and other teams around the country were beginning to take notice. For the first time since 1935, the 1938 Badger squad went undefeated in dual meets. But apparently due to a scheduling conflict, the Badgers could not compete in the 1938 NCAA championship tournament. As incredible as this seems, recall that the tournament then was not nearly what it later became, in terms of team and fan interest. "They didn't travel a lot," Madison sportswriter Butler recalled. "Money was tight." (Indeed, the next year, when the NCAA finals were held in Madison, was the breakout year from both a publicity and financial standpoint.) A March 30, 1938, article in the campus newspaper, the *Daily Cardinal*, stated that "none of the Wisconsin fighters will be able to compete in the nationals because of the fights Monday night"—the Badgers had a dual meet slated against Washington State on April 4 while the NCAA tournament finals were held April 3 in Charlottesville, Virginia.

Everyone in Madison treated the Badgers' match with western power Washington State as the real 1938 national championship, and they might have been right. The *State Journal* headline April 5 read, "Record-Breaking Crowd of 14,300 Sees Badger Boxers Defeat Cougars." There was a picture of the jam-packed Field House below another headline, "When Badgers Won National Title." It wasn't, not really. But the Badgers and their fans knew what they had accomplished. It was Truman Torgerson, the Badgers' 175-pound fighter, who clinched the victory with a knockout over Washington's Tom Tarbox in the second round.

McCormick wrote: "When announcer George Lanphear informed the crowd that Torgerson's victory had clinched victory and a mythical national championship for Wisconsin, the crowd let out a roar that shook the steel girders."

For the record, the '38 team settled for an undefeated dual meet record and looked to next year, when they would host the NCAA tournament for the first time. It would prove a year worth the wait, for in 1939, history embraced Wisconsin boxing, once and for all.

c h a p t e r   3

GLORY DAYS

The great chronicler of Wisconsin boxing, *State Journal* sports editor Henry McCormick, declared it no contest.

"Wisconsin's greatest boxing team was that of 1939."

Many years after McCormick wrote those words, his colleague Butler agreed: "My impression was that the '39 team was the greatest of them all."

They raced through their dual meet season with a record of 8 wins and 0 losses. Only 2 matches were even remotely close—the two fought outside of Madison. The Badgers decisioned Penn State 5½–2½ and then Washington State, in Pullman, 5–3.

The Badgers were absolutely dominating. Later, in the NCAA tournament in Madison at the Field House, one of the eight Wisconsin fighters to qualify for the tourney, heavyweight Nick Lee, was defeated and afterward Walsh was overheard complaining that the decision should have gone Lee's way.

"My God, John," someone said. "Do you want to win every fight?"

"Yes," Walsh replied.

Butler recalls that there was a wonderful mix of personalities and styles among the Badger boxers that year.

First among equals, of course, was Crocker, "The headline star of Wisconsin's greatest boxing era," as a 1973 tribute magazine, *Badger Boxing Legend*, put it.

Walsh said of Crocker: "He was the greatest of all the boxing representatives we ever had. [On other occasions, Walsh said his best was Harman, or another member of the 1939 team, Gene Rankin.] A real gentleman. He not only distinguished himself at Wisconsin, but also in war, where he was a great soldier."

Crocker was born March 25, 1916, in Norcross, Minnesota, and won the Minneapolis Golden Gloves before coming to Madison. He became a college boxer like no other, a star on the Madison campus, and a mythic figure in the boxing ring. "The collegiate boxing brass was afraid of Crocker," Butler said. "They were afraid something drastic was going to happen because he hit so hard."

Crocker's aura was described this way by author Wallenfeldt: "For people in Wisconsin in the uncertain times of the late 1930s with another world-engulfing war emerging on the horizon, Crocker's positive and decisive actions in the ring represented a strength and certainty everyone

9. This display at the Field House in Madison gives an indication of the incredible success of the UW boxing program: 8 NCAA team titles and more than 30 individual championships.

could understand. His good looks, confident air, and reassuring smile were ideal for the kind of hero America wanted. . . ."

After his birth Crocker's family had moved to the Upper Peninsula of Michigan, where he was raised. Crocker came to boxing because of an older brother, Charles Crocker, who actually turned pro and had some 75 bouts around the Midwest before Omar Crocker came to Madison. Charles Crocker taught his younger brother the ropes, including the vicious overhand right that became Omar Crocker's trademark.

By the time of the 1939 NCAA tournament, held in Madison for the first time in late March, Crocker had turned twenty-three. Fighting at 145 pounds, Crocker had been tested early during the Badgers' unbeaten regular season. Though Wisconsin easily dispatched West Virginia, 7½–½, in the year's second match before twelve thousand fans at the Field House, Crocker's bout at 145 pounds with West Virginia's Guice Tudor

10. Nicknamed "The Haymaker," Omar Crocker was perhaps the hardest puncher ever to enter the ring for the Badgers. A fan favorite, his only loss was the result of a judge's scoring error.

was a classic. Tudor was only a freshman in 1939, but he could box. *Badger Boxing Legend* would declare the "three terrific rounds" fought by Crocker and Tudor as "one of the greatest bouts ever fought in the Field House."

Crocker won the decision, and later, he graciously called Tudor the best all-around fighter he had ever faced. Two years later, Tudor would lose in the semifinals of the national tournament to Belaire of LSU, then depart western Virginia for service in the Army Air Corps. That loss was Tudor's last college bout and his joining the service was not untypical. Crocker himself was in the National Guard during his boxing days in Madison and left for the army following the 1940 boxing season.

That was still a year off when Crocker and the Badgers hosted their first NCAA championship tournament in March of 1939. It was a three-day event: Thursday, March 30, were the preliminaries, followed on Friday by the semifinals, and the finals on Saturday, April 1. Twenty-four schools were represented in Madison. They came from Miami to North Dakota, California to Syracuse. It was the fifth NCAA boxing tournament and the first one for the Midwest. The tournament program explained that the first tournament, in 1932, had been held basically to qualify college boxers for the Olympics. That's one reason there was a four-year lag until the next tournament, in 1936, which was held for the same purpose. The next year the NCAA decided the boxing championship tournament should be held annually.

There was some apprehension that the Field House crowds in Madison, large and raucous as any in the country, would not conduct themselves in a sportsmanlike way and this concern was actually addressed in the tournament program, which stated the NCAA's worry whether "spectators could be held to the standards of decorum which, in the East, are deemed essential to the welfare of college boxing."

A local paper noted: "Specifically, they had in mind Wisconsin's ability to secure compliance with the rule of silence during the progress of the rounds."

The introductory notes in the program made the following request: "The management requests that spectators at the 1939 tournament co-operate by refraining from applause—except between rounds and at the conclusion of each bout."

The NCAA felt strongly enough about it that the back cover of the program—prime advertising space—was devoted to a few hundred words

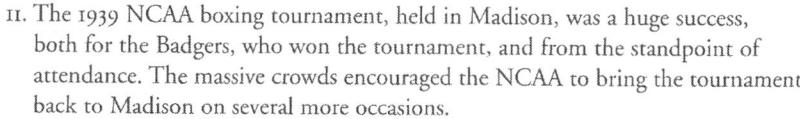

11. The 1939 NCAA boxing tournament, held in Madison, was a huge success, both for the Badgers, who won the tournament, and from the standpoint of attendance. The massive crowds encouraged the NCAA to bring the tournament back to Madison on several more occasions.

"to our tournament guests" which both explained some of the collegiate boxing rules and also reinforced the fan conduct recommendations.

"Intercollegiate boxing must be kept as a fast, clean sport," the program noted, "good fun to play, in which speed and skill are emphasized. This can be done with your cooperation, and it is worth doing for, as a game, nothing can compare with boxing to foster self-control, coordination and courage.

"A correct attitude on the part of spectators during a boxing meet can do much toward developing good sportsmanship, both in and out of the ring. In fairness to the contestants, silence must be maintained during each round. This silence, in addition to its many advantages of fairness, also enables the referee to be heard without difficulty by the boxers. The proper time for applause is between rounds and bouts.

"Boxing officials are experienced and thoroughly indoctrinated in college rules. They conscientiously strive to arrive at honest decisions. Spectators, facing less responsibility, are inclined to render what is known as a 'popular decision' based upon sympathy and similar factors outside the rules. Spectators expressing derisive protests usually represent 'poor losers.'"

In college boxing outpointing an opponent was supposed to be as applauded as knocking him down. Knockdowns were not encouraged, at least under the rules, which were awarded for clean hitting and aggressiveness to a fighter on the offensive—but a fighter on the defensive could also score points for cover blocking, making an opponent miss, and being prepared to counter attack. Clinching and holding and rules infractions caused points to be removed. "General" points were also awarded for a fighter who seemed in control of himself and the bout.

In each two-minute round, the fighter judged to have won the round received 10 points. The opponent would receive a number less than 10 depending on how close he came to winning or tying the round—in the event of a tie in a round, each boxer received 10 points. The final score of a match would be the added total of all 3 rounds.

It is possible to read between the lines of the extensive program notes for the 1939 tournament in Madison. Clearly the NCAA Boxing Rules Committee was already, at this early date, sensitive to the criticism of boxing as barbaric. Bloodthirsty crowds and the dirty back room deals of pro boxing were never to taint the college game. That became the religion of UW coach John Walsh, and he preached it often. Walsh never gave an interview from the 1930s on when he didn't talk about strategy and tactics (as opposed to brutalizing and knocking out an opponent) and how much he disliked the pro game. He always mentioned that almost none of his fighters turned professional. When one did, Walsh said, inevitably the young man came to regret it. Fadner, the Badgers' very first national champion in 1936, was one of the handful who gave the pros a shot. "Someone talked him into it by telling him how much money he would make," Walsh said.

The coach recalled: "The only time I saw him after that was walking on the street. He saw me and crossed to the other side. He did it because he knew how I felt about pro boxing." Fadner, Walsh said, lost a couple of pro fights and then quit. When he did he sought out his former coach. "He came to me," Walsh said, "and said, 'Now, coach, I want you to use me as an example of what not to do.'"

"What do you mean?" Walsh replied.

"Well," Fadner said, "I turned pro. You told me not to. You were right and I was wrong. Use me as an example of what not to do if anybody else is going to turn pro."

Late in his life, Walsh was again asked what it was about the pro game he disliked. "I just don't like the people in it," he said.

Another story Walsh would tell about pro boxing concerned one of the greatest college boxers of all time, a young man to whom Walsh grew very close, though he didn't box for Wisconsin.

Chuck Davey made his NCAA tournament debut in Madison, but he wore the uniform of Michigan State. It was March 26, 1943—a truncated tournament because of the war, but the fan support at the Field House (eleven thousand for the finals) was still impressive—and Davey decisioned Virginia's Jim Miragliotta in the semifinals. Author Wallenfeldt's description of Davey the night of his first NCAA fight in Madison is of a green youth, a "blond, curly-haired, high-foreheaded seventeen-year-old [who] conveyed anything but the impression that he was to become the epitome of college boxing."

Still, Davey beat a Badger, John Werren, in the 1943 finals, and with that captured the first of what would be four NCAA individual championships, though his second was delayed until 1947 because of World War II. At seventeen, Davey was the youngest ever NCAA champ. Davey was born in 1925 and credited his father for teaching him how to box.

"I never went hungry," Davey told *Detroit News* columnist Joe Falls in February 2000. "My dad worked at Ford and he had other jobs, and what I remember is that we moved a lot . . . I guess you could say my father taught me to fight. I had an older brother and we got into a fight one day playing ball at the front of the house. My dad saw it and took us down to the basement and told us to have it out. That was OK, but we didn't have any gloves and we went at it bare-knuckled. I learned a lot that day. When we were done belting each other around, our dad gave us each a whipping."

It was Davey who administered the whippings once the war was over and he was back at Michigan State in 1947. In four years of college boxing, Davey was never defeated, never even tied. His four national championships are an unprecedented record. Naturally, he was a fan favorite, and there was great anticipation of him turning pro.

Yet Walsh claims Davey once asked the coach to stop him if he ever tried to become a professional. This was in 1948, Walsh was the U.S. Olympic coach, and the final tryouts for the team were held in June in Boston.

Davey did not make the Olympic team. In the trials he had 2 bouts in one day. The day before he'd had one fight and outpointed Edwin Muffin, also a college boxer at Navy. The next day, Davey first fought New York Golden Gloves champ John Saxton. Davey won that decision but later that day he got in the ring with Bud Smith of Chicago, who beat him. Saxton and Smith both turned pro and eventually each would win a world title, Saxton as a welterweight and Jones as a lightweight, meaning Davey had fought two eventual world titleholders on the same day.

Walsh said that after his loss to Smith, Davey, who was exhausted, asked something of Walsh and Woodward, the Wisconsin assistant who was helping Walsh coach the Olympians.

"Vern and I were helping Chuck back to the dressing room," Walsh recalled. "He was absolutely petered out. He said, 'If you ever hear of me thinking of turning pro, tell me about tonight and change my mind.'"

Six months later, Walsh read in a newspaper that Davey, the great Michigan State boxer, was considering turning professional.

"I wrote him a long letter," Walsh said, "which he didn't answer."

Six months later, Walsh and Davey ran into each other. By that time Davey had turned pro.

"Chuck, I'm mad at you," Walsh began.

"You have every right to be, John," Davey replied. "I didn't answer your letter because I'm sure you are right. And I am just Irish enough to want to see if I'm as good as people say I am. I promise you that the first match that I lose, that I take a licking, I'll quit."

Even though Davey turned professional, he and Walsh stayed close. Audrey Walsh, John's wife of more than sixty years, remembers traveling twice to Chicago to watch Davey in a pro bout. The second time was February 11, 1953, for a bout that was ranked as one of the top ten in Chicago in the twentieth century by the *Chicago Sun-Times*. Davey fought the welterweight champion Kid Gavilan at Chicago Stadium, and Gavilan dispatched the collegiate great with relative ease. Davey took a punch to the Adam's apple in the third round and when the bell rang to announce the start of the tenth, Davey couldn't answer it. The worst part of the fight was the way Gavilan toyed with Davey, turning around on several occasions and fighting left-handed.

There was one light in the darkness of the Gavilan fight. According to Audrey Walsh, the nurse who administered to Davey's bruises after that fight was a young woman named Pat. Davey and Pat were married later in 1953 and eventually had nine children.

A long time later, Walsh was honored to be invited to a resort in northern Michigan for a reunion of the Michigan State boxing team. "I was the only outsider invited," Walsh said.

The stories and memories flowed. "It was beautiful and we had a ball," Walsh said. It developed that Davey had gone into the insurance business and enjoyed tremendous success. In fact, Walsh later told friends that Davey had the largest New England life insurance agency in the country. "He put his education to the right use after he quit pro boxing," Walsh said. "I am very proud of that boy."

In a 1984 letter to author Wallenfeldt, Davey, perhaps the greatest college boxer who ever lived, spoke for many when he set down his thoughts on what boxing had brought him: "It has given me a lot of confidence in myself and has enabled me to meet a lot of people both in my business and private life. It has enabled me to stand on my own two feet and not rely on others to solve my problems. It has also helped in shaping my philosophy of life. I consider myself competitive, self-reliant, optimistic, realistic, God fearing and loving, and pragmatic. All of these traits, I believe, were shaped to a greater or less extent by my boxing experience."

Davey told Wallenfeldt that his toughest college opponent was a UW boxer, Don Dickinson, whom he beat in the 1949 welterweight finals of the NCAA tournament.

There are no certainties in boxing or life. Less than a decade after he retired a wealthy man from his insurance business, on Thanksgiving Day 1998, Davey was body surfing with his wife Pat in Costa Rica. He was riding a wave when the water curled and swept him under, the undertow smashing his head against the sea bottom. Davey was knocked unconscious, and his neck was broken. The incident put Davey in a wheelchair for the rest of his life.

Falls, the well-known Detroit sports columnist, went to visit Davey the following February at the former boxer's home in Birmingham, Michigan, outside Detroit.

"Davey speaks clearly but slowly," Falls wrote. "A gulp of air from the ventilator, a few words, another gulp, a few more words. It is remarkable how much of his life he remembers and how easily he recalls all the memories. He loved talking about his boxing days."

Davey chuckled and said, "If you ever wonder if I was afraid in there, I was. Every single time." Then he paused, and the laughter stopped. "I never thought anything like this would ever happen to me," he said.

Davey was one of the few fighters Walsh wasn't able to warn off the pro game. The well-earned stigmas attached to professional boxing had college boxing administrators constantly reiterating the difference in the two sports. Hence the program warnings about proper crowd behavior as the 1939 national college tournament prepared to open in Madison in late March.

If they were jittery about the crowd, the NCAA officials were nevertheless anticipating their most successful event yet. "This is the fifth NCAA tournament and it promises to be far and away the greatest ever held," wrote *State Journal* sports editor Henry McCormick in his column as tournament week began in Madison.

The next day, McCormick wrote: "If the NCAA tournament that opens here Thursday afternoon isn't the greatest in history, there will be a lot of surprised people. . . . The members of the boxing rules committee of the NCAA arrived Tuesday afternoon, and all of them are bubbling over with enthusiasm."

McCormick spoke with George Little, who was in Madison for the tournament as the Rutgers athletic director and a member of the NCAA Boxing Rules Committee. Little had a keener interest than most of the visitors in how Madison did as tournament host, after all, Little had supervised the construction of the Field House when he served as UW athletic director from 1925–31. He was thrilled with the potential of the 1939 tournament to break records and showcase Madison and the arena.

"I understand you have been filling it for boxing this year," Little said. "That's great. I hope it's filled for one of the tournament sessions. To see that would give me one of the biggest thrills of my life."

McCormick, the great proponent of college boxing, rose to the occasion in his tournament week columns. In the same column, two days before the tournament, in which he quoted Little, McCormick wrote: "Madison's guests this week—boxers, coaches, spectators, and NCAA officials—have heard fantastic tales of the ability of the Wisconsin boxers and the enthusiasm of the Wisconsin fans.

"Maybe it's wrong to say the tales are fantastic, but they must seem that way to one who hasn't seen for himself. They've heard that 14,000 people saw Wisconsin box Miami and Villanova, and that 15,000 saw the Badgers against Louisiana State. But it's hard for an outsider to believe such things until he sees the huge Wisconsin Field House jammed to the roof, until he witnesses with his own eyes the spectacle of people arriving two hours ahead of match time to obtain a favorite seat."

Madison fans did not disappoint—the total attendance for the tournament topped 37,000, and the crowd for the Saturday night finals was 13,252.

Along with the size and demeanor of the crowds, how Wisconsin's boxers would fare in the tournament was the hot topic around Madison early in the week. Eight Badgers had qualified.

McCormick again, two days before the tourney's first bell: "How many championships Wisconsin will win, or whether it will win any, is impossible to say, but it's a cinch that the boys in Cardinal will help put on some fistic fireworks."

Wednesday afternoon the Wisconsin state legislature passed a joint resolution of the Assembly and Senate, unanimously approved in both houses, praising the Badger boxers. Calling Walsh and his boxers "splendid sportsmen, fine personalities and remarkable scholars," the resolution stated that the citizens of Wisconsin were "justly proud of the team and of the coaches who have achieved the unique distinction of maintaining an unblemished record for two consecutive seasons against the finest collegiate teams in the country."

The tournament began at 1:30 p.m., Thursday afternoon. Only one Badger was scheduled to fight that first afternoon, and if Gene Rankin, the UW's entry at 135 pounds, won his first bout against Dick Bond of Centenary College, he would fight again Thursday night, against the top seed at 135 pounds, two-time NCAA champion Benny Alperstein of Maryland.

Author Wallenfeldt referred to Rankin as the "Mr. Enigma" of college boxing, a fighter who "fought poorly against mediocre competition, drawing with or looking bad in winning from boxers with half his talent and experience." But Wallenfeldt also noted that Rankin "battled magnificently against and defeated many of the best of his day."

Rankin was born in Duluth, Minnesota, on November 25, 1916, and grew up in adjacent Superior, Wisconsin. Northern Minnesota, Wisconsin, and Michigan produced a lot of good young boxers and an amateur circuit—sometimes not so amateur, with the fighters getting "expense money"—developed in the area in the early twentieth century. A Superior truck driver named Spike Dugan taught and trained boxers on the side. Rankin was one in his stable.

"I was too small to make any of my high school teams," Rankin said long after he had left the ring. "It felt good to come back to school on Monday with a mouse under my eye and say to the guys, 'Yeah, I won!'"

Out of high school he kept boxing—Rankin once estimated he had sixty-five fights as an amateur—though he didn't come to school in Madison immediately. It was the Depression and Rankin landed a job with the government's Civilian Conservation Corps in Ashland and Hurley in northern Wisconsin.

Rankin spent two years with the conservation corps and then moved to Milwaukee where he continued to box, making a name for himself in the southern part of the state and eventually representing Milwaukee at 135 pounds in the prestigious Diamond Belt tournament in Boston. Rankin won the Boston competition, and then a Badger boxer, Harman, whom Rankin knew from growing up in Duluth-Superior, suggested that Rankin might want to get a college education and box for the UW.

"I wanted to," Rankin said later. "That sounded like a deal."

When Rankin learned there were no boxing scholarships, his ardor cooled. But he kept an eye on the program and enrolled for the second semester of 1938, working two jobs—in Martin's restaurant and as a night watchman on campus—to pay for it.

Once in Madison, Rankin started sparring with Crocker and Swancutt and went from being a good boxer to a superb boxer, good enough that Walsh once said if he had to pick one fighter to put in the ring for one round, if you absolutely needed to win that round, he'd pick Rankin.

Later in his life Rankin seemed to express mixed feelings about his boxing years. In his lengthy *Smithsonian* piece on Mohr, Doherty quotes Rankin telling author Wallenfeldt that the object in boxing is "to hurt somebody. I couldn't break eggs, but I was out there all the time trying to knock them out."

12. Originally from Duluth, Minn., three-time NCAA champion Gene Rankin later coached the sport.

What Doherty didn't note is that in the 1949 NCAA guide, Rankin wrote—in the form of a hypothetical letter to a "Mrs. Jones," whose son is considering taking up boxing—a virtual love poem to boxing.

"You may wonder why I stress the importance of boxing above the other sports, Mrs. Jones," Rankin wrote. "Maybe I can explain it this way: In what other sport in our school, and most high schools, can your son stand or fall on his own efforts, his own merits, his courage and will to win, his self-discipline, and adherence to training rules as in boxing? In what other sport can he learn so well the art of winning or losing graciously? Where can he learn better to take it on the chin and come back fighting or show consideration to an outclassed opponent? Where can he learn to be 'on his own' more completely than in boxing for it has been said, 'There is no place so lonesome as a boxing ring for a tired boxer.'

"It is true, Mrs. Jones, that some of these values are to be attained in other major sports, but no so completely. In football the boy shares the victory with 15 or 20 others; his chances for the 'big head' are divided by 15 or 20. In basketball he shares the defeat with five or 10 others; his chances for the 'sore head' are also divided. In boxing it's 'I won'—or 'I lost'—and he learns to do both with grace or he finds he is just another spectator."

Whether his stellar college boxing career helped later or not, Rankin—like so many Badger boxers—was successful in his professional life. He taught physical education and social science at New Richmond High School in Wisconsin. He also coached boxing at the school and one of his students, Bob Meath, came to Madison and in 1954 won an NCAA championship at 156 pounds. Later, Rankin, too, came back to Madison. In 1978 Rankin was inducted into the Madison Sports Hall of Fame.

In his first NCAA tournament, in 1939, Rankin was hardly the favorite at 135 pounds. The weight class had the most entrants of any and they included the defender, Benny Alperstein of Maryland, and Joey Church of Miami, undefeated during the pretournament 1939 season.

Rankin himself had a record of 4 wins and 1 draw leading up to the 1939 NCAA championships. Dick Bond, Rankin's Thursday afternoon opponent from Centenary College, was no pushover. *State Journal* sports editor Henry McCormick was ringside and wrote, "the Wisconsin ace won, but only after a slashing, tiring fight. Rankin obviously was tense and

straining, handicapping himself by trying too hard." McCormick attrib-
uted Rankin's problems to first bout first round jitters, and said Rankin
settled down, "lost his nervousness after that first round, and he won with
room to spare."

That night, however, Rankin had to climb into the ring again—this
time against the two-time defender at 135 pounds, Alperstein of the University of Maryland.

McCormick again: "Alperstein made full use of the fact that Rankin
had fought in the afternoon while he had been resting. The Maryland
southpaw moved in fast and out the same way, and Rankin never seemed
quite able to catch him. Rankin never stopped trying, but Alperstein
invariably evaded him with a flashing retreat and a contagious smile. But
as the third round came up, Rankin went out to make Alperstein fight
his way, and he succeeded. It was no picnic for Rankin even when he
drew Alperstein into fighting his way, for the Maryland boy was a better
puncher than he had been painted a lot more durable. But Rankin had
enough of an edge at the finish in the opinion of the judges to grab the
decision."

The Maryland coach did not agree, and said so, in an interview with
a Washington, D.C., newspaper. In the time-honored tradition of non-
winners everywhere, Heinie Miller found reason to fault the officiating of
the bout. The fights had three judges and in the opinion of two, Rankin
carried the day, so naturally Miller cited the third.

"Johnny Behr was one of the judges and he had Alperstein winning by
a city block," Miller told the newspaper. "For two rounds that Rankin
didn't lay a glove on Benny and in the last round Alperstein goes out and
slugs with him and has all the best of it. Look at Ben, does he look like
he's been in a fight? He does not. There isn't a mark on him. Well, Behr,
and he's coached our last two Olympic teams, coached Chicago's Golden
Gloves teams, and been in the game ever since he was old enough to swing
a mitten, he said Alperstein put it all over Rankin. Maybe I'm biased or
prejudiced, but I don't think so in this case. If Benny lost I would call it
one of those breaks and let it go at that, but he didn't lose, and that hurts."

Madison *Capital Times* sports editor Casserly must have been watching a different fight. Casserly wrote: "The third frame was all Rankin. The
gallant Badger lightweight tore in ferociously as the bell opened the round
and with a terrific two-fisted attack to the head and body drove Alperstein

into corners and ropes. Ben again tried a counter-attack, but Rankin shook him off and drove in as hard and as fast as his tired arms would allow. In the closing seconds, both boys stood toe-to-toe and whaled away, with Gene finally getting the best of the exchange and the eventual and well-earned decision."

All told, seven of the eight Badgers in the tournament advanced to Friday's semifinals. The only losing Badger was Jim Walsh at 127 pounds—Jim and his brother Art, who came to UW from Janesville, Wisconsin, were the Badger co-captains. Jim lost to Carl Eckstrom of North Dakota.

Casserly wrote of the fight: "Eckstrom had an immense height and reach advantage on Jim Walsh and he piled up points with a flicking left hand, while he also landed two solid punches to the Badger boxer's jaw. Eckstrom lost points in the second round, on low blows, but otherwise was in complete command of the situation. The North Dakota boy hit Walsh low again in the third round, but the Badger wasn't hurt by the illegal punch. Eckstrom won the third and final round and the verdict."

Walsh's brother Art had better luck at 120 pounds. He decisioned Joe Colonna of Rutgers—"a Tartar," in the estimation of Casserly, writing the next day of the bout. "Walsh battered his foe about the ring but couldn't stop the game boy. . . . Art landed three hard lefts to Colonna's face and Joe's right eye began to close. Walsh also suffered a cut eye . . . Walsh switched to a body attack in the second round and drove Colonna about the ring."

Crocker's quarterfinal bout, at 145 pounds, was of heightened interest for a number of reasons. Crocker, to begin with, was the local fans' favorite. In the *Wisconsin State Journal,* Henry McCormick had begun referring to Crocker as "Mr. Destruction." A couple of days before Crocker's opening bout, against Sam Zingale of Idaho, McCormick wrote: "He hasn't been defeated or tied in his two years of competition, and out of the 13 straight fights he has won nine ended in knockouts."

Zingale, meanwhile, had a strong Wisconsin connection. He was from Milwaukee and had attended UW–Madison in the middle 1930s. Zingale had won a couple of interuniversity tournaments in Madison before transferring to Idaho.

Casserly on the Crocker-Zingale bout: "Crocker stalked Zingale about the ring but the latter . . . who had reports of Omar's sleep-producing punches back-pedaled through the first round. Crocker managed to land one left to the face as he chased the nervous Zingale. Starting the second round, Zingale tightened up his belt and tossed a couple of punches. Crocker, grimly determined, landed a left to the body and a right to the jaw and Zingale was down."

Casserly observed that the referee asked Zingale if he wanted to continue: "The answer was in the negative." It was one minute and three seconds into the second round.

If Crocker's quarterfinals victory was expected, Badger Ray Kramer, boxing at 165 pounds, was regarded as at least a slight underdog against J. L. Golsan of LSU. During the 1939 college season, Kramer had won 3 bouts and drawn 2; Golsan had 8 wins against 2 draws, as well as 3 consecutive Southeastern Conference championships.

The 1939 NCAA tournament program included this observation about Golsan, in a story on LSU: "The Bayou Tigers had one of the outstanding battlers in Southern collegiate history in J. L. 'Joe Palooka' Golsan, the only man ever to win three successive conference titles. Golsan was middleweight champion his sophomore season, light heavyweight title-holder last year and dropped back a division to take the middleweight crown a second time recently."

Kramer and Golsan had boxed to a draw the week before in a dual match in the Field House won 6½–1½ by the Badgers. In the NCAA quarterfinal, each came out with a burst of furious energy. Both scored points with hard right hands but Golsan was docked some points for clinching.

"Kramer blocked most of Joe's tosses," Casserly wrote, "in the second frame and scored the heaviest punches of the fight with a right and left to the head. Golsan was missing badly. Golsan opened strong in the final stanza, however, and backed up the Badger middleweight with a barrage of left hooks and rights to the head."

Kramer, though, battled back, and in the middle of the last round landed a left hook to Golsan's jaw, which, while not sending the Tiger star to the floor, took him off the offensive. Kramer finished the fight tired but still punching—and he got the decision, much to the delight of the Field House crowd.

At 175 pounds in the quarters, Wisconsin's Torgerson, unbeaten and untied in 1939, faced Don Rossi of Michigan State, who had a record of 2 wins and 1 loss. The loss was to Americe Wojciesjas of Syracuse, New

York, a formidable foe, as Torgerson would find out forty-eight hours later. Sixty years later I spoke to retired *State Journal* sportswriter Butler, who was in the Field House with his dad and brother for the '39 finals. Butler said of Wojciesjas: "You knew the guy possessed great inner strength and perseverance just learning to spell his own name at an early age."

Torgerson decisioned Rossi to win his quarterfinal bout. Truman was about as typical a son of Wisconsin as the state could produce. He grew up on a farm in Dunn County, got a degree from the College of Agriculture in Madison, and in his professional life became president of a dairy cooperative. "The original cheesehead," in the estimation of sportswriter Butler.

13. Truman Torgerson, a national champion, grew up on a dairy farm in Wisconsin and later became president of a dairy cooperative. Sportswriter Tom Butler called him "the original cheesehead."

Boxing had always intrigued him. With money earned from herding cows as a boy he bought gloves and a punching bag. The punching bag he installed in his parents' hen house. Young Torgerson took on all comers from Dunn County but really had no sanctioned boxing experience when he came to Madison for college. In high school he had lettered in football, track, and basketball—there was no boxing team—and after the football season in Madison he just showed up at the boxing team's drills one day in 1937, somewhat nervously asking to see Coach Walsh. He was impressed by Walsh's kindness, and Walsh clearly saw something in the Dunn County farm boy and asked him to try out. Before long Torgerson boxed his way to a varsity spot.

Years later, asked by author Wallenfeldt what the sport had meant to him, Torgerson replied: "An awful lot. First, it taught me above all other sports, self reliance. After all, you're one on one, no teammate to fall back on to pick up the slack, or cover your mistakes. It also taught self control. If one lost his head in a boxing match, it was a sure way to tightening up and becoming ineffective." Torgerson credited college boxing with broadening his horizons through travel and with making his name known outside his own circle of friends.

"As a high school teacher and coach it brought respect with the students and remuneration from the school board," Torgerson said. "Surely I had developed a self confidence that enabled me to take the lead on numerous new projects. It was easy to challenge the old established ways, there was always the courage to take on a scrap if I felt I was in the right. All the attributes found in boxing together with the notoriety captured for me numerous offices and leadership positions in the business world. My philosophy of life—give one's all, be fair and understanding."

Two more Badgers won quarterfinal bouts Thursday night, and they couldn't have been more different. Swancutt won a tough 3 round decision at 155 pounds while Lee, the UW heavyweight, won by knockout in the first round.

Swancutt fought Truman Southall of Virginia (the two would meet the next year in the NCAA tournament finals). On that March night in 1939, Swancutt, according to Casserly in the *Capital Times*, "did a fine job polishing" Southall. "Swancutt cut loose with a two fisted body attack in the first round, but the Virginian was willing to trade punches and the boys had a merry time pummeling one another. It was Swancutt's round.

Southall landed a hard right to Woody's right eye in the second round and another to the Badger's jaw, but again Swancutt battled back and in the third round put the decision on ice as he hit his foe with a barrage of rights and lefts."

Swancutt, of course, would become perhaps the most celebrated Badger boxing outside the ring, later in life, the only one deserving of a lengthy obituary in the *New York Times* upon his death in 1993, at seventy-eight.

He was born July 4, 1915—the day altogether fitting for a man later described by his son as "very patriotic. He believed in the United States totally."

The birthplace was Edgar, Wisconsin, near Wausau in the central part of the state. Later his family moved to La Crosse, on the Mississippi River, where Swancutt attended Central High School. After school he came to Madison for college and originally studied premed while making a name for himself in the ring as one of the Badgers' best boxers.

14. Many Badger boxers went on to extraordinary careers outside the ring, perhaps none more so than Woody Swancutt, a career Air Force officer who piloted the plane that dropped an atomic test bomb on Bikini Atoll and, later, helped found the Strategic Air Command.

In November 1940, his college boxing career over, Swancutt was preparing to enter medical school, but the world—and before long the United States—was at war. Woodrow Swancutt III, his son, would say later, "He was due to enter medical school but he enlisted in the war instead." More precisely, the United States Army Air Corps. After earning his wings in July 1941, at Camp Kelly in San Antonio, Texas, Swancutt began a storied military flying career. He flew a total of forty-nine combat missions during World War II, many over China, India, and Burma and was the first to fly a daytime attack on Japan, leading a raid on the steel mills in Yawata. When Lord Mountbatten, the Allied Supreme Commander of Southeast Asia, was to be flown across the globe for a conference in Washington, D.C., it was Swancutt who was chosen to fly the plane. His many war honors included the Distinguished Flying Cross with oak leaf cluster.

Swancutt always flew with the black-and-white checkered towel he carried with him from the Field House locker room to the ring. It was in the plane Swancutt piloted carrying an atomic bomb, the fourth ever atomic explosion, and the first ever announced in advance. The first, of course, had been in the New Mexico desert in July 1945—a Manhattan Project test. Subsequently atomic bombs were exploded in the Japanese cities of Hiroshima and Nagasaki. On July 1, 1946, Swancutt's plane dropped its bomb on the island of Bikini atoll in the Marshall Islands.

Swancutt never made it to medical school. The air force would become his life's work, and he logged some seven thousand flying hours during his lifetime. After the war Swancutt became a wing commander at Lockbourne Air Force Base, deputy director of operations and plans at the Strategic Air Command headquarters, division commander at Turner Air Force Base in Georgia, and director of operations at Air Force Headquarters. He flew himself into Madison in 1963—in a single engine jet—when he keynoted a UW alumni club annual dinner.

"He was," Swancutt's son said, after his dad died suddenly in 1993 of a heart attack after jogging, "the kind of guy you would want in your corner."

At the 1939 NCAA tournament, Swancutt won his quarterfinal bout on points. Badger heavyweight Lee won by knockout. His opponent was Walter Watson of the California Aggies, the 1939 Pacific Coast champion.

The fight lasted only one minute and forty-five seconds. After the opening bell the fighters circled warily for only a moment, then Lee connected with two hard rights to Watson's midsection. Watson tried to flail back but got himself out of position and Lee connected with what Casserly in the *Capital Times* called "a crushing right flush to the button. Watson was out like a light and was dazed for a minute after he had been counted out."

Lee, who would go on to help Walsh and Woodward as an assistant coach in the boxing program (and with the Little Badger Boxers, the clinics for Madison kids), had other things on his mind the weekend of the '39 tournament. On Sunday, the day after the finals, Lee had decided to go public with news he had withheld for nearly a year. The previous June, Lee had married Idelle Boyce, a speech instructor at Randall School in Madison. The marriage was announced the Sunday after the 1939 tournament at a tea given by the school principal. The bride was a Phi Beta Kappa, a UW graduate, and very active in Madison theater groups. The revelation of the couple's marriage made the *Wisconsin State Journal*'s front page.

With Lee's win in the quarters, Wisconsin had seven fighters in the semifinals Friday night, slated to begin at 7:30 p.m. Sixteen bouts were scheduled—first up, the Badgers' Art Walsh against Loyola of New Orleans fighter Sewele Whitney, the pretournament favorite at 120 pounds, and a boxer with one of the most fearsome left hooks in the college division. He was too much for Walsh, and the Badger boxer was eliminated. It was nearly the UW's last loss of the night. The only other Badger to lose was Kramer at 165 pounds. Five others successfully advanced to the finals.

Rankin was first, in the night's fifth bout. The Badger 135-pounder, who had boxed twice the day before, had a tough match with Danny Falco of Temple University. The tournament's biggest crowd so far, over ten thousand people, was in the Field House, and it was Rankin's match that first got them on their feet "with a roar of acclaim," according to Henry McCormick in the next day's paper. Falco and Rankin split the first 2 rounds and then in the third and deciding two minutes, Rankin dominated, scoring on a dozen punches to Falco's three, winning the decision handily.

Crocker was next up for the Badgers Friday night, and in the second round he had Lawrence Harmon of LSU on the canvas twice. He didn't have a chance to fall in the third because as Crocker began to administer punishment, the referee stepped between the fighters and raised Crocker's right hand—the Badgers' star was in the finals, by technical knockout.

Swancutt then faced Mississippi's Steve Wilkerson at 155 pounds. Wilkerson was the defending champion, the only Ole Miss fighter ever to win a national title. Swancutt fought a brilliant fight, winning all 3 rounds against Wilkerson, leading McCormick to say that in Friday night's bout, Swancutt was "like Caesar's wife in that he could do no wrong." Not so Torgerson, who won the first 2 rounds of his semifinal match with Al Passic of Idaho but had to withstand a furious charge by Passic in the third. Torgerson hung on. Heavyweight Lee, soon to be found out as a newlywed, boxed the last match Friday night and dispatched Larry Adams of Superior State a minute into the second round, the referee stopping the fight, McCormick noted, because "Adams appeared helpless."

Adams didn't agree. "Back in his corner Adams made faces like the whole thing was silly," McCormick wrote, "that stopping the fight was utterly ridiculous, but he convinced no one but himself—if he did that."

The finals were Saturday night. The *State Journal* headline told the story that morning: "Five Badgers Fight for National Titles Tonight."

The deck for the report that followed read, "Feat Never Equaled Before" and McCormick's piece opened with this lead: "They'll be settling the national college boxing championships of 1939 tonight at the Field House, and Wisconsin will have representatives in five of the eight divisions. The show opens at 8:00 o'clock, and everything points to a capacity crowd of 15,000."

One oddity: the team championship, which looked like it might well go to Wisconsin (LSU, with three fighters in the finals, also had a shot), was not yet officially recognized. Followers of college boxing kept an informal tally that gave a team 5 points for an individual weight-class champion, 3 points for winning in the semifinals and reaching the finals, and 1 point for making the semifinals and losing there. When the team championship began to be recognized officially, the impetus came from Madison. A large and well-connected booster club for UW boxing, the Madison Downtown Seconds Association, purchased a trophy in 1947, which they named after the Badgers coach, Walsh, and that cup went to the champion team.

Still, everyone knew the informal score in 1939, and the Field House crowd—not quite the 15,000 McCormick had predicted, but a healthy 13,500—was fired up as the Badgers sought their first national title. Never before had any school won more than two individual championships. Wisconsin had its sights set on five.

Incredibly, they nearly pulled it off. The first Badger fighter in the ring was in the night's third bout, at 135 pounds. Rankin faced Henry Davis of Mississippi State, in a match that McCormick, the next day, said had "action all the way." Davis was a well-known name in amateur boxing circles, having once made the semifinals of the prestigious Chicago Golden Gloves tournament.

Rankin eventually beat Davis on points and may have been pushed over the top by three penalties assessed to Davis for low blows. Wisconsin had its first 1939 champion.

In the very next bout, at 145 pounds, Crocker faced Anthony Guida of Temple University. Guida had cruised to the finals without throwing a punch. He had no quarterfinal foe, and his opponent in Friday's semifinals, Ashby Barksdale of Virginia, had to drop out due to an infection. That's not to say that Guida didn't deserve to be in the ring with Crocker. The Temple University fighter had won his division at the Eastern Collegiate Boxing Conference tournament.

"Guida looked like a pretty tough boy," McCormick wrote that night. But he was facing the Badgers' "Mr. Destruction," a fearsome puncher who going into the finals had won 15 straight fights. Crocker didn't disappoint, though at the end of the first round Guida staggered him with a flurry of punches. The bell for round two brought Crocker quickly from his corner. A little less than a minute into the round, Crocker caught Guida with a hard left hand, and before the Temple fighter could recover Crocker countered with a right that actually knocked Guida's mouth protector to the canvas. They kept boxing. Crocker threw another punch and this time Guida himself, not just his mouth guard, almost hit the canvas as he stumbled backward. A minute remained in round two. Crocker glanced at the referee, O'Donnell, and when O'Donnell didn't stop it, Crocker shuffled in and finished it with a right that put Guida down. "It took a matter of some minutes to revive him," McCormick noted, and the Badgers had their second 1939 NCAA champion.

As Crocker left with his title, his friend and sparring partner, Swancutt, stepped into the ring. Swancutt's opponent was Heston Daniel of LSU. Daniel was the favorite, having handed Swancutt a rare loss when the two met a week earlier, in the Badgers' last dual meet of the season. Daniel might have expected to meet Wilkerson, the Mississippi boxer he had clashed with three times—"three of the finest bouts ever seen in a college ring," according to the 1939 NCAA program—prior to the tournament, but Swancutt had knocked off Wilkerson, the defender at 155 pounds, in the semifinals.

McCormick on the Swancutt-Daniel final: "It was a fast, flashing battle with neither catching any damaging blows. Swancutt was the aggressor all the way and he proved the more capable of the two at long and short range."

The 1939 Badgers had their third national champion.

Two Badgers were left to box, but first, at 165 pounds, Frederick Stant of Catholic University fought Washington State's Ed McKinnon. McKinnon, the defender, was considerably ahead on points when a glancing blow from Stant opened a cut near McKinnon's left eye. A doctor examined the gash and stopped the fight, the decision going to Stant.

That set the stage for the championship at 175 pounds, an extraordinary bout that has passed into legend. The match between the UW's Torgerson and Wojciesjas of Syracuse has been called the most exciting fight in the entire annals of college boxing. Certainly the tournament's admonishment to the fans to observe decorum was quickly discarded. They were on their feet almost from the outset.

Wojciesjas, an honor student, was undefeated in 8 dual meet bouts during the year. Save for a match against Army, all had been by knockout. He was no stylist, but his punch was ferocious. The *Capital Times'* Casserly had written that of the five Badgers to reach the finals, Torgerson was the least likely to emerge with a national title. Up against perhaps the best amateur light heavyweight in the country, Torgerson had also picked up a twenty-four-hour flu bug. In the minutes before the bout, Walsh, the UW coach, told Torgerson that at all costs, he shouldn't get in a slugging contest with the Syracuse fighter. Keep moving, Walsh said. If you stand and trade blows, you'll lose.

So, as often happens to the best laid plans, Torgerson—in his last college match—spent the first 2 rounds in a vicious slug fest with Wojciesjas. "Action was the keynote of the bout," Casserly wrote, "with both boys tossing leather at all times. There was never a dull moment."

McCormick, writing in the rival *State Journal*, was even more taken by the bout. "The most hair-raising battle on the championship card was the one everyone expected," the editor wrote. "Here was a fight to quicken the pulse of the most blase, a crashing, smashing battle such as you seldom see."

Butler, soon to be a *State Journal* sports columnist, but in 1939 a fifteen-year-old thrilled to be in the Field House watching with his brother and dad, remembered Wojciesjas looking "like a coal miner from Pennsylvania." Butler said the back and forth blows in the fight were as vicious as any he ever witnessed: "And John Walsh told me Torgerson was suffering from a cold that night." Butler's recollections were close: Wojciesjas actually worked in a steel mill, not a coal mine, and Torgerson didn't have a cold but was getting over the flu.

Most observers felt the first round went to Torgerson—"he caught him early," Butler said—but the Syracuse fighter didn't relent. He kept "walking in," as McCormick wrote that night, "catching punches most of the time, and once in a while landing them to do his share of damage."

Into the second round, McCormick felt Torgerson had the bout unless, in the editor's colorful prose, "he got careless and caught a smash to the whiskers." In that round, McCormick related, Wojciesjas kept "moving in like an automaton, and he's mighty hard to keep away with anything short of a baseball bat." Casserly wrote of the second: "The Syracuse wild man refused to quit and carried the fight to the Badger." But Wojciesjas paid a price for his aggressive style—near the end of round two he was staggered by a flurry of quick punches from Torgerson.

Then the bell sounded, ending the round, and an extraordinary thing happened. Wojciesjas returned to his corner, sat down—and missed his stool, sprawling on the canvas.

"He recovered in a hurry," McCormick noted, "and he was fully as strong as Torgerson in the third. In fact, he might have been stronger." Some observers felt Torgerson had wearied himself in the first 2 rounds—"punched himself out," was how the Associated Press (AP) man on the scene called it—and Torgerson remembered years later how his opponent just "kept coming on." But the Badger fighter had enough in his tank to finish, and the decision went his way. The crowd roared. Torgerson was the fourth UW champion.

Then it was time for the last bout of the tournament, the heavyweight final, and it proved something of a let down, especially to the wild Wisconsin crowd, after Torgerson's heroics. The Badgers' Lee faced LSU's Rene Trochesset. The two had met the week before in a dual meet at the Field House, and in that bout Lee had knocked the LSU man out in the second round. The title fight began as if the same scenario might unfold.

Lee punched open a small cut under Trochesset's eye and the Wisconsin fighter won the first round. In the second, however, Lee went to the canvas, in what McCormick, in a column written a few days later, called a "debatable knockdown," which gave points and indeed the round to the LSU boxer. McCormick claimed the fighters were tangled near the ropes when Lee slipped and fell. "In accordance with national college rules," McCormick explained, "Lee had to take a nine count even though he was up immediately and waiting impatiently for a chance to get at Trochesset."

The decision, after an even last round, went to Trochesset. Butler recalled that afterward, Walsh felt Lee had been robbed. Still, it had been a wonderful tournament for the Badgers—winning the unofficial team title with 25 points (4 firsts for 20 points, a finals loser for 3 points, and 2 semifinalists, worth 1 each). LSU was next with 14 points. The big crowds, the largest by far in tournament history, had NCAA officials smiling. Madison was the official epicenter of college boxing.

The UW and the city of Madison could not wait to honor their 1939 heroes. Monday night, two days after the end of the tournament, a banquet was held at the Loraine Hotel, just off Madison's Capitol Square. The toastmaster was Madison retail businessman Bill Purnell and 350 fans and friends of the team paid a dollar fifty admission that included a dinner, which McCormick noted, "by any other name would still have been modest."

Planning the banquet, Purnell had promised to keep it as brief as possible, but it's hard to keep people from making speeches. And Purnell remarked that the great tournament success of the team meant "there is so much deserved enthusiasm for the Wisconsin team and its coach that we will not try to cut the program short. Instead we will keep it moving rapidly and while we may have quite a few speakers, all of them will be brief."

The banquet ran three hours and fifteen minutes. "An unwieldly length," in McCormick's estimation.

Highlights included large ovations for the departing seniors—Art and Jim Walsh, and Torgerson—and the naming of Crocker as the captain for the following season. Crocker shyly admitted to being nervous when asked to speak, but quickly added, "I am tickled pink."

One oddity from the 1939 season: It wasn't over with the banquet. Even though the Badgers had their mythical national championship, and

4 undisputed NCAA champions, there were 2 dual meets left in their season. A week after being feted at the Loraine Hotel, Walsh and his crew left for the west coast and matches against Washington State at Pullman and San Jose State in San Jose, California. It would have been a shame for the Badgers to end their most brilliant year with a loss, and they didn't, though the Washington State match in particular was close. UW prevailed 5–3, with national champions Swancutt, Crocker, and Torgerson winning their bouts. Rankin lost a decision to Les Coffman, who would reach the NCAA finals himself the following year.

15. Left to right, the individual champions of the 1939 NCAA tournament in Madison: Sewelle Whitney, Loyola (125 pounds); Ted Kara, Idaho (125 pounds); Gene Rankin, Wisconsin (135 pounds); Omar Crocker, Wisconsin (146 pounds); Woody Swancutt, Wisconsin (155 pounds); Frederic Stant, Catholic University (165 pounds); Truman Torgerson, Wisconsin (175 pounds); and Rene Trochesset, Louisiana State, heavyweight

From Washington the Badgers traveled to San Jose and this time their winning margin was 6–2. Crocker won by first round knockout but Swancutt drew his match with Bill Bolich and Bolich's brother, Pete, decisioned Torgerson. Rankin, this time, was victorious, as were the Walsh brothers, and heavyweight Lee won in a first round knockout.

With that the spectacular season really was over. In a column summing up the remarkable year, McCormick listed all the records the team had shattered and then noted that 1940 held potential to be an even better year for Badger boxing.

"Returning are three national champions in Gene Rankin, Omar Crocker and Woodrow Swancutt, along with a national runnerup, Nick Lee, and a semi-finalist in Ray Kramer." There was also a promising freshman class anxious to move up. "Stir them together, let John J. Walsh handle the supervision and you may have a team to outclass even the Badgers of 1939."

McCormick concluded with an open note to Walsh: "Don't I fix the easy assignments for you, chum?"

chapter 4

THE FORTIES

The 1940 season started with a jolt—Rankin, the NCAA champion at 135 pounds, was ruled academically ineligible to compete. Fortunately, the Badger program was now so well established, with as many as 125 young men coming out for the team in the fall that Walsh had talent to fall back on.

Eventually filling the void left by Rankin's classroom trouble was Warren Jollymore. "Jolly," as everyone called him, was born in Proctor, Minnesota, November 20, 1919. His dad was a railroad conductor for a line based in Duluth, and Jollymore began boxing early, before his teens, because an older brother was immersed in the sport. Jollymore was a sophomore journalism major in 1940 and out of college worked for the *Wisconsin State Journal.* In 1953 he joined General Motors and eventually worked his way up to the number two public relations job in the company. He and his family settled in a Detroit suburb, and it was there that Jollymore died, in February 1975, after suffering a stroke. He was fifty-five.

Madison *Capital Times* columnist Harry Sheer profiled the young Jollymore when word leaked that Rankin was going to be ineligible for the 1940 boxing season. Jollymore, Sheer noted: "has come up the hard way [and has] been working at one job or another since he was 14 years old. Right now—if it's lunch or supper time—he's waiting on table at the Memorial Union dining room on the campus. His only recreation is an occasional jaunt on a basketball court."

Friends insisted Jollymore was quite a campus Romeo but the fighter shrugged and said, "Haven't got time for women." Sheer called him "exceptionally polite and curious. Never has a bad word to say about anyone—except himself, when he loses." That wasn't often—after all, like so many UW boxers, Jollymore had fought probably his toughest opponent in the all-university tournaments on the Madison campus. Rankin had dispatched Jollymore twice so it made a certain sense for Jollymore to step in when a chemistry professor knocked Rankin out of the ring. He was a fine boxer from the go: "Easily the classiest on the squad," according to Sheer. Eventually Jollymore would win a national individual championship as well as the John S. LaRowe Trophy that went to the boxer who best matched sportsmanship with success in the ring.

Jollymore's first varsity bout for the Badgers actually came in the second match of the 1940 season. The Badger at 135 pounds for the season opener against Michigan State was Tom Delwiche. "Tommy Delwiche will have to carry the load for the Badgers," McCormick noted, "with only a little more than a week of training. Gene Rankin is ineligible for the season and Warren Jollymore won't be able to clear his eligibility until [the day after the Michigan State match]." Walsh was nervous about the Spartans—a State Journal headline in the week leading up to the match read, "Wisconsin Mitt Record Menaced"—and matters were further complicated, in a reflection of the UW program's growing fame, by the presence that week of photographers from Life magazine. The most prominent magazine in the country shot the Badgers' training sessions and stayed for the Michigan State match, which if UW won would make 15 straight dual meet victories.

Walsh need not have worried. Though Michigan State came to Madison after giving Syracuse all it wanted in a match the week before—that one ended in a 4–4 tie—the Badgers won easily. Delwiche was the only UW fighter to lose in the 7–1 trouncing. The crowd at the Field House was announced at 12,500, setting the stage for an all-time national record for college boxing attendance in a single season. More than 84,700 fans watched the Badgers' 6 dual meets in 1940.

Opening night against the Spartans included a typical performance by Crocker at 145 pounds. Michigan State's Don Wagner for some reason decided to go at Crocker head on and in less than a minute he was on his back on the canvas, victim of a Crocker knockout. Swancutt needed a few seconds less to knockout his opponent at 155 pounds. "Never has

Swancutt fought with as consummate fury," Henry McCormick wrote that night.

The Badgers finished the 1940 dual meet season with only 1 loss, a road trip to Baton Rouge where LSU got the best of them, 5–3. Crocker won—Crocker always won, or so it seemed—but Swancutt was tied and two other stalwarts, Jollymore and heavyweight Lee, lost.

The 1940 NCAA tournament was in Sacramento's Memorial Auditorium. The defending champion Badgers looked like the early favorite—along with Southwestern Louisiana, the Badgers were the only team to have eight boxers in the tournament. Some of the names were new: Clay Hogan, Bobby Sachtsdale, and Billy Roth joined Crocker, Swancutt, Lee, Jollymore, and Kramer in Sacramento.

Neither Madison newspaper staffed the tournament but the *State Journal* contracted with assistant coach Woodward to file reports back to Madison. In his first effort, Woodward reported that Coach John Walsh had the UW boxers doing drills in the baggage car of the train on the ride west. "They also got brief outdoor workouts at North Platte, Nebraska, and Ogden, Utah," Woodward said.

Four Badgers won their quarterfinal bouts. The veterans Swancutt, Crocker, and Lee advanced as did newcomer Sachtsdale at 120 pounds. Jollymore's loss at 135 pounds was particularly tough. Jollymore faced former UW student Zingale, now with Idaho. Zingale had lost to Crocker the year before in a higher weight class. Against Jollymore, Zingale scored a knockdown in the first round, and Jollymore returned the favor in the second. It was close in the third when a cut opened up over Jollymore's eye and the referee stopped the bout, decision to Zingale. It hurt doubly because it appeared Idaho would be the Badgers' toughest foe in the team competition, with five of their boxers advancing to the Friday night semifinals against the Badgers' four.

Madison readers woke up Saturday to a shocking report from assistant coach-turned correspondent Woodward.

Woodward's lead: "Capt. Omar Crocker of Wisconsin tasted defeat for the first time in his brilliant three-year intercollegiate boxing career here Friday night when he dropped a split decision to Snyder Parham of Louisiana State."

When Woodward sent his dispatch back to Madison Friday night, the coach didn't know the story behind that huge upset, involving a bureaucratic mix-up of large proportion. Yet reading Woodward's analysis it is clear, even allowing for a little emotional bias, he felt Crocker had won. "The first round was fairly even," Woodward wrote, "Crocker forcing the fighting but Parham keeping pretty well away from him until near the end when the Wisconsin captain smashed a hard left hook to the body that made Parham clinch." Of the next 2 rounds, Woodward wrote: "Crocker appeared to have a clear edge in both."

The referee agreed, scoring the bout 30–25 for Crocker. One judge, Wes Frye, gave the decision to Parham by a whisker, 30–29 (meaning he had 2 rounds tied and 1 round 10–9 for Parham). It was with the second judge Jack Downey that the trouble began. Downey turned in his card showing 30–29 for Parham; the ring announcer subsequently announced that Crocker, for the first time ever, had lost a fight.

The problem was this: Downey had attempted to score the fight in Crocker's favor but had somehow written it wrong on his card. In the immediate aftermath of the bout, error compounded on error because Downey then either assumed or was told that both the other judge and the referee had the fight for Parham, which would have meant that even if Downey had marked his card correctly, Parham would have won the decision 2–1. It wasn't until hours later that Downey learned the truth: the referee and the other judge had split, and Downey's judgment decided the fight. His judgment was that Crocker had won, but of course his card did not reflect that.

At that point, sometime in the wee hours of Friday night or Saturday morning, Downey alerted the NCAA officials to what had happened. The NCAA Boxing Rules Committee went into an emergency session, emerging with the issuance of a statement saying Downey realized "to his chagrin" that he had marked a win for Parham on his card "when in fact he meant to record a win for Crocker."

The *Capital Times* went to press a little later that Saturday so that while its early-closing sports pages reflected only a Crocker loss, the banner page-one headline told the story of what really happened: "Crocker WON But He LOST—Judge Admits He Made MISTAKE."

The fight story in the paper was written by *Sacramento Bee* sports editor Rudy Hickey, who wrote: "Crocker fought a cautious fight, entirely different from his usual slugging style, and was unable to uncork his terrific right hand. The bout was dull, neither landing any telling blows.

Parham flicked a few gloves into Crocker's face in the first two rounds, but Crocker carried the battle all the way and in the third round tried hard to connect for a knockout. He couldn't tag the elusive Parham with a solid punch."

Still, even before the scoring controversy came to light, many felt Crocker had won. Badgers head coach Walsh said, "I thought Crocker won the second and third rounds on aggressiveness, if nothing else."

Though the Crocker mess would remain the talk of the tournament, there were other bouts being fought. Two Badgers advanced Friday—Swancutt and Lee—while Sachtsdale lost at 120 pounds to Bill Sellers of San Jose State.

The finals on Saturday in Sacramento drew only 5,500—quite a comedown from the huge crowds the year before in Madison. It was announced that the following year's event would be hosted by Penn State, but privately, NCAA officials said they would like to bring it back to the Field House as soon as possible.

The individual championships by Swancutt and Lee gave the Badgers' second place in the mythical team national championship race. Idaho took first. Swancutt knocked his opponent, Southall of Virginia, to the canvas in the third round and the referee, finding a cut over Southall's eye, stopped the fight. Lee decisioned Herbert Kendrick of Louisiana State.

In the days after the 1940 tournament concluded, McCormick and Casserly, the deans of the Madison sportswriting corps, continued to carp at the injustice done Crocker. Casserly called it "a bit difficult to understand," adding, "We have the deepest sympathy for Crocker and his coach, Johnny Walsh, for the unfortunate incident. We know many a fighter, placed in Parham's boots, who would have retired and given his place to Crocker. Apparently that's not an L.S.U. custom."

McCormick was even more bitter: "Let's get it down in the records right now that so far as this writer is concerned, Capt. Omar Crocker of the Wisconsin boxing team is still undefeated in college competition and still is national 145-pound champion."

A few days later McCormick noted that the Crocker controversy was all Madison was talking about. "Probably never before has any city displayed as universal rage as Madison did over that Crocker verdict. The net result of the affair has been to make Crocker more popular than ever and to make Thursday night's boxing banquet a must affair for all fans who can get tickets."

The banquet itself—held the week following the tournament—sold out two days early. In fact, five hundred tickets had been sold for the event at the Marine Club, which held a little more than half that. "First come, first served," banquet chairman Gil Bach said. He added, "We are obtaining prize beef from Chicago for the meat course." University of Minnesota athletic director Frank McCormick was booked as keynote speaker, though doubtless most of the fans wanted to hear from Crocker, the departing captain.

At the banquet, Swancutt and Lee were announced as co-captains for the 1941 team. Coach Walsh praised his team and its fans, and McCormick, from Minnesota—the state that let Walsh slip away—saluted Walsh as "a great coach, a great teacher, and one of the finest gentlemen in the coaching game."

Walsh, in his talk, had referred to Crocker as the greatest all-around fighter in Wisconsin history. No surprise, then, that when Crocker was introduced at the banquet, the fans went wild, standing as one.

Crocker was visibly nervous, but he did his best at the microphone.

"You fans," he said, "have provided the incentive for us boxers."

The crowd roared.

"What boy wouldn't work a little harder," Crocker continued, smiling, "and be just a little better, with the incentive you fans give us? On behalf of the Wisconsin team I want to tell you something that each member of the team would like to say: That is that I want to thank each and every one of you from the bottom of my heart."

Having lost only Crocker, speculation around Madison was that the 1941 Badger boxing team might well regain the mythical national championship. Their dual meet mark did nothing to discourage such optimism. The Badgers fought 6 matches and won them all, the closest being a 5–3 win over Idaho before 14,500 fans on March 24 at the Field House. Badger winners that night included familiar names like Rankin, Jollymore, and Roth—Roth had come on strong at the close of the 1940 season—along with some newcomers in the 1941 season, among them Phil Prather at 165 pounds and heavyweight Verdayne John. With John fighting heavyweight, Lee had dropped to 175 pounds.

Prather was particularly impressive against Idaho, decisioning Laune

Erickson, who hadn't lost all year and would in fact win the NCAA title later that year. Lee would call Prather the toughest sparring partner he ever had, but for some reason Prather never delivered in the NCAA tourney itself.

The 1941 NCAA tournament at State College, Pennsylvania, however, was a disappointment for the Badgers. Lee went out in the quarterfinals, ousted by Fred Spiegelberg of Washington State. Prather and Gibson also dropped first round bouts.

The bright spot was Rankin. He caught a break when the fearsome West Virginia fighter, Tudor, entered the NCAA event at 155 pounds. In a dual meet at Madison in February, Tudor had inexplicably weighed in at 135 pounds and drawn Rankin for the bout later at the Field House. Rankin was stunned. Tudor, after all, had gone toe-to-toe with Crocker and nearly won. Rankin determined to dance and stay away from Tudor during the fight, and the strategy worked to an extent. When the ring announcer in Madison read the name of the winner, Rankin misheard the first name—or maybe the announcer said "Gene," that was never clear after—Rankin jumped to his feet in elation. In fact, Tudor had won, the only loss the Badgers sustained that night.

At the NCAA tournament in Pennsylvania, Rankin was relieved when Tudor weighed in out of the 135 pounds division. No Madison paper staffed the tournament that year, but Jollymore, the Badger boxer, was an aspiring journalist and contracted with the *Wisconsin State Journal* to file reports on the event, including this dispatch concerning Rankin's bout in the finals with Coffman of Washington State:

"Rankin won his crown almost as he won the same title in the NCAA meet in Madison in 1939," Jollymore wrote. "He used clever, cool ring generalship, taking a clear, but close decision . . .

"Coffman was unable to get set against the fast-moving Rankin and Gene spiked the West Coast champion's heaviest guns with a sharp left jab that sent Coffman's head back time and time again.

"Gene, boxing like the champion he is, and wearing a continual smile on his face, took the fancy of the crowd of 5,000 as he made his opponent miss repeatedly, countering with lefts and rights. Never was the outcome in doubt. Rankin grabbed a slight lead in the first round and increased it in the next two, to win his second crown in as many years of collegiate competition."

Though 1941 was far from the Badgers' best NCAA tournament performance—Roth made the finals at 165 pounds but lost to Belaire of LSU—a team that faired very well, Southwestern Louisiana Institute (SLI), had a UW connection. Southwestern, which finished second to Idaho in the mythical team championship, was coached by a man named George "Gee" Mitchell. Mitchell had been coaching boxing at SWI for three years—his primary position at the school was as an assistant football coach—when in 1938 he came up to Madison to pursue a graduate degree in American history. The UW boxing program was just poised for launch—their great first national championship team was just a year away—and Mitchell used his year in Madison to take some private boxing lessons from Badgers assistant Woodward.

The Badgers themselves fared better in the next year's tournament. The 1942 squad had gone undefeated in dual meets—Mitchell's SLI team gave them their toughest match, a 5–3 UW win at the before the season's largest crowd, an estimated fifteen thousand.

The tournament was to be held in late March at Baton Rouge, Louisiana. Seven Badger fighters were entered; of the seven, four were undefeated in the dual meets. Rankin, the UW captain, had the most on the line as the Badgers boarded the train to New Orleans on Wednesday, March 24. If Rankin could win he would become the first college boxer ever to win 3 national individual championships in the same weight division—135 pounds. Idaho's Teddy Kara had three, but had fought in both the 120 and 127 pounds weight classes. The other Badgers had a lot riding on the outcome, as well. On the train ride down, boxing writer Henry McCormick had told the team that if they won, dinner Sunday at the famed Antoine's in New Orleans was on the *State Journal.*

"You can order that dinner right now," Rankin said.

Walsh, boarding the train in Madison, had been a little more cautious. "So much depends on the class of the field, and on breaks, that you can't reasonably predict championships."

In terms of the strength of field, the 1942 tournament was among the smallest of all time. There were just thirty-six boxers from twelve schools in the field. McCormick cited economic reasons—the last NCAA tournament to make any money and kick it back to the schools was the 1939 event in Madison—but there was also the grim reality that little more than three months before the United States had been bombed and was now at war.

The import of boxing or any sport paled against the sweep of world events. Washington State, a powerful team in the dual meet season, did not send a single boxer to Louisiana. As a consequence of the small draw, many boxers received quarterfinal byes and went straight to Friday's semifinals.

But if the field in Baton Rouge was small, there were still plenty of talented fighters—with seven each, Wisconsin and LSU had the most. In front of just fifteen hundred fans at Thursday's opening session, Rankin and Cliff Lutz advanced for the Badgers. In Friday's semifinals, four Badgers advanced. Losing in the semifinals were Johnny Collentine at 127 pounds, Ray Crandall at 120 pounds, and heavyweight John.

John in the ring was a bit of a contradiction. Years later Madison sportswriter Butler would remember John as "a big handsome guy from Milwaukee. He could hit, but the thing was he had a bit of a glass jaw."

In the exciting 1942 dual meet match in Madison against SLI, John had come into the ring for the heavyweight bout, the last of the evening, knowing that the score was 4–3 Badgers, and John needed a win for UW to remain unbeaten. SLI hadn't lost a dual match since 1940, winning 15 in a row before coming to Madison. John fought SLI's Wilson Broussard. It lasted only sixty-four seconds. The crowd was quiet at the outset, McCormick noted, but "John jerked them to their feet at full throat. John jabbed twice with a spearing left and then smacked a heavy right high on Broussard's head.

"From there on it was swift destruction. John fought with unaccustomed savagery and he gave Broussard a sound lacing. When [the referee] finally stopped the fight, John had Broussard against the ropes and was systematically cutting him to ribbons."

No doubt John was hoping for a similar outcome in Baton Rouge. He didn't get it, but John's loss in the 1942 heavyweight semifinal is regarded as one of the great bouts in NCAA tournament history. His opponent from Syracuse was a football player named Salvatore "Toots" Mirabito.

McCormick's report from ringside was breathless: "Verdayne John of the Badgers and beetle-browed Salvatore 'Toots' Mirabito of Syracuse put on a grand heavyweight fight, a fight that John lost when he was dropped to the deck in the second round. John took the first round when he speared his squat opponent repeatedly with a sharp left hook, but Mirabito took the second by a bigger margin as a result of scoring a knockdown. However, it was after the knockdown that big Verdayne showed courage that flamed as brightly as the Cardinal jersey on his back. Gallantly, John fought back as he had gotten to his feet, and at the end of the second round, the Badger was picking up points with his sharp left. The third was a rabble rouser, culminating a great fight. John was only a shade behind at the finish."

Four Badgers advanced to the finals—Lutz, Makris, Jollymore, and Rankin. There was another boxer in the finals who would one day be a Badger—Dick Miyagawa, who in Baton Rouge in 1942 was boxing at 127 pounds for San Jose State. Walsh would eventually convince Miyagawa to transfer to the UW, but that was years off. A Japanese American born in Hawaii, Miyagawa would be sent to a relocation center not long after the 1942 tournament.

Miyagawa had grown up poor on the island of Maui and like many other disadvantaged youths, had turned to boxing as both an outlet and a way to protect himself. He boxed Amateur Athletic Union (AAU) and in

16. Dick Miyagawa, who boxed for both San Jose State and the Badgers, and would sometimes play the ukulele in the locker room to settle his nerves.

high school events. His coach had attended San Jose State and encouraged Miyagawa to enroll there, where he came under the tutelage of a coach named DeWitt Portal, who later grew to near legendary status for his innovations in physical conditioning and psychological tactics in the ring. In 1942 Miyagawa had a chance to become Portal's first national champion and he did it, decisioning Ray Fontenot of SLI.

Miyagawa's transfer to UW came out of his respect for Walsh and also his desire to attend such a prestigious academic institution. Miyagawa eventually earned a master's degree at UW–Madison in 1950 and from there became recreational director at Shorewood Elementary School. He eventually moved into residential real estate sales in the Madison area and enjoyed a long and successful career. Like so many other UW boxers, Miyagawa saw his college boxing days as instrumental in his later success—in Miyagawa's case, because it gave him a university education. In a 1984 interview with Wallenfeldt, a tape Wallenfeldt shared with me for this book, Miyagawa discussed the relationship between academics and athletics: "If the purpose of educational institutions is to get the fullest potential of a human being, to get him to produce to his utmost and cope with society, then if sports can do it for a person, you shouldn't deprive him of that privilege to go through college and become a college graduate and compete in society."

Miyagawa won the 127-pound title in 1942. The first bout of championship night went to Don Harper of SLI at 120 pounds. From that point on, the Badgers "blazed a trail of brightest Cardinal across the ring of Louisiana State University's Coliseum," as McCormick put it in the next day's *State Journal.*

Rankin, trying for an unprecedented third title at 135 pounds, was first. Rankin and his opponent, John Joca of Florida, knew each other well. Rankin, in Baton Rouge before Joca, had actually met his opponent's train. They shook hands warmly and then each tried to psyche the other out. "You came a long way for a beating," Joca said. "It may have been a long trip down," Rankin grinned back, "but the ride back will be short—as champion."

Rankin's was the more accurate prediction. "Rankin won in a sharp boxing contest," McCormick noted. "Rankin stuck a left in Joca's face throughout, and he landed a few more hard punches, too." Rankin had also defeated Joca in the 1941 semifinals.

Jollymore was next. Jollymore not only beat tough Bob Baird of Penn State in the 145-pound final, he won the John S. LaRowe Trophy for sportsmanship and competitive excellence as well. Baird, according to McCormick, "fought true to form in that he was rough and guilty of many rules infractions, but Jollymore didn't even need those demerit points for a clear win." Jollymore stayed above the rough stuff, and won the trophy named for LaRowe, the late Virginia boxing coach. Inscribed on the trophy were these words: "Awarded to the athlete whose sportsmanship, skill and conduct perpetuates the finest attributes of college boxing."

Jollymore's win of the John S. LaRowe Trophy was all the sweeter because the crowd in Baton Rouge was not predisposed to the Badgers.

17. National champion Warren Jollymore later went to work for General Motors in Detroit, and wound up as the number 2 man in the company in public relations.

Success will do that. The fans were particularly rough in the 175-pound final, where Wisconsin's George Makris was a decided underdog against Leon Coe (indeed, Coe had defeated Makris a week earlier in a dual meet) of SLI, and some one thousand SLI fans had traveled to Baton Rouge for the finals. Coe was introduced to a thunderous cheer, while Makris's introduction brought a sustained boo.

Makris had come to boxing through football. Originally from Rhinelander, Wisconsin, he played in the offensive line on the Badger football team and only started boxing when a buddy in gym class told him he could be a natural. They put on the gloves and Makris knocked his friend out. The friend, Stan Kozuszek, was a Badger middleweight. Walsh got wind of that informal bout and before long Makris, although already a junior, was a Badger boxer.

His first "official" bout was in December 1941 at the campus Contender's tournament, which served as a benefit for the *Wisconsin State Journal*'s Empty Stocking Club. Makris won that bout, and he kept winning right up through the NCAA finals.

Makris's upset win over Coe might have been unpopular in Baton Rouge—the fans booed again when his trophy was awarded—but it was well earned. McCormick saw the first round as almost even, maybe a shade to Coe, but then Makris came back in the second, "a rough round with Coe trying to intimidate Wisconsin's light heavyweight. Well, there's no scare in Makris, not an ounce of the likeable Wisconsin boy that isn't full of fight."

The last round started with the tally sheet even: "And into that third round went Makris," McCormick noted, "with a fiery determination to defeat Coe and even matters for the dual meet defeat he had suffered at Madison a week ago. Coe got rough a couple of times in clinches, and Makris cuffed him stingingly for his pains. Late in the round, Makris had Coe pretty well convinced of who was the tougher of the two in this meeting."

Makris had fought that night with a heavy heart. Just a few weeks earlier, his younger brother, Pete, who had played end on the Rhinelander High School football team, went down with the United States cruiser *Houston* in the Java Sea during a fierce battle with the Japanese navy. By the time of the NCAA tournament, nineteen-year-old Pete's status was "lost and unaccounted for," and it was clearly not looking good. McCormick had run into Makris in the Badgers' locker room prior to the UW's March 16 dual meet with Penn State. "I guess all I can do is hope," Makris had told the sports editor. "Yes, I guess that's all I can do." It was as grim as possible a reminder that larger events than boxing were taking place. McCormick, who wrote a column about George and Pete Makris, said, "To me, George Makris is typical of the boys who will carry the banner of this country against the Axis nations. I never knew his brother Pete, but I imagine he was of the same type as George. Here's why I like to think of George as typical of the boys who will carry our nation's banner. He's a product of America's melting pot, being of Greek extraction. He's one of those boys who has unquestioned courage, who never goes out of his way to look for trouble but who never dodges it. And George Makris is the kind of a boy who never will be a trouble-maker on any team or any other organization."

Prior to Makris's bout, the Badgers' Lutz had fought the 155-pound final against Gus Boughan of Purdue University. Lutz came from Appleton, Wisconsin. In a 1970 interview with Gard, who was writing a history of the UW, Walsh recalled that Lutz had shown up in Madison and said, "Just put me anywhere coach," so Walsh put him at 155 pounds. Eventually he would win two national championships.

"He came here literally without a shirt on his back," Walsh said of Lutz. "Today an athlete can get room and board, tuition and books. In those days our boys would thank us very much if we could just get them a board and room job. Usually, I would tell the boys: 'Now don't come until I get you at least a meal job.' But Cliff came down anyway, and we didn't have a job for him. Later I found out that he ate for eight days on one dollar and fifty-six cents. When I asked him how he did it, he said: 'Graham crackers and milk.' We told him to go to Toby and Moon's restaurant, but Cliff forgot the name and was too bashful to come up and ask me about it. Later, of course, we got him a job, and he had an excellent career from that time on. I mention Cliff because today he makes at least $50,000 a year, outstandingly successful. From a boy with a dollar and fifty-six cents, he became a great boxer and a great all-around man."

In McCormick's view, Purdue University's Boughan produced "no trouble" for Lutz in the first round of their championship fight: "Lutz cuffed Boughan with lefts and rights to the jaw that would have felled a boy not as strong as the Boilermaker." Boughan used that strength in the second:

"Boughan threw Lutz roughly away from him, the Badger stumbling and reeling. Back came [Lutz] with a mean glint in his eye and a thud in either fist. He rocked Boughan like a ship on a stormy sea, but the Purdue boy reeled and kept his feet." In the end, the decision went to Lutz.

The tournament ended with the Badgers boasting 4 individual champions and the mythical team championship with 23 points. It was the kind of performance Rankin had predicted when he told McCormick on the train ride to Louisiana to book the dinner at Antoine's. The sports editor did indeed take the team to the famed New Orleans eatery. They ate a huge noon meal before catching the Panama Limited back to Madison.

During the meal the talk centered on the matches just past, and also on the future of NCAA boxing during the war. The consensus was if there was going to be a 1943 tournament, it would have to be in Madison. In lean times, the Badger fans would still come out for the event. Plus, it was centrally located, accessible from both the east and west coasts. But was it proper to even have a national championship tournament, with American troops dying overseas? The mood lightened when McCormick pointed to a framed picture on the wall at Antoine's. The boxers were surprised to see the picture was of none other than McCormick's colleague Roundy Coughlin, the rustic *State Journal* sportswriter with the fractured English and national following.

As Coughlin often pointed out, he was very large at Antoine's. Long-time proprietor Roy Alcatoire made a fuss over him and gave him a special table.

Someone once said of Hollywood that underneath all that phony tinsel is real tinsel. You could say of Coughlin that underneath the act of a philistine lurked a real philistine. After dining at Antoine's the first time, Coughlin came home to Madison and wrote a column about it: "First there was oysters all you could eat and I ate two dozen. Then they brought some fish cooked in paper sacks the best I ever ate. For dessert they brought in some little pancakes all rolled up and damned if they weren't on fire."

The annual boxing banquet honoring the 1942 team was set for April 8. As dictated by the schedule that seems so odd today, the Badgers still had 1 dual meet left after the NCAA tournament. Some fourteen thousand fans showed up at the Field House April 4 to watch the Badgers crush Washington State 7–1. Only Crandall, at 120 pounds, lost for UW.

The banquet was at the Park Hotel on Madison's Capitol Square. The Park's largest banquet room could handle only three hundred people and the event sold out a week early. It was a special night for a number of reasons. Downer, the longtime director of UW athletic publicity and the man responsible for both starting boxing on campus and bringing Walsh to Madison, had died in 1941. A Madison businessman and boxing buff named Jack Ferguson had donated a trophy in Downer's name that would go annually to the best boxer on the Wisconsin team, "to perpetuate the memory of Mr. Downer and to commemorate the signal work he did in helping the development of the sport from an infant to its present status."

Rankin was given the Downer Memorial Trophy and the only three-time Badger NCAA champion happily accepted and introduced his father, Fred J. Rankin, down from Superior. Gene told the crowd: "I've been here a long time. I've had a lot of fun and I can't thank you too much."

Another departing senior, Jollymore, had his dad, John Jollymore of Proctor, Minnesota, in for the banquet. Jollymore spoke briefly and emotionally: "I'm dead serious tonight. I've often wondered how it felt when I saw other seniors give their final talks. Now I know."

John was named the captain for 1943 and he, too, introduced his parents, who had made the drive over from Wauwatosa, Wisconsin.

The keynote speaker at the banquet was Badger great Swancutt, who was now in the United States Army Air Corps and stationed at Bolling Field in Washington, D. C. Crocker, Swancutt's fearsome former teammate, had also been invited but his armed services schedule would not permit a trip to Madison. Instead, Crocker sent a wire: "Impossible to attend banquet. Congratulations to the team. Tell Woody instead of matching slap for slap, will match him Jap for Jap."

In his speech, Swancutt said, "I feel sort of silly—like the Axis powers at the next peace conference. This is just like coming home. I thought Omar Crocker would be here. I don't know where Crock is but I do know he's still champion. He wants to trade me Jap for Jap instead of slap for slap. If he does as well with the Japs as he did with his slaps, well, God bless them."

UW president Clarence Dykstra also spoke. "The president of a university has to look around and see the boys he's associated with," Dykstra said. "If we can produce boys like Woody Swancutt, now serving his country, certainly we are on the right track. We have reason to be proud of our

Wisconsin boys. Some are in the far east, some in the Philippines. Some are not coming back."

Football coach Harry Stuhldreher said: "Last year we sent an invitation for the national tournament to be held here, but it was turned down. Maybe it was better that way. Our boys went to foreign fields, did a great job, and left a splendid impression. The credit for this should go to [coaches] Walsh and Woodward."

Walsh spoke, and after lavishing praise on his boxers, had some fun with them, and the audience at the Park Hotel by mentioning the "Chin Up Club" he had founded as a way of reminding his fighters that the most basic rule in the ring is to keep your chin down and your hands up. The "Chin Up Club" was for boxers who forgot the rule, and Walsh said his assistant, Woodward, was one of the charter members until he took a few nasty shots to the chin. At the banquet Walsh laughed and named three current boxers as officers in the club: John, Lutz, and Collentine.

As Stuhldreher mentioned at the banquet, the NCAA had gone elsewhere in 1942, but they brought the tournament back to Madison in 1943. It was scheduled for March 25–27.

The 1943 dual meet season showed the effects of the war on college boxing. The Badgers fought only 5 dual matches, and one of those almost didn't come off. In late February the Washington State athletic director, Fred Bohler, contacted Walsh and said that their early March trip to Madison was in jeopardy because they had lost so many boxers to the armed forces. Bohler, however, had an idea. What if Washington State combined with Idaho? In that way they could field a team that might give the Badgers a run. Walsh agreed—though the result still wasn't close. The UW dusted the combined team 6–2 before thirteen thousand at the Field House.

The week before, on February 26, Virginia had come to Madison. The Badgers won that one handily, too, 7–1, the match marking UW's 17 straight dual meet victory. Against Virginia the Badgers star at 120 pounds was Jackie Gibson. A Gibson left hook had drawn blood from his opponent, Jim Elkins, in the first round. It's interesting to note that in his spoken comments on the round, which were presented to Gibson a couple of days after the fight, Walsh never mentioned that blow. He mentioned a good right hook to the belly and then said, "Jackie, you've got your hands too low." A perspective member of the chin up, hands down club, perhaps.

But Walsh delighted in Gibson. In his 1970 interview with Gard, Walsh recalled that Gibson, whose family lived near the Field House, had started coming to watch practices when he was barely out of grade school. "The nearest thing the boxing team had to a mascot was Jackie Gibson," Walsh said. "He was just so enthralled with boxing that he came out every time. He was with us for about seven years before he actually came to college, and our little mascot grew into one of the finest boxers we had."

Of course, it wasn't just Washington State that saw its ranks thinned by the war effort. As Walsh said of Gibson: "He was just at the point of winning the national championship when Uncle Sam took him, one week before the match."

Still, the Badgers entered eight fighters in the second national championship tournament to be held in Madison. Elmer Fisk took Gibson's spot at 120 pounds. The Badger veterans in the tournament included Collentine, Lutz, Makris, and John.

One of UW's tournament newcomers was a boxer who would fight a match that turned out to be one of the most memorable of not only the 1943 tournament, but in all the annals of college boxing. Walsh later called it one of the three best fights he had witnessed in a quarter century of college coaching. The Badger boxer's name was Don Miller.

Miller was born in Racine, Wisconsin, April 9, 1920. He boxed Golden Gloves in nearby Kenosha and then on the high school team at Racine St. Catherine. Miller's coach eventually wrote a letter to Walsh recommending Miller, and Woodward drove over to take a look. In the end both Miller and his younger brother, Myron, nicknamed Mick, attended UW–Madison, and both boxed for the Badgers in the 1943 tournament—Don at 155 pounds, Mick at 165 pounds.

Don Miller would go on to have one of the most distinguished careers, outside the ring, of any Badger boxer. After the 1943 tournament, Miller graduated the UW and joined the U.S. Army. He was sent to Europe, where he won the Silver Star, two Purple Hearts, and the hand of Katherine Juliano, whom he met while she was singing with the Glenn Miller Orchestra in a U.S.O. show for the troops. They'd eventually have two daughters.

Miller would spend twenty-six years in the army—rising eventually to colonel—and secure a reputation as a blunt, no-nonsense administrator, who, on retiring, was grabbed up by the United States Olympic Committee (USOC). Miller served the USOC as a fundraiser for four years and then, in 1973, he became executive director, a post he held twelve years. In the days before Miller, Olympic fundraising consisted of little more than selling one-dollar lapel pins. The USOC budget in 1969 was around two hundred and fifty thousand dollars. By the time he left, the annual budget was twenty-two million dollars. Miller shepherded the USOC through the difficult 1980 boycott of the Moscow Games by the United States and helped make the 1984 Games in Los Angeles a success, at the same time negotiating a piece of the profits—a revolutionary concept—for the USOC. The figure turned out to be about one million dollars. The great sprinter Jesse Owens signed a picture for Miller with the following inscription: "To the greatest man we've ever had in the Olympics. I'm proud to be counted as a friend." Through it all Miller smoked cigarettes, and in 1994 he was diagnosed with lung cancer. Miller died two years later, at seventy-five.

Miller almost didn't box in the 1943 tournament. He wasn't in the line-up until Wednesday of tournament week—the quarterfinals started Thursday—and he got in when Chuck Kidd, the Badgers' 155-pound representative, went out on what the *Capital Times* called "a scholastic technicality." The paper's sports editor, Casserly wrote: "The change doesn't materially weaken the Badgers, although Kidd was a rip-roaring battler, while Miller is more adept as a boxer."

Miller won his quarterfinal bout against Marvin Crowley of Superior State Teachers College. Miller knocked Crowley to the canvas in the first round—"to win the round by a country mile," Casserly noted—and then hung on for the decision. Miller's semifinal decision over Billy Richards of Penn State was regarded as an upset and the Badger was an underdog going into the 155-pound final, against Mike Melson of Washington State.

That final was the bout Walsh would remember as a classic. Casserly, writing that night in the *Capital Times* (the city's best boxing writer, the *State Journal's* McCormick, was by March 1943 off to war), did not give the impression of a man who had witnessed one of the greatest college bouts of all time.

Casserly noted that Melson was favored and that Miller had scored a clean cut upset. "Miller boxed nicely, spearing his foe with lefts and an occasional right, as Melson, tense as a bow string, couldn't get started. Melson didn't score a solid punch in the first round and appeared in a fog as Miller continued to outbox him, peppering his foe with lefts and looping rights. Miller won the first two rounds and the third was even, Melson emerging from the fog to score with a few rights, with Miller always on top with his better brand of boxing."

That last phrase may be the key to why Walsh remembered the fight as a classic. In Miller, he had found his ultimate tactician, a smart fighter who used strategy more than strength. Miller himself said, "I had the greatest trepidation about that particular match. I think in all considerations it was the toughest match because of his reputation and one thing and another, and it did take the development of certain skills and so forth to work with him effectively, much of which I attribute, of course, to John Walsh and Vern Woodward in preparing me for that match."

Walsh had studied film of Washington State and drew up a defensive game plan for Miller that worked to perfection. Miller scored points with his blocking and weaving and those boxing proponents who said that in some fundamental ways boxing could be compared to a chess match found in Miller their champion.

No doubt Miller's victory on points was well earned, but the Field House crowd in 1943 was doing its best in all cases to get the scorekeeper to see thing the Badgers' way. Indeed, some former Badger champions were in the crowd. Sitting shoulder to shoulder at ringside were the Badgers' very first national champion, Fadner, and the only college boxer to win three titles at the same weight, UW alum Rankin. Rankin in particular was vocal, calling out instruction to the Badger boxers as well as the referee. *Capital Times* columnist Sheer noted that Rankin was so loud he "now is accepting bids as either a hog-caller, sideshow barker or just plain foghorn."

If the past Badger stars were represented during tournament week in 1943, there was also, for those who knew where to look, a glimpse of the UW boxing future to be seen. On Wednesday of tournament week, before only a handful of interested onlookers, a half-hour sparring match took place in the Badger training quarters in the Field House. Dee Portal, the San Jose State coach, had stopped in Madison en route to his assignment in the navy (and Portal would eventually briefly coach the Badgers, when Walsh was away at war). Meanwhile, Portal's 1942 national champion at San Jose, Dick Miyagawa, was in Madison as well since he intended to enroll at the UW in June. Coach and pupil laced on the gloves that Wednesday afternoon and Sheer—whose *Cap Times*'s boxing column was called "The Punch Bowl"—said it was something to behold, noting:

"There was more leather flying around than the whole gang of tournament entries could produce in two days. It was classy boxing, hard punching and 'father, don't spare the rod.' Portal outweighed his former protege considerably and stood at least four inches taller, but the little 127 pounder stood toe-to-toe and slugged away giving as much as he took. Portal didn't pull any punches and Miyagawa didn't mind a bit."

Portal had come to Madison in part for the National Collegiate Boxing Coaches Association meeting and found himself elected president for the next year. Thursday night, only forty-five hundred fans showed up at the Field House for the 1943 quarterfinals. "Considering the difficulties facing the local committee," Casserly noted, referring to the war, that was still pretty good. Friday night's semifinals drew seven thousand and the Badgers established another record by advancing seven boxers to Saturday's finals. That was astonishing. Sheer noted that the other coaches for years had been threatening to mount an all-star team to take on the Badgers, and that's what the Saturday night draw resembled. Of the eight NCAA championship bouts, seven involved UW boxers. Only Fisk, at 120 pounds, had lost in a preliminary round.

Saturday night, the first Badger in the ring lost. Werren's defeat in a decision at 127 pounds was notable in that it marked the first of four NCAA titles for Chuck Davey of Michigan State. Badger Collentine was next and lost as well, to Dave Knight of Washington State at 135 pounds. But that was the end of the Wisconsin losses. The eleven thousand fans who turned up at the Field House saw the Badgers win the next five titles, starting with Lutz at 145 pounds, followed by Miller's upset win at 155 pounds; Miller's younger brother, Mick, at 165 pounds; Makris at 175 pounds, and heavyweight champion John.

The following week, the Wisconsin state Senate issued a resolution in praise of the Badgers and their 1943 season: "The most impressive performance of its kind in the history of collegiate boxing and tournament competition. These exciting and startling victories have resulted in nationwide applause and admiration of the team and the great individual performers and their competitive sportsmanship."

Speaking of sportsmanship, at the tournament John had captured the John S. LaRowe Trophy and said, "Thanks, there really should be eight of these, one for every champion."

Earlier, the war had been on John's mind when the Badger senior was asked to say a few words at the annual luncheon held in conjunction with the national tournament. Like it or not, the war was everywhere. John said, "If we can maintain the same fighting spirit we show inside and outside the ring, we can't help but come out on top of the Axis."

The annual boxing banquet, held the following week, again showed the impact of the war. Gibson, who won the Downer Memorial Trophy, had missed the tournament and was in San Antonio, Texas, with the Army Air Force when the award was announced. Walsh noted at the banquet that if Gibson hadn't been called up, there would have been a sixth national champion from Wisconsin that year. Gibson's father, UW Professor J. C. Gibson, accepted for his son at the ceremony at the Madison Club.

Walsh was little more than a year away from joining the service himself. The war, which had loomed large over the 1943 championships (one direct consequence was the allowing of freshmen into the tournament, which is how Davey and the UW's Mick Miller were able to box and win titles), would cause the suspension of the national tournament for three years.

Still, there was little doubt in anyone's mind that week in Madison that when the war was finally over, college boxing would return, and in a big way. Would it really be as big as it had been, or even bigger than ever? Time would tell, though the resumption of the tournament in 1947 would coincide with the first official rumblings against the sport on the Madison campus. Professor Walter Morton's criticisms would lead the UW administration to make a study of boxing and its appropriateness as a college sport.

That last week in March 1943, however, Casserly looked into the future and saw only roses: "When peace comes," Casserly wrote, "there is every indication that college boxing will become a major sport. More and more coaches are beginning to see the light regarding this he-man sport and the field will be combed for capable mentors. In fact there is liable to be a huge turnover of coaches when the boys and the younger men in the service are free to return to the coaching game. Boxing is spreading like wildfire and some of the strongest opponents to the sport have been won over and are ready to install the mitt game as an important part of the physical education program."

Even with Walsh gone and the NCAA tournament temporarily suspended, the Badger program kept going. The Badgers were unbeaten in

6 home matches in 1944, with attendance averaging about six thousand. Military training academies fielded teams and the next year, the Badgers dropped a home dual match for the first time in 51 starts. Iowa Pre-Flight prevailed 4½–3½.

According to *Badger Boxing Legend*, the magazine-style tribute to UW boxing put together in 1973 by Madison businessman George Holmes and sportswriter Bonnie Ryan, the following year was probably the leanest during the war period: "In 1945, during Walsh's first year in the service, the late Tom Kenneally, a CPO with the Navy Radio Training School at Wisconsin, and at one time a top-ranking professional heavyweight, was co-coach of the Badgers along with Vito Schiro, one of Wisconsin's best boxers several years before that."

Schiro, a Madison native, had competed in the 1936 NCAA tournament in Virginia, losing a first round bout.

In 1945, *Badger Boxing Legend* continued, "with only the Navy V-12 and radio trainees stationed on the campus, the available talent was meager and well below the usual Badger standards. The 1945 season record showed only two wins, two losses and three ties. The Navy transferred men so fast that the coaches, week to week, didn't know the talent available."

By 1946 the Iowa Pre-Flight team had moved its base from Iowa City to Ottumwa, Iowa. The Badgers were still looking for revenge when the two met in Madison in March. Still, how much bad blood could there be? The Iowa Pre-Flight coach in 1946 was none other than Woodward, the former Badger standout and assistant to Walsh, now serving in the Naval Reserves. The *State Journal*'s Hank McCormick, himself back from a stint in the navy, took the occasion of Woodward's homecoming to recall a ferocious knockdown the heavyweight had suffered at the hands of Ashby Dickerson of West Virginia. By 1946 Walsh, too, was back in Madison— Portal's one-year stint as coach was over. With the stars in that kind of alignment it figured that Wisconsin would win and the Badgers did, 5–2, before a crowd of thirteen hundred.

It also figured the next year that the 1947 NCAA tournament, scheduled for late March after a four-year war-related absence, would be held in Madison. The UW administrators knew how to put on the tournament and the fans in Madison would ensure good attendance. As much as anything, the return of *State Journal* sports editor Hank McCormick probably gave the first post-war tournament a chance for success.

Coughlin's rough hewn wit would always render the rustic columnist more fame and fans, but McCormick, by the late 1940s, had truly become the bard of UW boxing. Born in Madison, McCormick attended Madison High School (later Central) and graduated from UW–Madison in 1926. It was a toss-up whether football or boxing was his favorite sport. He joined the *State Journal* on graduating college and after a year on the police beat, McCormick became sports editor in 1927. His timing was pretty good. The campus intramural boxing tournaments were just beginning to draw crowds and Walsh's arrival in Madison was just a few years away. Walsh would find, in McCormick, his Boswell. Several decades later in Madison, another *State Journal* sports editor Glenn Miller would help turn the city onto college hockey. For boxing in the 1930s and 1940s, McCormick was the sage.

In August 1942 McCormick wrote a column that began, "This is 'Anchors Aweigh' for this writer." He had been called up by the navy for training in Virginia. He noted that he hated leaving Madison with fall approaching: "There is no more beautiful spot in the world than Madison on an October afternoon when the leaves are beginning to turn, when a soft haze floats through the air, and when the lakes toss back the sun's rays like mirrors."

McCormick and Walsh grew close enough that in that 1942 going away column, McCormick instructed readers with any complaints in his absence to see Walsh. "You may know Johnny as Wisconsin's boxing coach, but he's also my lawyer. I always figure that a guy like that will win for you one way or another. He always has for Wisconsin."

Both McCormick and Walsh were back in Madison for the 1947 resumption of the NCAA boxing tournament and the UW team did not disappoint as tournament week dawned. Seven Badger boxers were entered in a good field that included sixty fighters from seventeen schools.

It would be far from their best tournament performance, but the Badgers won the unofficial team championship with two individual titles and four boxers who finished runner-up. Lutz's win was unusual in that Lutz had actually lost in the quarterfinals to Dan Hickey of Michigan State, but Hickey's eye had been cut during the bout and when he couldn't box the next night, Lutz was substituted in. He decisioned Bob Anderson of San Jose State for the title.

Another oddity from the 1947 event in Madison: two of the boxers who won individual championships—one of them from Wisconsin—were destined to meet in the ring at the Field House less than two years later in what some observers would call the greatest single match in the history of the sport. The boxers were John Lendenski of Wisconsin and Herb Carlson of Idaho.

In the 1947 155-pound final, Carlson met Lendenski's Badger teammate, Dickinson, who Chuck Davey of Michigan State would later call his—Davey's—toughest opponent. Dickinson proved tough for Carlson, too—McCormick the next day called their bout a "savage melee"—but the decision went to Carlson. Lendenski, meanwhile, decisioned San Jose State's Wayne Fontes at 165 pounds. That was in 1947.

Now to that historic Carlson-Lendenski fight, some twenty-two months later. It was February 1949 and Carlson had moved up 10 pounds to 165 pounds, meaning that two past NCAA champions would be meeting when Idaho came to the Field House for a dual meet. There was a great deal riding on the match that night. Wisconsin had established another dual meet winning streak of twenty-one in a row, but if any team had a claim to be close to the Badgers as a college boxing power, it was the Vandals, whose boxers had over the years won eleven individual NCAA titles (compared to twenty-one for the Badgers). There was another streak of 21 straight wins on the line as well. Herb Carlson himself had that record going. Most likely one of those 21-straight streaks would be snapped. No wonder thirteen thousand fans showed up at the Field House to see what would happen.

The drama built as the evening progressed. Wisconsin had a 3–2 lead in the match when Carlson and Lendenski climbed into the ring.

Lendenski was from Pennsylvania, and had served in the Marine Corps during the war. He studied sociology at UW–Madison and later in life counseled kids who got in trouble. Carlson had been a bomber pilot during the war and later owned a sporting goods store in Idaho. Until getting in the ring in Madison that night with Lendenski, Carlson had never lost a match.

The Idaho fighter came out storming in the first round. His method in the ring was to mount such a ferocious offense that a defense was rendered unnecessary. You don't have to worry about keeping your chin down and hands up when your opponent is looking up from the canvas. Lendenski, in the Walsh pattern, was more of a boxer, willing to let his opponent tire himself and take his shots when an opening presented itself. As Carlson swung from the heels in the opening seconds of the bout, Lendenski, in McCormick's words, "measured him as methodically as a butcher going about his work."

Lendenski countered Carlson's offensive mainly with a series of left jabs that kept the Idaho fighter at least at arm's length. The crowd roared as the first round ended because it appeared the upset-minded Lendenski had a small lead on points. The bell sounded for the second round and somehow the crowd got louder. The noise, McCormick noted, "all but lifted off the Field House roof." In the corner between rounds, Walsh had praised Lendenski for staying away and using his left. But the Badger coach had also said he felt Carlson might be vulnerable to a hard inside right. Lendenski used his quick, punishing right hand in the second and

18. John Lendenski, who in 1949 fought what some observers say was the greatest college bout ever, against previously unbeaten Herb Carlson of Idaho. Lendenski won by TKO.

according to McCormick: "If you sat a few pews from ringside it didn't look like a hard punch, but up close you could see what it was doing to this tough Idaho boy."

In the middle of the round Lendenski followed a spearing left jab with a right cross that staggered Carlson enough that he fell backward, catching himself above the canvas with his hands. Still, referee John O'Donnell deemed it a knockdown.

The bell sounded to end the second, and Lendenski had furthered his lead, at least in the view of the raucous Madison crowd. (Portal, the San Jose State coach who spent a year at UW in Walsh's absence, had long suggested tallying the scores and announcing them at the end of each round. "In what other sport don't you know who's winning at halftime, or for that matter at any time during the contest?" Portal asked. It didn't happen, and McCormick, for one, was glad, noting that all the announcements would do was give fans three chances to boo and express their dissatisfaction with the scoring rather than just one.)

Carlson, though, was convinced he was behind, and he began the third round with a fury. In the face of that charge, McCormick said, Lendenski "was never better." He caught the advancing Carlson with a right that again staggered the Idaho boxer. This time O'Donnell's call was no knockdown, and the Badger crowd reacted angrily. "It's a cinch Carlson didn't stumble over a rose petal," McCormick noted tartly. But it was nearly over. "Carlson came back with renewed savagery," McCormick wrote, "and this time Lendenski brought over that right hand again. Carlson went down sprawling and Referee O'Donnell signaled the bout to be stopped." Carlson wasn't pleased, feeling he was fine to continue, but he showed some class later when asked about the fight. "I really got beat," he said of the technical knockout, his first loss in a college ring. "I didn't think it was a knockout, but I have only myself to blame."

A day or two later, with the benefit of hindsight, McCormick said it just may have been the greatest bout ever in the Field House. Every fan had to judge that for himself, McCormick noted, but Lendenski-Carlson had all anyone could ask: "There was sharp boxing, hard punching and cagey footwork. And there was impeccable sportsmanship."

Back in 1947 both Lendenski and Carlson had won individual titles. That year's team championship, won by the Badgers, was the last one that would be considered unofficial. The boxing booster club in Madison, known as the Madison Downtown Boxing Seconds, had purchased a trophy and proposed to the NCAA Boxing Rules Committee that it be named for Walsh and presented annually to the team champion. The committee liked the idea, and points toward the team total were designated in roughly the same way that the press had crowned a "mythical" champion in previous years: five points for winning an individual title; 3 points for winning a semifinal bout; and 1 point for each win leading up to the semifinals—since some weight divisions had more entrants, this was deemed fairer than giving a boxer defeated in the semifinals 1 point.

The following year, 1948, was an important year in college boxing for other reasons as well. It was an Olympic year—Walsh would be one of two coaches of the U.S. team that summer—and all individual NCAA champions would be invited to the Olympic trials. It was also the year that perhaps the first sustained voice questioning boxing as a proper collegiate pursuit was heard on the Madison campus, this despite the fact the NCAA tournament was once again slated for the Field House, in early April.

It was April 5, 1948—two days after the tournament concluded—that the UW Faculty Senate requested the UW Athletic Board "to furnish the Faculty with the facts pertaining to boxing as an intercollegiate sport." It was presumed the impetus had come from Walter Morton, a UW economics professor who had actually made a motion in the Faculty Senate to abolish boxing as a varsity sport. Morton later claimed he only made the motion because he had been urged to do so by a physician, a former UW Athletic Board member named Lorenz. Morton said Lorenz had too many close friendships with former boxers and others in athletic circles to dare be point man against the sport. "He did not want to take the initiative," Morton said, so the economics professor made the motion and took the heat. Sometime later, when this version of events was reported by *Capital Times* editor William T. Evjue, another UW physician, Dr. William J. Bleckwenn, who had served on various boxing committees and was close to Lorenz, said Morton was talking nonsense. Lorenz, Bleckwenn said, would not support abolishing boxing. Morton said Lorenz had kept his opposition from Bleckwenn. In any case it was Morton who went public with the motion and it was Morton who took tremendous heat from the powerful boxing lobby in Madison. In 1948, after all, the sport was at its zenith. Morton was roundly criticized in the letters columns of local newspapers. Still, he was not without some support. On April 21, 1948,

Morton got a letter from Alfred W. Swan at the First Congregational Church in Madison, who lamented the "out of proportion place boxing now holds in our university culture." Another medical school professor, physiologist Walter Meade, wrote Morton and noted, "Gene Tunney knew enough to get out of the game . . ."

Boxing people, the college coaches in particular, could sense the opposition marshalling its forces. Badger boxer Dick Miyagawa would recall a conversation he'd had with Portal, who coached him at San Jose State and later came to Madison for a year while Walsh was in the service. The most insistent and perhaps effective argument against boxing, Portal said, was that it was the only sport in which inflicting punishment on an opponent, indeed, knocking him to the ground, was the stated goal. Fans of boxing could point to the often brutal nature of football, and to the death, in 1944, of a UW player following an injury during a game at Camp Randall, but the boxing critics would not be swayed. As Arthur Steinhaus, dean of Chicago's George Williams College, told *Sports Illustrated*: "My feeling on football is that there are dangers in it, but in football if someone gets hurt both sides are sorry. In football it's a straight accident. In boxing it is part of the sport to injure the opponent. Boxing stands alone in that regard."

Either hearing or at least sensing that sentiment, Portal told Miyagawa he sometimes thought college boxing should change its rules to make the goal of a bout primarily defensive: draw a circle in the ring, perhaps, and award points for the amount of time a boxer holds onto that turf, in a version of the "king of the hill" game played by school children.

Portal never followed through on those musings, but his intuition was right. Boxing never did figure out a way to counter the "intent of the sport is to injure" argument.

There had, in fact, been an earlier study of boxing on campuses, one that was eventually ridiculed in *Sports Illustrated* magazine and not taken seriously by the boxing fraternity—at least not until it was almost too late. This was a 1940 study titled "The Evaluation of Boxing as a College Activity," published in the *Research Quarterly* by three members of the University of Illinois physical education department. It was based on questionnaires sent to both medical and athletic officials, and it was harshly critical of boxing and the number of "punch-drunk" former fighters the sport produced. Martin Kane of *Sports Illustrated* cited the study's contention that college bouts are "impossible to control" as proof of its sloppy scholarship—if nothing else, college boxing matches were closely officiated and indeed stopped at the first sign of trouble for either fighter. The professors had in fact asked questions and raised concerns related to *pro* boxing and then used the results, which were based only on opinion in any case, to impugn the sport at colleges. The study, not widely circulated when published, would be resurrected later when the abolishment argument became more serious.

When Morton made his motion in Madison in 1948, nobody was about to abolish boxing on campus, not then. What the Faculty Senate did do was pass the buck to the athletic board, asking them for the "facts" about boxing. The athletic board knew just enough to know it couldn't properly handle the assignment, and called in the deans of the medical school and the school of education for advice. The result: John W. Brown, professor

19. Walsh and Woodward discuss strategy in 1948. The two were good friends as well as coaching colleagues.

of preventive medicine and director of the Department of Student Health, was named to head the study of the medical aspects of boxing in college. Two professors from the Department of Education, A. S. Barr and C. W. Harris, would look at the scholastic aspects. Woodward, the former Badger heavyweight and now assistant coach to Walsh, would poll former boxers on their attitudes toward the sport and also list their achievements since leaving the program.

The scholastic aspect of the study was finished first. In that aspect of the report, dated July 1, 1949, Barr and Harris had two stated goals: to determine whether significant differences existed between the classroom performance of college boxers and a group of nonathletes on campus; and whether a difference existed between boxers and a mixed group of athletes. The study found that the nonathletes achieved a slightly higher average grade point than the boxers but the boxers scored a small percentage higher than the group of mixed athletes.

Woodward's study of the accomplishments of former boxers and their subsequent attitudes toward the sport on campus, was dated May 29, 1950. Ninety-two former boxers responded to the mailed questionnaire. Four of the former boxers had gone on to box professionally. Sixty-nine of the ninety-two earned university degrees. All ninety-two respondents, Woodward reported, said they felt that boxing was a worthwhile college sport, though more than half felt the pro game was dangerous. Ten felt boxing aroused "undesirable emotions" in spectators at the matches.

A portion of the medical aspect of the study had the same 1950 date as Woodward's report. In its report, the medical team said it had used the boxing seasons of 1949 and 1950 and scrutinized 188 bouts involving 376 contestants. The matches included the UW dual meet season, the Northwest Intercollegiate tournament and the NCAA tournament in both years.

For what physicians believed to be the first time, electroencephalograms, or brain scans, were performed on 135 boxers immediately following their bouts. Of the 135, 19 had been dazed during their fights, and 2 had been momentarily unconscious. None of scans proved abnormal. (The study also noted that 12 former UW boxers had volunteered to have the scans, and all those proved normal, as well.)

The doctors wrote: "In the experience of the observers there were no episodes during which a contestant received a series of hard blows to the head after becoming dazed or unable to defend himself. Contests were stopped quickly when a hazard of this kind developed. Blows which resulted in the knockdown of an opponent were infrequent."

The Wisconsin study physicians also fired a shot directly over the bow of the University of Illinois 1940 survey when they noted: "Various aspects of the controversy relating to the acceptability of boxing for the collegiate athletic program have been studied. . . . All are deficient in factual information of real value. The lack of information on the changes in the brain as a result of boxing, especially college boxing, is a handicap. Many theses have been based upon information obtained from questionnaires which were sent to interested officials, pathologists, physicians of experience and others. Most investigators will agree that the use of questionnaires is not a satisfactory method for obtaining reliable data. This is undoubtedly especially true of an area of popular interest, such as boxing, where opinions are so likely to be of influence."

The doctors conceded that their study could not shed light on any cumulative, long-term effects of boxing on the brain. With that caveat, the medical report concluded that its study indicated "that acute injuries of serious nature do not occur frequently during boxing in college under the supervision of the NCAA."

The athletic board's recommendation came down squarely in favor of continuing the sport at Wisconsin: "It is believed there will always be differences of opinion regarding the desirability of intercollegiate boxing, and the relation of the sport to the cultural standards of the University. . . . In keeping with the principles of the University, it is believed that intercollegiate boxing is being conducted in an exemplary manner. It is possible that the conduct of intercollegiate boxing at Wisconsin may lead to general progress in the sport."

Reaction to the report was predictably mixed. Walsh liked it so much he included an edited version of it as the last chapter of his 1951 book, *On Boxing*. Morton, whose motion in the Faculty Senate had led to the study and the report, called it a farce.

The report had been commissioned on the heels of the 1948 NCAA tournament, the fourth national championship event to be held in Madison and the last until 1952. The 1948 tournament may have been the most memorable of all—the total attendance was 49,800, an all-time NCAA record, and the Badger team's performance led observers to remark that if any UW team stood up against the "greatest ever" squad of 1939, the 1948 team might be it.

The 1948 Badgers were undefeated in 6 dual meets and sent seven boxers to the early April tournament. All seven won their quarterfinals bouts at the Field House Thursday night and four—Steve Gremban, Dickinson, Cal Vernon and Vito Parisi—won national championships Saturday night. The new official team point competition showed the Badgers with 45 points, a knockout by any measure, as second place Michigan State tallied nineteen points.

Vernon, at 176 pounds, was the first African American to win an NCAA championship. Vernon came to Madison from Milwaukee Lincoln High School, later known for its outstanding state champion basketball teams, and he played halfback for the Badger football team. In the 1948 tournament, Vernon opened Thursday with the quickest knockout of the day—sixty-six seconds over George Smith of Michigan State. He faced Ralph Shoaf of Virginia in the semifinals, "a tough, game and dangerous foe" in McCormick's estimation. Vernon took the early lead in the bout, coasted a bit in the second round and then came out blazing in the third, catching Shoaf with a short right uppercut to the jaw that sent the Virginia fighter to the canvas. The referee stopped the fight. In the Saturday night final, Vernon won a unanimous decision over William Diehl of Idaho when the fight was stopped one minute into the third round when a cut opened over Vernon's eye. Under the college rules, Vernon suffered no penalty because he was the one cut, and the decision went his way since all judges had him ahead on their cards.

After Vernon's semifinal victory on Friday night, McCormick called him "the most devastating puncher the tournament has produced." He eventually took that aggressiveness into another arena for on graduating, Vernon enrolled in law school and later became a practicing attorney in Chicago.

"That was my dad's influence," Vernon told me when we spoke early in 2003. "He said I always seemed to have an excuse for everything, so I should be lawyer."

While Vernon spent his senior year in high school in Milwaukee, he actually grew up in Mason City, Iowa. Out of high school he joined the navy, traveled to several bases, and at the one in Pensacola, Florida, he first put on boxing gloves. He had no real training for the ring. As much as any Badger boxer ever, Vernon was a natural.

"One day in Florida someone on the base asked if I wanted to participate in a smoker," Vernon said. "I didn't know what it was." It was a boxing match. Vernon liked it, but he still felt football was his sport. Out of the navy he came to UW–Madison, and it was on a football practice field that Makris, who himself had both played football and boxed at UW, asked Vernon if he might want to come out for the boxing team.

"Count me in," Vernon said.

In the ring, few were tougher. "I wasn't a boxer," Vernon told me. "I ran over people like a lawnmower."

I asked him if race was ever an issue. "We didn't travel south much," Vernon replied. "Our road trips were west and I never really had a problem."

There were some small incidents. At the 1948 NCAA tournament in Madison, Vernon said, a Southern boxer whom he might have met in the

20. Cal Vernon was the first African-American boxer to win a national championship. Later an attorney in Chicago, Vernon also played halfback on the Badger football team.

semifinals came up to him after the quarters and said, "I'm glad I lost. I told my mother I would never get in the ring with a Negro." Vernon shrugged it off. He'd heard worse on the football field.

Vernon actually felt his race gave him an edge. "Vito Parisi told me I had an advantage just by taking my robe off. There were no other blacks out there." Then, too, of the blacks who were known in boxing, like the professional heavyweight champion Joe Louis, many were regarded with awe if not actual fear.

In his semifinal bout against Shoaf of Virginia, Vernon recalled Shoaf saying, "I don't care what color your are. You are in for a boxing match tonight."

More than a half-century later, Vernon chuckled and said, "He was right. He was tough." But Vernon won the bout.

Of the cut that stopped his fight in the 176-pound final, Vernon said his opponent, Diehl of Idaho, had head-butted him. The decision went to Vernon.

Vernon eventually turned pro and had a number of fights before turning to the law. He recalled that Walsh had tried to talk him out of it but Vernon had later gone to dinner with Woodward and Woodward had said, "You're good enough. If you want it, do it." Vernon would eventually become the fifteenth ranked light-heavyweight in the world, and spar with Ezzard Charles and Archie Moore. "I got fan mail from Australia," he said.

Besides Vernon, the other Badger champions in 1948 included Dickinson at 147 pounds and Gremban at 118 pounds. But the most memorable fight of the tournament, a stunning upset and one of the most talked-about bouts of all time in college boxing, came when Wisconsin heavy-weight Vito Parisi met Art Seay of Miami.

Parisi was a Madison kid whose dad ran a saloon on the city's near west side. Parisi went to West High School, just up Regent Street from the Field House. I reached Parisi in Aurora, Colorado, in the late summer of 2002, and he recalled sneaking into the matches at the Field House before he himself became a Badger boxer. Parisi had boxed in the Contender's tournament on campus in 1944 when he was seventeen, after that he entered the service. The 1948 season was the only full year Parisi boxed for the Badgers (though he fought in some dual meets in 1950). He told me he let himself get out of shape after that and, of course, after April 1948 what could he do for an encore?

Parisi's quarterfinal opponent Thursday night was Art Hughlett of Michigan State. Henry McCormick's younger brother, Monte McCormick, now a *State Journal* sportswriter himself, said, "this was a battle in which there were no dull moments as both boys mixed freely and willingly." McCormick called the decision, which went to Parisi, "clear cut." In the semifinals Parisi faced Don Schaeffer of San Jose State. Again a facial cut wound up going the Badgers' way when Schaeffer started bleeding thirty-three seconds into the second round and the fight was stopped with Parisi ahead on points. The stage was then set for the Saturday night heavyweight final, the Badgers' Parisi against fearsome Seay of Miami. It was a bout for the ages.

More than half a century later, sportswriter Tom Butler told me: "People who were there will tell you that to this day, that's the loudest they ever heard the Field House."

21. Vito Parisi, a Madison kid who boxed for the Badgers, pulled off one of the great upsets in tournament history when he beat fearsome Art Seay of Miami for the national championship. Fans said it was the loudest they had ever heard the Field House.

Butler was there. His wife to be went with him—she had been a West High School classmate of Parisi's. Of course the Field House was packed and buzzing as loud as it ever had. The only attendance question may have been whether Parisi would show to take on the fearsome Seay. Butler recalled: "Vito Schiro told me Walsh had assigned him to make sure Parisi showed up that night." When we spoke in 2002, Parisi recalled meeting both Schiro, himself a former Badger boxer, and Chuck Davey early that day at the Field House. Parisi didn't know Schiro had been tabbed as his shadow but he talked to both of the veterans about how he might best fight Seay. "They were both southpaws," Parisi told me, "and they said use the left, use the left."

Of course, Walsh had always called the left hook a boxer's best friend. The night of the finals Schiro brought Parisi into the locker room and presented him to Walsh. "John, here he is. He's yours now." Butler again: "That fight proved to me what a great coach Walsh was. He told him how to handle Seay."

Parisi, more than half a century later, told me he couldn't remember much of the now classic fight. "I do remember the Field House was louder than I ever heard it." Butler said that when Seay took off his robe, the women in the audience went crazy. "He was an Adonis. From Miami and it looked like he spent most of his spare moments at the beach. The Field House was rocking."

Hank McCormick, writing that night, was in agreement. "That was the bout that brought one of the most ear-splitting roars you've ever heard in the Field House, for Seay had been reckoned virtually a certain winner. However, Parisi not only outpointed Seay but did it so decisively that there was no possible room for doubt. Fighting a perfectly charted battle, Parisi stabbed Seay with long lefts, then cuffed him soundly on the chin with looping rights." Both fighters were exhausted at the end. With the final bell they congratulated one another and then each lay on the ropes for several seconds, too tired to move to their corners.

The announcement of the decision for Parisi brought a sustained roar that became even more deafening when the Badger heavyweight was sent back into the ring to receive the team trophy. For UW there were four individual titles—Parisi, Vernon, Dickinson, and Gremban—and its fifth team championship in the eleven years the tournament had been held. Walsh would say that in his estimation the 1948 team, while not the equal of the 1939 team in talent and accomplishment, may have been his favorite. "I'm probably prouder of this bunch of kids than any I've ever had because I think they have done so much better than anyone had any right to expect of them."

Walsh had been named co-coach of the American boxing team for the 1948 Olympics. John Mendoca was the other. Walsh may have hoped and expected some of his Badgers to travel with him to London, but it was not to be. At the tryouts in Boston, in late June, Gremban, Dickinson, and Vernon all lost. Davey, the great Michigan State boxer and friendly rival of Walsh, lost as well.

Walsh's 1948 Olympic experience was a mixed bag. The games were held in London, and Walsh spent two months overseas, leaving in late June and returning the end of August. He returned full of praise for the experience and the overall spirit of the Olympic Games, but no American boxer won a gold medal. Walsh felt the fact that the tryouts had been conducted using AAU rules hurt the Americans. Using collegiate rules in the tryouts, collegiate rules being nearer to those used in the Olympics, might have had the American squad better prepared. As it was no college boxer made the team. The officiating itself, Walsh said on getting back to Madison, was desperately uneven.

"Many of the judges didn't know the rules or interpreted them differently," Walsh said. "One referee would let you do everything but bite while another would warn you if you looked cross."

Walsh continued, "One of our boys was fighting in a bout that had a Spanish referee. I was standing in our corner chewing gum, when the referee suddenly pointed at me and made the sign to indicate I was to cease coaching. He had seen my mouth moving and thought I was coaching."

Still, Walsh was proud of his team and the Olympics in general. "The sportsmanship among the competitors was of the highest order. They were even stricter on such things as in-fighting and butting than we are in college bouts. For harmony and fostering finer international relations, the games were wonderful."

Walsh was in Ireland, after the games, when word reached him that his law office required his immediate presence in Madison. Walsh and his Olympic boxers had traveled to Dublin for 2 matches against an Irish team. The Americans won them both, 6–2, but Walsh would later laugh about taking a team to his home country: the referee for the matches was named, like the coach, Walsh. "The Irish heavyweight was also named Walsh," he recalled.

The coach had sailed for Europe the previous June aboard the *SS America*, but in August the legal business required he fly home. His plane, a four-engine Constellation, almost didn't make it. "We started on an air trip from Dublin to Shannon, and about 75 miles out, one of the motors conked out completely. I was sitting right where I could see the motor die. We limped back to Dublin and it didn't make me feel very good to see the ambulances and fire trucks lined up in case of a crash." He finally made it to New York and a train brought him to Madison in time for his legal emergency and for the start of the 1948–49 school year.

It would not be the Badgers' best season, not by any means. But the 1949 season did bring the first appearance in the ring of a boxer who would become one of the Badgers' best, a raw but talented heavyweight from Wyoming. His name was Bob Ranck.

"Cody was a cowboy town," Ranck said when we spoke in the fall of 2002. "Cowboys did a lot of fighting." He was in Madison for a reunion of the 1952 Badgers and visiting with his old teammates seemed to spark a flood of memories.

"I was always boxing," Ranck said. "As a little kid my dad would get down on his knees in the living room and we would get the gloves on." That continued into high school. Ranck's high school football coach, Bill Waller—ninety-one years old as of fall 2002—had been an assistant football coach at the University of Illinois before coming to Wyoming. At the small Cody high school Waller was also the basketball coach, and he was a boxing buff.

"At halftime of the basketball games," Ranck said, "he'd have a boxing show. I was always in it. After the half I'd run down and change back into my basketball uniform." Ranck recalled boxing at all the service clubs around Cody. "Anytime there was a boxing show going on I was part of it."

One of the most important shows came Ranck's junior year in high school when some promoters from Denver came to Cody and announced a Wyoming-Montana Golden Gloves championship. There was a training session every evening after dinner for two weeks leading up to the event. The promoters told Waller, Ranck's coach, "This kid can box." Waller agreed, and so did everyone else after Ranck won all of his three Golden Gloves bouts by knockout.

Waller, remembering his years at Illinois, said to Ranck: "I think you have some real talent. Have your heard about the boxing program at the University of Wisconsin?"

Ranck had not. College wasn't really on his radar screen. "My dad was a barber," he said. "Twenty-five cents a haircut. He couldn't send me to college." But one day Waller, Ranck, and Ranck's dad were in the barber shop talking and Waller again brought up Wisconsin. The shop didn't have a phone so they walked around the corner to the Cody sporting goods store and Waller placed a call to Madison. He reached Walsh.

"I've got a kid here who I think can fight."

"Send him along," Walsh said.

22. Bob Ranck, a heavyweight from Wyoming, excelled against fighters who later had successful pro careers. Ranck himself went into law and became a judge.

There was no scholarship, but there was a promise of a job. Ranck got a ride to Madison from a Midwesterner who had summered in Cody. Ranck was dropped at the Park Hotel on Madison's Capitol Square. He had twenty dollars in his wallet and a heart that was pounding in his chest. He was seventeen and knew nobody. Woodward, the kindly Badger assistant, came by the next morning and took Ranck over to John and Audrey Walsh's place near the Field House.

"I had never really had quality boxing training," Ranck said. "John Walsh opened my eyes. He wasn't bossy, but neither did he equivocate. He was particular about how you did things."

They worked on technique: "I was throwing my left hook with my thumb down," Ranck said. "That's how Jack Dempsey did it. Walsh said that was a fine way to break your thumb."

Ranck's first college bout came in the Badgers' first match of the 1949 season, at Penn State. The Nittany Lions had a fearsome heavyweight, Chuck Drazenovich, who would later play pro football for the Washington Redskins. In 1949 he was the EIC heavyweight champ and Ranck went to State College knowing Drazenovich outweighed him by nearly 50 pounds.

"I was 178 and he was maybe 225 and this was a fight I was supposed to get shellacked in," Ranck said.

The day of the match, Walsh and Ranck happened to be walking into the locker room together when a car drove up near the door. "This guy pulled up in Hudson," Ranck recalled. "He hops out and he has fancy clothes and an air about him. I asked Walsh, 'Who's that?' He said, 'That's the guy you're fighting.'"

In the locker room Ranck sat down on one of the benches that were bolted to the floor in front of the lockers. He looked over and saw Drazenovich sitting on a similar bench across the room. The Penn State boxer was reading a letter.

Ranck walked over and said, "Hi, Chuck. I'm Bob Ranck."

"Who?" Drazenovich said.

A half-century later, Ranck still remembered his reaction. "That upset me."

So Ranck replied, "I'm the guy who is going to whip your butt tonight."

Ranck did win the fight and the Badgers beat Penn State 6–2. They went on to have an undefeated dual meet record—drawing fifteen thousand people to the Field House for the final match, against San Jose State, on April 1—but the 1949 NCAA tournament proved disastrous for the Badgers.

The tournament was held in East Lansing and for the first time in their history, the Badgers entered boxers into an NCAA tournament and came away without a single national champion. Only one Badger made it so far as the semifinals: Dickinson, who made it to the 145-pound final where he lost to the host school's Chuck Davey. For Ranck, the news was even worse. For him the end of the decade brought news that he was scholastically ineligible for the 1950 season. "I was stupid," Ranck said. "I thought I was just supposed to win every fight. I flunked out."

It was a bitter pill for the heavyweight sensation, who would return to Wyoming and spend a semester at the University of Wyoming, getting his grades in shape so he could return to Madison. Ranck would eventually do just that, and become a good enough student to attend law school. In time he would become a distinguished district judge. But as the new decade dawned, Badger boxing was in as uncertain shape as it had been since Walsh came to town in the early '30s. The coach felt confident he could turn it around, and he did. There were plenty of glory days ahead. No one could have guessed that darker days also lay not so far ahead, days that would threaten the very existence of boxing on college campuses.

chapter 5

THE FIFTIES

The decade began inauspiciously. Worse than that, really. The Badgers went up to Minnesota on February 11, 1950, and sustained their first dual meet defeat since 1945, when the Iowa Pre-Flight service team dusted UW 5–3. The Gophers' 4½–3½ win ended a string of 28 straight dual matches without a loss. "They were up for the match and we weren't as sharp as we could have been," Walsh said. "They deserved to win."

There was one bright spot. Joe Hendrickson, covering the match for the *Minneapolis Tribune,* was greatly taken by the Badger fighting his first college bout for the red and white at 165 pounds. "The Badgers had the consolation of defeating a national intercollegiate champion," Hendrickson wrote. "Dick Murphy, a battling Irishman, scored a tremendous upset in the 165 pound class when he piled up an early lead and decisioned Minnesota's Cody Connel, who won the NCAA crown the previous spring in East Lansing."

Murphy came from Milwaukee. The Golden Gloves were big there when Murphy was growing up but his parents didn't want him to have anything to do with boxing. He could run track, that was fine, but boxing was out, or so his parents decreed. It was out for Murphy but it was not out for Patrick O'Reilly, the name of a pal that Murphy borrowed for his young ring career. The fake name was in case he won something and wound up in the newspaper. He won all right and the trouble turned out to be not with the newspaper but with the Golden Gloves official summoned to present "O'Reilly" his winning medal. This same gentleman had presented Murphy a track medal the previous spring. "They caught me," Murphy recalled. His parents were notified and, perhaps because he was winning and none the worse for wear, finally gave their permission for him to continue boxing.

It was at a later Golden Gloves tournament that Murphy caught the eyes of Walsh and Woodward, who regularly scouted the Gloves for possible college talent. "They asked if I'd be interested in coming to UW," Murphy recalled. This was the late 1940s and Murphy wasn't sure. School had not fascinated him. He waffled. Eventually Murphy joined the armed services and when he got out he went to work for the phone company. Still, Woodward had never lost touch. "I want you to come to Madison," Woodward said. This time Murphy said yes.

23. Dick Murphy was a national champion from Milwaukee. Years later, Murphy would host reunions of the boxing teams at his home in Madison.

"John and Vern really took an interest in you," Murphy recalled fifty years later. "At the time I'm sure I didn't appreciate it, but they cared about you. They cared that you do well in school. They insisted that you do the work. The same was true with boxing. They had a great training program. They knew if you weren't in shape you weren't going to win."

After his stunning upset at Minnesota in his first bout, Murphy and the Badgers came back to Madison the next week to face Idaho. Walsh moved Murphy up to 165 pounds, and the young fighter knew exactly what that meant. He would be facing Herb Carlson, Idaho's two-time national champion. Murphy remembers being extremely nervous before the bout. Exactly how nervous? Sitting on a bench in the locker room, Murphy realized he had taped his hands before putting on his boxing shorts and shoes. He muttered to himself, "What the hell am I doing?" Carlson could do that to people. Carlson's Field House loss to UW's Lendenski one year earlier remained one of the great bouts and most stunning upsets in college boxing history. Carlson did not want to lose in Madison again—and he didn't. Carlson beat Murphy, one of only two times Murphy would lose in the Field House in his career.

The Badgers fared better as a team, besting Idaho 5–3. But the 1950 dual meet season would be remembered as one of Walsh's worst. On the heels of losing at Syracuse on March 3, the Badgers came home to face Michigan State a week later and the truly unthinkable happened. For the first time ever, after 74 home matches, the Badgers were defeated in a dual meet at home.

The Spartans came to Madison undefeated and would have been favored on form; only the aura of invincibility the Badgers had attained in winning 71 matches and tying 2 in the past two decades at home cast Michigan State in less than the favorite's role. The Spartan coach knew the Field House well. George Makris was a student of Walsh and a national champion for the Badgers in the early 1940s. Makris knew every rafter in the Field House.

It was an exciting match. After 7 bouts it was tied at 3½. Only the heavyweight bout remained—the Badgers' Parisi against the Spartans' Gabriel "Gabby" Marek. The first round was even but then thirty-six seconds into the second round Marek threw a hard right hand that landed on Parisi's jaw and knocked him down. The referee, Johnny Tighe, stood over Parisi and when the count reached seven the Badger struggled to his feet. But it was over. Walsh called to Tighe to stop the bout and he did.

"We were tough," Walsh said. "But we weren't quite tough enough."

Flush with his record-smashing win, Makris said only, "It was a great match. A great match."

The Badgers ended the season with a losing dual meet record of 3–4. "It is a case of the law of averages catching up and taking its full measure," wrote Harry Golden in The *Capital Times*. The season final, a 5–3 win over DePaul, drew only nine thousand fans and Golden used his column to scold fans for grumbling. Maybe everyone had been a bit spoiled by Walsh's success. So overwhelming was that success that as the teams gathered in State College, Pennsylvania, for the 1950 NCAA tournament, no one was yet counting out the Badgers.

Henry McCormick was there for the tournament and noted that Walsh "has been 'The Champ' too long for them to be thoroughly convinced that he won't be a factor in the tournament."

24. The atmosphere in the Field House for Badger boxing was electric. Coach John Walsh said the local fire department had once threatened to stop the matches unless the crowd sizes could be contained.

The Badgers had four fighters entered in the event, which began March 30. Of them, Murphy at 155 pounds was viewed as probably having the best title shot. Murphy saw himself as a counter-puncher, a stylist rather than a home run puncher, and the referee of his last dual meet bout against DePaul, Kenneally, assessed him the same way:

"Murphy didn't get hit once in all three rounds against his DePaul opponent. The boy weaves away from 90 percent of the punches thrown his way. He also has a fine two-fisted attack that scores heavily. When he punches with both hands to the body he gives his college opponents plenty of grief."

Murphy, who would go on to a very successful career as an executive with the Miller Brewing Company in Wisconsin, always said that his toughest opponents were usually the guys he sparred with during Walsh's practices. Murphy and Ranck, the great heavyweight, came out early for practices. In the first weeks of a new season Walsh only required first- year boxers attend, but Murphy and Ranck figured the extra work might give them an edge. They were frequent sparring partners and developed a large mutual admiration. Fifty years later, they remained the closest of friends.

During the substandard 1950 dual match season Murphy had brought a smile to everyone's face on St. Patrick's Day when he wore a green necktie under his robe for the match in Pullman against Washington State. Walsh, Irish to the bone, laughed harder than anyone but asked "Murph" to remove it before his fight with Milt Wilson, whom Murphy beat. Murphy had to remove the necktie, but he kept the green shamrocks he had drawn on the side of his boxing shoes.

If Murphy looked like the Badger with perhaps the best 1950 title shot at the NCAA tournament in State College, the least likely Badger had to be Ted Kozuszek at 165 pounds. Perhaps for that reason, McCormick, covering the event for the *Wisconsin State Journal,* took a special interest in him. Kozuszek, a senior from Peshtigo, Wisconsin, best known around the state for the devastating fire in the early years of the century, had been a last minute addition to the Badger contingent when co-captain Dwaine Dickinson decided not to make the trip. Dickinson had a good excuse: the week before his wife had given birth to an eight-pound baby girl. The girl was born on a Friday afternoon; that night Dickinson knocked out DePaul's Bill Conrad twenty-four seconds into the second round. But going down the street for a Field House bout was one thing. Dickinson passed on going to Pennsylvania for the NCAAs.

Kozuszek drew a bye into the semifinals at State College. That was the good news. The bad news was he had to face the winner of the Raul Diez-Herb Carlson quarterfinal bout, almost certainly Carlson. Sure enough, on Thursday Carlson decisioned Diez, of San Jose State, 3–0. Carlson, of course, was the two-time defender, the Idaho fighter who had given Murphy his only loss of the year earlier in Madison (Murphy dropped a weight class before the tournament). But Kozuszek was not in awe of Carlson. McCormick was lounging around his hotel Friday morning when he ran into the Wisconsin team physician, John Bentley, and the subject of that night's Carlson-Kozuszek bout came up.

"He told me that he's going to beat Carlson," Bentley said. "And I don't think he's just talking. If I ever saw a boy that was thoroughly convinced that he's going to win, it's Kozuszek." McCormick was intrigued enough to seek out the Badger boxer and hear for himself.

"He is better than I am," Kozuszek said. "I figure if we fight 25 times, he beats me 24. But this is one fight and I have a feeling."

McCormick walked away impressed with Kozuszek's confidence. It was more than that. McCormick had never heard a boxer express such quiet determination. The sports editor was still marveling at it when he ran into Ike Deeter, the coach of Washington State. Part of the fun of the NCAA tournament week was renewing old friendships with members of the fight game you may only see once or twice a year.

"Kozuszek has no more business beating Carlson than I do," McCormick said. "But I have never seen a boy as calmly confident. The one thing I do know about him is that when they measured him for heart they gave him the biggest one in the place. And I know they didn't short-change Carlson when it came to the ticker equipment." McCormick paused and asked Deeter: "What do you think?"

"Don't sell your kid short," the Washington State coach said. "I have been at these tournaments a long time and one thing I have learned is never to underestimate a boy's own estimate of himself. That kid of yours is as game as they come, and boys that are toughest to beat in tournaments are these tough, game kids who are sure they can win."

He very nearly pulled it off. "In this writer's book," McCormick wrote late that night, "Kozuszek won from Carlson, but that's not how the officials saw it." All three scorers had Carlson the victor. But McCormick was unswayed: "Kozuszek went in there against Carlson Friday night, and it was a tough battle from the start. He was hitting Carlson with rights and lefts, and he was brushing off Carlson's counters as though they carried no sting when anybody who knows Carlson will tell you that the Idaho boy with the icy blue eyes hits with extreme authority."

The day of the Kozuszek-Carlson fight, Friday, papers around the country carried a small item from the AP that said the NCAA Boxing Rules Committee would begin an investigation "of all aspects of college boxing." The story read: "The investigation will enlarge upon a two-year study conducted by Wisconsin physicians which has disclosed no harmful effects of boxing."

The announcement came from UW's Dr. Bleckwenn, who had been named chair of the committee the year before. Bleckwenn, who had served on General Douglas MacArthur's staff during World War II, liked boxing well enough. The study was as much as anything a pre-emptive strike against those who would condemn it. The Wisconsin study had shown no serious side effects from boxing and the NCAA "expansion" of that study would produce similar results. What is important in hindsight is that the NCAA thought an expansion of the Wisconsin study was necessary at all. A UW football player had actually died on the field at Camp Randall in the 1940s and no one suggested an investigation into all aspects of football. "The stigma of boxing has always been there," Murphy said. He remembered undergoing brain wave tests after sparring in practice. "Always negative," he said. "But the stigma is that the purpose of boxing is to hurt someone. That's not really true."

At State College, for the first time, no Badger made it to the finals of the NCAA tournament. It said something for the Badger fans that when the annual year-end boxing banquet was held the next week in Madison, the crowd at the Park Hotel on Madison's Capitol Square was the largest ever. There were too many people for the banquet room and many attendees wound up in the Park Hotel's regular dining area. It prompted Walsh to go to the microphone and proclaim, not for the first time, that UW had the greatest fans in the country.

It was a big night for Murphy. The Milwaukee native won the Downer Memorial Trophy signifying progress during the season and the highest standards of sportsmanship. Murphy was also named captain for 1951. Parisi "won" the "chin up and hands down" award and got a laugh when he said he was glad he wouldn't be back the next year to go for three in a row. Jollymore, the former NCAA champion, keynoted the banquet and paid tribute to Walsh: "Johnny is the greatest coach in the country and the best guy. I would rather have been a third stringer at Wisconsin than a national champion at any other school."

Walsh began the 1951 season determined to bounce back from the disappointment of the year before. The great heavyweight, Ranck, was back after getting his grades in order in Wyoming. Murphy was strong and getting stronger. They were the anchors.

Arriving on campus that year was a kid who was about as green as any future national champion could be. Bob Morgan grew up in Duluth, Minnesota, part of a strangely amalgamated family that had both a lot of love and a lot of dysfunction. Morgan was raised by his grandmother, a strong and remarkable woman, and her son (Bob's uncle), an alcoholic who talked to chickens and hunted rats with a shotgun when in his cups.

25. Bob Morgan, a national champion in 1951, spoke about how much boxing had meant to him at a Downtown Rotary Club meeting in Madison 50 years later. Morgan also became a published author.

One night, World War II had just ended, young Morgan picked up the Duluth newspaper and noticed that there were going to be tryouts for an all-city boxing tournament at the YMCA. "Everyone is welcome," the article said. Morgan read it out loud to his grandmother.

"Think I could go?"

His grandmother took a while to answer. "Go, but I want you home as soon as it's over. If you use this as an excuse to run around I'll put a stop to it just like that."

"I promise I'll come right home."

"Go, then. And if you're going to be a fighter, be a good one." She paused and added, "Once you start, keep at it. If a job is once begun, never leave till it's done."

There was a coach, Bob Gerber, who took an interest in Morgan. The youngster sensed Gerber was "someone who knew what he was talking about." That night Gerber showed Morgan three boxing basics: how to throw a left jab, a straight right hand, and how not to trip over his own feet. Morgan learned and won a few fights at the YMCA. He became a regular at the gym, and he got better. He fought on the Duluth Golden Gloves team and ran up a record of 19 and 5. Then one day Gerber asked him to come upstairs to the lounge.

"Is anything wrong?"

"I've known you a couple of years," Gerber said. "You can box. But I happen to know you're not doing that great in school."

Morgan didn't say anything. Gerber had never talked about school or studying before. Gerber said, "I think you have a chance to get a boxing scholarship to college."

"I hate going to high school," Morgan said.

Gerber spent the better part of an hour selling Morgan on why college was important. He mentioned Madison and the huge Field House crowds. Later, he wrote letters on Morgan's behalf. In the fall of 1950 Morgan caught a bus for Madison.

He was met at the station by Jollymore, the former Badger, and NCAA champion, who was also from Minnesota and knew Gerber. "I have a room for you at the YMCA," Jollymore said.

Morgan was eighteen and scared. His room was tiny and the radiator was loud and the only window was long and narrow and near the ceiling. "They have put me in jail," he said to himself. The next day, Jollymore took Morgan over to meet Walsh, whom Morgan regarded as a larger than life legend. "What struck me most about him was his kindness," Morgan recalled a half-century later.

Walsh secured Morgan a construction job and an apartment just a few blocks from the Field House. He wouldn't officially enroll at UW–Madison until February 1951, but he worked out with the boxing team. One member of the '51 team who did box, and who would come to think of Morgan as something of an inspiration—as well as the guy who, in later years, kept the fraternity of UW boxers together by encouraging reunions—was Madison native Tom Zamzow.

Though he grew up in the city, Zamzow would recall that he didn't really know anything about the storied history of UW boxing until he was a junior at East High School. One night his older brother, lacking a date, asked if he wanted to go to a match at the Field House.

"I fell in love with it," Zamzow said, a half-century later.

Zamzow would fight at 130 pounds for the 1951 Badgers. Another member of that team also came to the sport via a brother. Pat Sreenan's fraternal initiation to boxing was rather more direct that Zamzow's. Sreenan was from Beloit and his older brother, Jim Sreenan, had been a UW boxer for several years starting in 1949. Sreenan recalled that one Christmas break his brother was home and feeling not really prepared for the annual all-university tournament, which preceded the varsity-boxing season and would be held when school reconvened. "He enticed my brother and myself to work with him getting into shape," Sreenan recalled. "As you might suspect, we both, having never boxed, at least with gloves, were punching bags for Jim." But Sreenan learned, more in self-defense than anything, and when he arrived on campus he was surprised to learn that he himself was signed up to box in the all-university tournament. "My brother had signed me up without my knowing," Sreenan said. His brother knew what he was doing: Sreenan won at 156 pounds as a freshman and a year later, when he was eligible, he joined Walsh's varsity.

The 1951 team, McCormick would write on the eve of that spring's NCAA tournament, was talented but maybe a year away from peaking. He was right. The Badgers turned around the losing season of 1950, finishing the dual matches with a record of 4 wins, 1 loss, and 2 ties. Heading into the NCAA tournament the first week of April a *State Journal* sports headline read, "Wide Open Battle for Team Title Predicted in NCAA

Boxing Meet." The host school, Michigan State, was one of the favorites, though having tied the Spartans 4–4 in the last dual match of the season the Badgers could not be ruled out.

"There is a feeling among the coaches that this is Wisconsin's year," McCormick wrote right before the event. "My own feeling is that Wisconsin is a year away, that the Badgers will be ready for a smashing effort in 1952."

Five Badger boxers were on the train to East Lansing for the tournament—Murphy, the captain, Ranck, the fearsome heavyweight, Sreenan at 145 pounds, Zamzow, who would go at 130 pounds, and at 135 pounds, Carroll Sternberg. Zamzow drew a first-round bye so four Badgers would find themselves in action Thursday.

26. Pat Sreenan, from Beloit, was younger brother of another Badger boxer, Jim Sreenan. Pat later became an attorney in Rockford.

The crowds at East Lansing were disappointing—no more than a couple of thousand spectators for any of the sessions. Speculation was that the tournament would be moved back to Madison in 1952. But the spectators who did show up were treated to some excellent boxing.

It started well for Wisconsin—all five Badgers advanced to the semifinals, four with victories and Zamzow with a bye. Sternberg's bout at 135 pounds was the fight of the night—"a savage brawl," in McCormick's estimation. Sternberg fought Michigan State's Pearce Lane in front of the Spartan fighter's home fans; a week earlier in Madison, the two had met with a close decision going to Lane. The rematch was full of action from the go, with the first round going to Lane, and the second to Sternberg, despite the Badger boxer being staggered at one point in the round. In the third round Lane appeared to tire. Sternberg landed three punches for every one thrown by the Spartan and much to the crowd's disapproval, the bout went to Sternberg and he was into the semifinals.

Friday night, only two Badgers, Murphy and Ranck, advanced to the finals. Sreenan went down in a tough bout that was interesting in part because his Michigan State opponent was actually a young man named Jed Black from Janesville, Wisconsin, one of the few state boxers to get away from Walsh and Woodward. Maybe he got away because he wasn't pursued. Black had done no boxing in high school but a friend of Michigan State coach Makris sensed the young man's potential and recommended him. Makris, himself a former Badger boxing star, took a chance on Black and it paid off.

Sreenan, who became an attorney in Rockford, Illinois, would remember Black as one of his toughest ever opponents. Their bout in 1951 was regarded as one of the best of the tournament. Black won the first 2 rounds and Sreenan, sensing he needed a knockout, came storming back in the third but while he won the round easily on points, he couldn't put the Spartan away. The result was a decision for Black, who would go on to win the championship the next night.

Two other Badgers also fell in the semifinals. Zamzow lost a third round technical knockout at the hands of Washington State's Jackie Melson, and Sternberg, too, lost to a Washington State fighter, Everett Conley, by a 3–0 decision.

That left Murphy and Ranck. The two boxers were already best of friends, sharing a flat on Frances Street and going out early to practice each fall with the first-year boxers, as a way of getting in the best possible shape. Later in life the friendship would continue, with frequent visits, letters, and calls after Ranck had returned to his native Wyoming to practice law and, later, to a seat as a district judge in the state. Murphy would remember one trip in particular when he went to visit his friend and they wound up taking a 250-mile snowmobile trip through the Yellowstone National Park.

At the 1951 tourney, Murphy advanced to the Saturday finals with a unanimous decision over Bill Miller of Syracuse (actually, one of the three judges had it a toss-up but tipped his card to Murphy on "ring generalship"). McCormick saw Miller as a "a southpaw who is built like a fireplug and who hits savagely with his left hand." He may have been a favorite of the East Lansing crowd because when the decision for Murphy was announced, there was loud booing. That could also have been due to the Spartan faithful inherent wariness of any boxer wearing the colors of the always-powerful Badgers. One observer noted that the Michigan State crowd was against Wisconsin even more than they were for the Spartans.

There was no disputing Ranck's victory in the semifinals over George Fuller of Maryland. Ranck sent him to the canvas a little under two minutes into the second round. The official record called it a technical knockout but Fuller never reached his feet. He was groggy and wobbling when the referee reached the count of nine and at that point the medical officer in attendance signaled the timer to strike the gong, stopping the fight.

Two Badgers had then advanced to the Saturday night finals. Wisconsin had not had an individual champion since 1948, the longest dry spell ever. Murphy was first up Saturday. His opponent was Len Walker of Idaho, who was looking for a third straight NCAA individual championship, with this caveat: the year before Walker had won at 145 pounds, and in 1949 he was in the 135 pound class. So by 1951, fighting Murphy at 155 pounds, Walker was a full 20 pounds heavier and 2 weight classes higher than when he won his first NCAA championship. Still, the senior from Wallace, Idaho, had an overall college record of 27–3 and would be tough to beat. It was also an important match in the battle for the Walsh team trophy— Idaho and Michigan State looked to be neck and neck for that honor. Murphy, as it turned out, was up to the challenge, but it was close. He was awarded a 2–1 decision when one judge had it for Walker, a second for Murphy, and the third had it even on points but gave the nod to the Badger boxer on "ring generalship," the second night in a row Murphy had earned a judge's vote that way.

In the heavyweight bout, Ranck fought Jack Scherberies of San Jose State. Scherberies was as tough as they come. A year later, in the 1952 Olympic trials, Scherberies knocked out Zora Folley, who was just a year or so short of being ranked in the top ten professional heavyweights.

When I asked Ranck about the fight fifty years later, in the fall of 2002, he said: "Scherberies was a tough guy. Really tough. He didn't move a lot except straight forward, right at you. I know it was a close fight. I'm glad I won."

Observers at the time were kinder to the Badger—a *New York Times* account said Ranck "easily defeated" the San Jose boxer. The judges gave it to Ranck unanimously, 3–0. But McCormick noted there was a moment in the second round when Ranck, who had dominated the first, may have gotten a bit careless and let himself get hit with three punishing rights in succession. Maybe that's what Ranck remembers as Scherberies coming at him like a runaway train. In any case the judges gave it to Ranck 30–27, 30–27, and 29–27. The Badgers had their second individual champion of the tournament and Ranck's win gave them a team total of 20 points, just short of Michigan State's 21 points. The Spartans, at long last, had captured a team title and Makris was elated.

The 1951 team banquet, back in Madison the next week, was again at the Park Hotel on Madison's Capitol Square. No surprise that Murphy and Ranck were named co-captains for the next season. Sreenan won the Downer Memorial Trophy, and the outstanding freshman was a young man from Gary, Indiana, named Ray Zale, a nephew of a famous pro fighter, Tony Zale, once world middleweight champion. Toastmaster was a state senator from New Richmond named Warren Knowles. In the next decade, Knowles would be elected governor.

Knowles was one of several speakers the night of April 11, 1951. The future governor said: "We legislators who come here to enact laws actually are passing restrictions for the few. The vast majority of people do not need laws, for they live by a code of decency and fair play." Boxing taught that as well, Knowles said.

Athletic director Guy Sundt said, "We feel keenly that boxing belongs as a part of our intercollegiate program."

UW professor Nate Feinsinger, chairman of the athletic board, used his brief talk to praise Walsh: "He was an old student of mine, and I want to say that Johnny Walsh was a boxing champion, he's an outstanding coach and above all, he's a fine gentleman."

Bleckwenn, chair of the NCAA Boxing Rules Committee, praised the 1951 Badger squad: "If there ever was another all-out war, which heaven forbid, and I should ever go to war again, I would ask nothing more than that I should have with me every member of this year's Wisconsin boxing squad."

Walsh was equally gracious when he stood and assessed the 1951 team: "This was not the very best boxing team we have had at Wisconsin," the coach said. "But it won more matches on sheer spirit than any other we have had, and I believe that is a greater honor than winning on extra ability."

Much was expected of the 1952 Badgers. Prior to the 1951 tournament, McCormick had speculated that the team was a year from peaking. Well, that year was up. The Badgers, again led by Murphy and Ranck, weren't going to sneak up on anybody. They would be favored wherever they went and in April, the NCAA tournament was coming back to Madison, to the Field House, for the first time since 1948.

The Badgers finished with a dual meet record of 5 wins, 0 losses, and 2 draws. The first of the 4–4 ties came February 15, in Pullman against Washington State. The Badgers took a train to Spokane and then boarded a bus to Pullman. At some point word arrived that the much anticipated heavyweight match between UW's Ranck, the defending national champion, and Washington State's Pete Rademacher would not come off because Rademacher had been ruled ineligible for college boxing. Rademacher had violated the NCAA rule, which stated that once a young man reached his eighteenth birthday, he could fight only high school or intercollegiate bouts—anything else would render him ineligible for college competition. With Rademacher ineligible, the Washington State fans would be deprived of a potentially great heavyweight match-up. A plan was conceived: Washington State would concede the heavyweight point to the Badgers, but Rademacher and Ranck would box a 3-round exhibition.

"It was fine with me and OK with Walsh," Ranck recalled fifty years later. But when the bell sounded for the "exhibition," Ranck sensed his opponent was out for blood. "He was trying to knock me out," Ranck said. "I thought it was an exhibition."

Rademacher was a considerable fighter—some years later he would box Floyd Patterson for the world heavyweight championship. Ranck went back to his corner at the end of the first round and Walsh said, "I think the exhibition is over."

Ranck replied, "I'm convinced of that."

"Go out there and wait for him to throw a left jab," Walsh said. "Just slip under it. When he throws his jab he drops his right hand. Duck the jab and you can get him with a left hook." The left hook that Walsh had always said was a boy's best friend.

"OK," Ranck said.

Round 2 began and the fighters circled for the first minute. "Then he threw a jab at my forehead," Ranck recalled, "and I hit him with the left hook and I think his head went out of the ring. He was out for over a minute. I was getting concerned. But he got up and was fine."

For Ranck, it was a tremendous, if unofficial, victory. The heavyweight was probably one of the three or four best boxers ever to fight for Walsh. Later that year, he would try out for the 1952 Olympic team and lose a 1-point split decision to Ed Sanders, who went on to win the gold medal with a victory over Sweden's Ingemar Johannson in the finals. Later on as a pro Sanders would fight the fearsome Sonny Liston.

The importance of the college game to his development as a person could simply not be overestimated, Ranck said.

"I can't tell you how important it was," Ranck said. "It was hugely important. Your teammates. They talk about boxing being an individual sport, but when we went into a match we went in as a team. Every guy was pulling for every other guy. I think Walsh and Woodward instilled in us that we were a team. You fight together, you train together, and after fifty years these guys are still my close friends."

Ranck felt that among Walsh's best characteristics was his ability to impart a sense of class in his boxers, a way of carrying themselves that extended beyond the ring and their time in Madison. "He instilled these things in each of us. Simple things but big things. 'Be on time. Think before you speak. When you do speak, do what you say you are going to do.' Great qualities—and he helped put them in every kid he touched."

The second dual match draw of the season came in the last match before the NCAA tournament, when Michigan State, the defending national team champion, came to Madison. More than thirteen thousand fans, easily the largest crowd of the year, packed the Field House. The 4–4 tie left fans wondering about the big event the following week: could the Badgers claim their first team title since 1948?

A day before the tournament began, with the national boxing fraternity arrived and raring to go in Madison, McCormick related in his column a conversation that had taken place a few years earlier when the tournament had been at East Lansing. It was the night before that tournament was to begin and around a corner table in a friendly hotel bar sat some of the best coaches and boxing minds in the country. Someone threw out a question: "Who would be on the all-time best NCAA boxing team?"

At the table besides McCormick were Badger coaches John Walsh and Vern Woodward, Dee Portal of San Jose State, Roy Simmons of Syracuse, Al York of Virginia, Ike Deeter of Washington State, Frank Young of Idaho, and Leo Houck of Penn State.

Three fighters were immediately agreed upon as having a place on any list: Kara of Idaho, Davey of Michigan State, and Crocker of Wisconsin. Each had fought at more than one weight class and Simmons of Syracuse quickly said that which weight division didn't matter. "You can put Kara at any weight within reach, and the same goes for Crocker and Davey. They were the best." Still they found weight classes for them: Kara at 125 pounds, Davey at 130 pounds, Crocker at 145 pounds.

Deeter of Washington State nominated another Badger: Swancutt, for 155 pounds. "That carried," McCormick noted. The sports editor turned to Houck. "Who do you like at 135?"

Before Houck could answer, Walsh said, "How about Gene Rankin of Wisconsin?"

There were dissenters, and one at the table said: "Baloney! I saw him get beat three times in one tournament and still win a championship!"

"Well," Walsh said quietly, "he won three championships at 135 pounds, and the judges couldn't have been wrong all the time."

Somebody else at the table said: "I agree with Walsh. I was just thinking and realized that a couple of boys I had been going to mention were both defeated by Rankin." The table, somewhat grudgingly, chose Rankin.

The discussion shifted to heavyweights. It was interesting, but the heavyweight division, the one which received so much media hype on the professional level—at times it seemed there was no other pro boxing other than in the heavyweight division—was not particularly respected among

27. The program from a UW match against Michigan State in 1952. Wisconsin had great rivalries in the ring with many schools, perhaps none more spirited than with Michigan State. One Spartan boxer, Chuck Davey, considered one of the best college boxers ever, became a personal friend of Badger coach John Walsh.

the college boxing fraternity. Maybe it had something to do with the college aficionados' love of the smart boxer rather than the brawler. In any case in the hotel bar in East Lansing that night when the call went out for the greatest college heavyweight ever, a coach at the table said, "They are so bad their own relatives won't pay to see them."

And another: "College heavyweights are like guards in football and third basemen in baseball. They ought to pay to get in the show." Finally Houck of Penn State said, "Let's have nominations. We're picking a full squad."

When nobody spoke immediately, Houck continued: "I'll make a nomination. I'll name that Lee of Wisconsin. He wasn't very big, but he never seemed to have much trouble dumping the big boys."

Another coach, not Walsh: "I guess he's about the best, at that. But wait a minute. That gives Wisconsin four of the eight."

It was left for Deeter of Washington State to admit the obvious: "Have you noticed who has been winning all of the championships lately?"

It was, of course, just barroom banter. Except that the people around the table were the most knowledgeable minds in amateur boxing. It was a great tribute to the success of Walsh and Wisconsin. If there was never any real "all-time" team of NCAA boxers chosen, that night in East Lansing could suffice.

And as the man said, Wisconsin had four of the eight.

But that debate had taken place on the eve of the 1949 tournament. By April 1952 three NCAA tournaments had come and gone without the UW taking home the team trophy. In Madison, the feeling was that losing streak was about to end. In anticipation of the large Field House crowds, the NCAA rules committee put out a plea for sportsmanship that was widely circulated in the Madison media. It was a five-part guide to good spectating that included withholding applause and comments until a round was over; a reminder that the officials know the rules; a suggestion that spectators keep their own score by rounds and remember that the punches in the last round count for no more than punches in the first two; a reminder that reasonable people can disagree on scoring; and finally, if you are happy with a decision, cheer, if you are unhappy, keep quiet. Silence, the committee said, is an effective way of showing disapproval. "And you won't annoy your neighbors."

That the plea was given front-page display in both daily sports pages indicates some felt there was a problem with sportsmanship at the Field House. There is some disagreement about this among people who were there. Remembering back fifty years, many of the fighters and fans I spoke with recalled how well mannered the Badger boxing crowds were. Excited, certainly, but never rude. "It was like a tennis match at Wimbledon," said Audrey Walsh, the coach's wife.

Others were less certain. "I learned that many fans were fickle," Badger boxer Pat Sreenan said. Sreenan recalled 2 bouts with opponents whom he had knocked out in earlier meetings. In each case, in the rematch at the Field House, Sreenan said he saw "definite fear" in their eyes and so he did not look to throw a knock out punch, safe in the knowledge he could win without it. "When I did not press for a repeat knockout," Sreenan said, "some fans voiced, to say the least, their disappointment."

Charlie Magestro, a freshman boxer in 1952, loved the atmosphere at the Field House and thought Badger fans were the epitome of a fair sporting crowd. But Magestro recalled one fight against a highly touted LSU boxer named Calvin Clary when the Madison crowd turned ugly when the decision went against the hometown fighter. "Even Clary came up to me later and told me I got robbed," Magestro said. The Field House fans booed and threw whatever wasn't nailed down into the ring for "the next two or three fights," Magestro recalled.

Even more ominously, a UW professor named David Fellman, who in a few short years would lead the effort to remove boxing from the Madison campus, had an experience in the Field House bleachers that he never forgot.

"I went to see one of the boxing matches just to see what it was like," Fellman said. "It was at the Field House. In one match, the Wisconsin boxer had the boxer from the other team on the ropes. He was obviously beating him up. All around me people were standing on their feet yelling, 'Kill him! Kill him!' I said to myself, 'That's a heckuva college sport, where you shout, 'Kill him.' It doesn't sound like higher education."

One thing was certain in 1952: the Field House crowds for the tournament, while large and noisy and far more impressive than one would see anywhere else in the country, were down significantly from the last time the NCAA showcase event came to Madison. The 1948 tournament drew 59,800 spectators to 5 sessions over three days. The 1952 event's attendance would total just over 37,000.

Still there was plenty of excitement in Madison. NCAA rules committee chair Bleckwenn hosted a party for the tournament visitors that Wednesday night at the Madison Club. There was a great turnout and Fred Gage of WIBA radio did his late sports round-up from the Madison Club. It was also announced that WIBA would provide reports from the Field House at the conclusion of each session of the tournament. Two Madison writers, Henry McCormick of the *State Journal* and Golden of the *Capital Times,* were voted honorary members of the National Intercollegiate Boxing Coaches Association. As for the contestants themselves, there was a full field in Madison, seventy-two boxers altogether, including two from the University of Hawaii, five thousand miles away.

The Badgers had seven fighters entered: Bob Hennessy at 119 pounds; Terry Tynan at 132 pounds; Sreenan at 139 pounds; Morgan at 147 pounds; Murphy at 156 pounds; Zale at 165 pounds, and heavyweight Ranck. Thursday's quarterfinals broke pretty well for Wisconsin: of the seven, only Tynan and Murphy lost. Murphy's was a particularly hard defeat. He was the defending NCAA champion and had beaten Miller of Syracuse on three earlier occasions. When the decision went to Miller tears streamed down Murphy's cheeks as Walsh and Woodward led him to the locker room. "I just didn't have it tonight," Murphy said. Writing that night, Henry McCormick would call the Murphy-Miller bout "the most dramatic event of the quarter-finals." It was destined to be Murphy's last college fight. The *Capital Times* report the next day echoed the fighter's own judgment that he was not at his best against Miller: "Murphy was far off form and appeared tight and tense. He failed to loosen up with his famed left and at times appeared to be falling right into the type of scrap that Miller sought. . . . The Syracuse scrapper is a southpaw and packs a lethal punch.

"Murphy appeared better in the second canto but after socking Miller with a left, caught a short right cross on the chin and went down for a nine count. Murphy was not hurt but the knockdown lost him valuable points."

Badger great Gene Rankin was watching at ringside and said the knockdown was the difference in the fight. In any event it was a tough way for Murphy to end his college career. It was more than that. There was speculation Murphy would try to qualify for the Olympic team but a job offer from the Miller Brewing Company kept that from happening: Murphy was done as an amateur fighter.

With five fighters advancing, the Badgers held a slim lead heading into Friday's semifinals. And Friday proved to be a great day for Wisconsin boxing. In a meeting at the Park Hotel, the coaches' association elected Woodward president of the organization for the next year. In the semifinal tournament bouts, meanwhile, the Badgers wound up almost clinching the team title. Only freshman Hennessy went down to defeat, and that in a split decision that saw Hennessy battle valiantly from behind in the third round. "He was the toughest fighter I've ever fought," said Penn State's Sam Marino, who was undefeated at that point.

Four other Badgers advanced to the finals, and going into those Saturday bouts UW held a commanding lead with 17 points. Defending champion Michigan State and LSU were next with nine, but each of those schools had only two fighters left in the tournament. Mathematically, if one Badger could win a championship, the team title would also go to Wisconsin.

More than thirteen thousand were on hand for the finals and two Badgers came away with individual championships. One was not much of a surprise: UW's fearsome heavyweight, defending national champion Bob Ranck, scored the only knockout of finals night, over Evans "Blackie" Howell of LSU.

"The Badger co-captain had to stalk Howell from the start," McCormick wrote, "and it wasn't easy catching up with the fast moving Louisiana State boy, but Ranck did it in the first minute of the second round and it ended quickly. Ranck lashed out with a right to the chin, and Howell started to reel; as he was slipping to the canvas Ranck dug a savage left hook into the pit of Howell's stomach. That was the end of the fight."

Two Badger finalists lost in tough split decisions. Sreenan lost to Chuck Adkins of San Jose State. The next day's *State Journal* called Sreenan's effort "magnificent." Years later, Sreenan would single out Adkins as "the best college boxer that I knew and also fought." Adkins would win a gold medal in the 1952 Olympics. UW's Zale also lost, at 165 pounds, to Gordon Gladson of Washington State.

The other Badger 1952 champion, in something of an upset, was Morgan at 147 pounds. "I barely survived the first two fights to get into the championship," Morgan admitted later. "I was tense and utterly exhausted by the end of those two fights." The title bout was against Dick LaForge of Michigan State, and Morgan pulled off a unanimous decision. His win also clinched the team title for the Badgers.

The *State Journal* noted: "Morgan paced himself well in the championship tussle against the heavy-hitting LaForge. He was in just as good a
condition at the finish as when he started. In his previous two bouts,
Morgan indicated a tendency to tire perceptibly in the final round." Jollymore, who had met the young Morgan at the bus station when he first
arrived from Duluth a few years earlier, clipped the *State Journal* story and
sent it up to Minnesota where it was published in the *Duluth News Tribune*. It was quite a moment for Morgan, who remembered it a half century later in his autobiography, "Goodbye, Geraldine," with these words:
"In the championship fight, it was as if I had purged myself of all the
clumsiness and mistakes and was free now for that once in a lifetime performance. It all happened so fast. The fight barely started and it was over.
There was the spontaneous, thunderous roar from the crowd. I couldn't
absorb all the feelings that flowed through me, but it seemed a chance
for the Wisconsin boxing fans to come together for 60 seconds of feeling good, a release from the tension of the fight, a continuation of 'the
flow' that was the fight that night. It was sixty seconds of later-in-life-day-
dreams, of joyous freedom and redemption for the badly fought and
barely won fights of the previous two nights. It was a depth of feeling I
would only know in quieter times years later."

Fifty years after his championship, Morgan would return to Madison for
a reunion of the 1952 team and he would be asked to speak to Madison's
Downtown Rotary Club. Several hundred listened raptly as Morgan spoke
about what the sport had meant to him, about how, when he suffered ups
and downs in life—and Morgan had some downs, including alcoholism,
but he also built a successful company—he always returned to the simple
verities he had learned from boxing: do your best, tell the truth, don't make
excuses, and honor your friends. His quiet talk to Madison's movers and
shakers was quite poignant. Anyone looking for the best that college boxing could bring out in an individual could do worse than look at Morgan.

The John Walsh Trophy, for the champion college boxing team in the
country, was back in the possession of Walsh for the first time since 1948,
so the 1952 team banquet at the Loraine Hotel was a festive occasion. Jollymore served as master of ceremonies and no less than Governor Walter
Kohler showed up to pay tribute to the champions. The Downer Memorial Trophy went to Ranck. Sreenan was named captain for 1953. Another
highlight: A dozen former individual national champions attended, from

28. Pat Sreenan boxing Herb Odom of Michigan State in a 1953 bout. Because the
fights consisted of only three, two-minute rounds, college boxing was fast and
furious.

Fadner, the Badgers' first ever NCAA champ (in 1936), to Crocker and
Parisi. It was a great night.

For all the talent Walsh and Woodward had brought to Madison in the
first two decades of the boxing program, it should also be said that the
teams never lacked for colorful characters. The 1953 squad would feature
a few more.

First among equals in the colorful category was Bobby Hinds, who
grew up poor in a broken home in Kenosha. Hinds would follow in the
steps of Lee and Ranck as a fearsome Wisconsin heavyweight, though
circumstances would conspire to keep Hinds from an NCAA title. That
would bother Hinds over the years but it wouldn't keep him down long—
nothing could. Hinds, who stayed in Madison after his boxing days were
done, was as irrepressible as ever when the new millennium dawned in
2000. Into his 70s, if you were to run into Hinds at one of the Madison
watering holes where he liked to hold court, he would tell you a funny
story, try to sell you something, buy you a drink, and show you pictures
of the famous person he was hanging out with the week before—all before
you had your coat off. His wife, Joy, could still count on answering the
phone and hearing someone on the other end say, "I got this number from
the craziest guy I met the other day." Hinds had another friend.

It hadn't always been easy for Hinds—far from it. He was not a dedicated student in high school in Kenosha but he cracked the books enough
to stay eligible for football. His senior year Hinds lived with the family of
his close friend, Alan Ameche, who was a pretty fair football player himself. Fair enough to win the Heisman Memorial Trophy a few years hence
playing for the Badgers in Madison. Their senior year in high school, the
Hinds and Ameche led Kenosha team was the top-rated high school squad
in Wisconsin.

Hinds had begun boxing Golden Gloves in 1945, when he was thirteen.
In subsequent years he boxed Golden Gloves tournaments all over the
state and in the Chicago area, accumulating titles and making a name for
himself in boxing circles. Word got back to Hinds that the Wisconsin
boxing team was interested in him.

He knew about the Badger program: "Of course we had heard about
it," Hinds recalled fifty years later. "We had this guy in Kenosha—he later
became sheriff—who was a great admirer of John Walsh, and this gentleman wanted me to go to Madison. Walsh by that time had a reputation

29. Bobby Hinds was a tough kid from Kenosha who became a tough Badger
heavyweight and, later, a colorful character on the Madison scene with his
portable exercise gym business. There were few celebrities Hinds hadn't met at
one time or another, including the gangster John Gotti, with whom Hinds
enjoyed a lengthy correspondence.

that was just incredible. It was almost mystical, if you know what I mean. But going to college was the farthest thing from my mind. I wanted to turn pro."

Their senior year at Kenosha, Hinds and Ameche wound up taking the bus up to a Badger boxing match. Woodward had been down to scout Hinds at a couple of Golden Gloves tournaments and extended the invitation. At the time, before Hinds moved in with the Ameche, Woodward took one look at his living circumstances and went directly to the grocery store. "He came back with $50 worth of groceries," Hinds said. Today that would get a program put on NCAA probation. Then it was a gesture of sincere kindness that Hinds never forgot. Nor did Ameche, when Hinds told him about it. Hinds would say later he felt Ameche was so impressed with Woodward that he came to the UW to play football in part because of Woodward.

That first trip up in 1950, Hinds and Ameche were overwhelmed by the spectacle at the Field House. "I had always drawn good crowds at my amateur fights but we walked in there and there were, what, 13,000 people? The enthusiasm blew my mind. Ameche looked at me and, 'Holy God, will you look at this!'"

They got a tour of the boxing workout room at the Field House and that also left an impression. Hinds recalled, "They had three beautiful rings and 21 speed bags across the back and the whole wall was nothing but mirrors. People came from all over the world to look at it. Boxing gyms as a rule were the pits. For a young kid this was mind-boggling."

That first trip, Hinds and Ameche were going to take the bus back but Woodward offered to drive and, on arriving in Kenosha, wound up buying groceries. In the end there was no way either Hinds or Ameche were going anywhere but the University of Wisconsin.

Hinds's freshman year, 1952, he still hadn't committed to studying. He wound up academically ineligible for the second semester, which of course included almost the entire boxing season. He did box the Badgers' first match of 1952, a road trip to LSU in late December, a well-publicized match in New Orleans that was held in conjunction with the Sugar Bowl football game. It was Hinds's first college match and it was a trip that he would never forget.

Hinds was fighting not as a heavyweight, as he would later, but rather a light-heavyweight at 175 pounds. Fifty years later he could still remember the date—December 27. Hinds was scheduled to box George Peyton, a highly regarded LSU fighter. Hinds recalled that prior to the bout, Walsh told him that college boxing was like the Olympics, in that when the fighters came out of their corners for the first round, they didn't touch gloves, as is the custom in professional fighting. Walsh told Hinds about that but Hinds, excited in the extreme before his first college fight, did not hear. At the bell he went out to the center of the ring and extended his gloves toward Peyton, who may or may not have grinned when he threw a vicious right that hit Hinds on the chin and deposited him on the ring's canvas floor.

"I wasn't really hurt," Hinds recalled later. "I got right up. And Walsh is yelling: 'Bobby! I told you!' Anyway I rolled up and the referee parted us and Peyton sort of got behind the ref and before I knew it he nailed me with a left hook. I went down again. It's not even 15 seconds into the first round and I've been down twice. I'm sure Walsh couldn't believe it."

Say this for Hinds: He came back and won the fight. That first bout could serve to capture Hinds in a nutshell: irrepressible, naive, exuberant, and tough. "A better fighter than even he realized he was," is the way one of Hinds's teammates, lightweight Terry Tynan, put it to me. Hinds never did lose a dual match in college. Tynan said that when he sparred with the much heavier Hinds, Tynan couldn't lay a glove on him. "He was that quick." Hinds may have been the best of the Badger boxers to never win an NCAA title—circumstances conspired against him. In one instance he withdrew due to illness. Another he lost in the finals in a controversial split decision.

Away from the ring, Tynan recalled, Hinds was always "totally uninhibited." That first road trip to New Orleans was, Hinds told me, "like being a kid in a candy store." If Walsh had known what was going on he would have followed Hinds around with a butterfly net. Hinds ran into UW athletics administrator Ivan Williamson and football coach Milt Bruhn on Bourbon Street and would have given them a big wave if he hadn't had a girl on each arm. As it was, he grinned. In one New Orleans saloon a stripper came up to Hinds and asked what brought him to town. "I'm a boxer," Hinds said proudly. "I was watching on TV last night," the girl said, "when a guy got knocked down twice in 15 seconds."

"You're talking to him," Hinds said.

Roundy Coughlin, the redoubtable *Wisconsin State Journal* columnist, never missed a chance to go to New Orleans and was down with the team for the 1952 Sugar Bowl match. "He took us to Antoine's," Hinds recalled. Coughlin, as we've heard, was very large at Antoine's.

"It was fantastic," Hinds said. "There were people lined up around the block to get in. Roundy just walked right by them and in the door. We were treated like kings. Roundy orders hors d'oeuvres: Oysters Rockefeller. Of course I've never heard of Oysters Rockefeller. The oysters come and they are sitting in hot white sand to keep them warm. Then they bring this basket that was actually bread—the bread is woven into a basket. I'm sitting a couple of chairs from Roundy and I don't know what I'm doing. What do I know? I don't realize the oysters are sitting on sand and I think the sand is part of the hors d'oeuvre, so I spoon up some sand. Roundy is watching and his eyes are wide and he says, 'Bob, how do you like it?'

"I said, 'It's a little bland.' Roundy almost fell on the floor he was laughing so hard. And of course he never paid."

There was usually laughter around Hinds. When his boxing career was over he parlayed his street-smart athleticism and natural born hustler's panache into a highly successful gym equipment manufacturing company. Hinds started with jump ropes, laying claim that simply jumping rope was the best exercise anyone could do. To prove it he would jump rope on an airplane, in a restaurant, and once, memorably, in front of Johnny Carson on the *Tonight Show*. Celebrities liked him, both for his zest and because—after he had moved from jump ropes to his portable Lifeline Gym—Hinds' equipment, which consisted of light rubber tubing, traveled well. This was in an era before hotels had fitness rooms. A celebrity on the road could break out Hinds's portable gym and get a strenuous workout without leaving his suite. Sylvester Stallone was a fan. So were the artist Leroy Neiman and the famed author Jim Harrison. As I mentioned earlier, Hinds even tried to send a portable gym to the notorious gangster John Gotti in federal prison in Illinois. The gym came back but Gotti initiated a correspondence that continued until the mobster's death. Hinds could get emotional talking about the ink drawings Gotti sent him. But then, Hinds could get emotional at a K-Mart opening. He wore everything on his sleeve and later in his life there was no subject that could move him like UW boxing and Walsh. "A man of great class," Hinds said. "He was in life like he was in the corner of the ring."

30. One of the great chroniclers of Badger boxing, Joseph "Roundy" Coughlin, shown here with legendary heavyweight Jack Dempsey. For years Coughlin gave out an award for the Badger fighter he considered the most spirited.

The early 1950s era of Badger boxing was not short on scrappers. Tynan was a lightweight from Chicago who, like Hinds, came to Madison as a freshman in 1952. Tynan had grown up on Chicago's far north side and fell in love with boxing before he was a teen. Tynan sparred with his father and pored over a sports magazine that included a boxing instructional piece by the great Billy Conn. When he was twelve Tynan rode the El train downtown to some boxing classes the Catholic Youth Organization (CYO) held at the Congress Hotel. "Until boxing," Tynan said, "there wasn't anything I felt I could do really well. I played other sports and I was OK. But boxing I loved."

Tynan went to high school in Evanston and got lucky: His first year was the first year they fielded a boxing team. He won a Catholic school tournament and remembered that in his very first CYO bout, he scored a knockout win. "It was my first and last clean knockout," Tynan said. When he was fourteen Tynan showed up at a gym on Division Street that held weekly fights that were televised in the Chicago area. A boy needed to be fifteen to get an AAU license to box but that wasn't a problem if you knew somebody selling fake baptismal certificates, like Tynan did. It cost a quarter.

Between the CYO and the AAU fights, Tynan was making a name for himself in Chicago boxing circles. "My mother was totally against it, of course," he recalled. "She was horrified. She went to exactly one of my high school fights and kept her head down the whole time."

His senior year in high school, a referee suggested that Tynan might want to try college boxing at Michigan State. But someone else suggested Wisconsin, and as Tynan recalled, "Once I looked at Madison I didn't even go to East Lansing."

Like so many of the boxers, Tynan retains vivid memories of his Field House experiences. A half-century later he could get misty-eyed talking about it. "People in Madison lived for boxing, some of them," he said. "The Field House—you know, the place would be packed and it would go completely dark. The spotlight would come on, and the other team would run up into the ring. Then the spot would swing to our dressing room. The band would start playing." Tynan paused. "It was quite an extravaganza."

Tynan was greatly impressed by the caliber of boxers Walsh had assembled. "I came thinking I was the cat's meow," Tynan said. "I was rudely

31. Terry Tynan, a Badger boxer from Chicago, remembered being swept up by the crowds and the atmosphere in the Field House. "It was quite an extravaganza," he said.

awakened." Still, he did pretty well. Tynan never won a national title but he fought a lot of varsity bouts as well as some epic fights in the all-university tournament against his teammate Charlie Magestro.

Magestro fit the profile of many of that era's Badger fighters: tough, up-from-not-much guys, self-made, unvarnished, young men with something to prove in the ring. Magestro was born in Cudahy, Wisconsin, and moved early with his family to south Milwaukee. "I was so poor I couldn't afford to window shop," Magestro said. But he found himself in athletics. Magestro was an all-city quarterback at Milwaukee's South Division High School and he lettered in track and baseball as well. As a freshman, he won the Milwaukee Golden Gloves at 135 pounds. Makris, the former Badger great who went on to coach at Michigan State, recruited Magestro to box for the Spartans. He considered it, but wound up in Madison, seduced by the kindness of assistant coach Woodward and the administrative and organizational talents of Walsh.

32. Charlie Magestro grew up poor in Milwaukee but found himself through athletics, first as an all-city high school quarterback and then as a UW boxer.

Magestro, like Tynan and Hinds, was not destined to win an individual NCAA championship, but he had a stellar college career, especially in light of a secret he kept from Woodward and Walsh: In a 1953 dual match with Syracuse, Magestro seriously injured his right hand in a bout against the Orangemen's John Granger, who would win two NCAA titles at 139 pounds before his career was over. Magestro decisioned Granger in the fight, a great victory, but fluid gathered and hardened under the skin between his knuckles and wrist—fifty years later, the large lump is still there. That was February 27, 1953. The Field House had more than ten thousand fans and the Badgers beat previously unbeaten Syracuse 6–2. Magestro's win at 139 pounds was an upset. Writing in the campus paper, the *Daily Cardinal*, Arlie Schardt said the bout "was everything it had promised to be and then some." Simmons, the Syracuse coach, said later he "didn't like the way the Granger fight was scored"—a decision for Magestro—but followed that with the odd remark, "I'm not saying Magestro didn't win. He's an excellent boxer."

He was better that night than anyone knew. Magestro remains unsure of the exact extent of the injury to his hand suffered against Granger, but it was serious enough that Magestro said later, "I could have been much better if it had never happened."

As it was, Magestro kept the injury to himself. Three weeks after the Syracuse fight in 1953, the Badgers were scheduled for a road match at Miami. "What poor kid doesn't want to take a trip to Miami in March?" Magestro said. "If I had told Walsh or Woodward my hand hurt, someone else would have fought in my place. That's just the way it was." But Magestro wondered if he was doing the right thing. "I didn't want to hurt the team," he said. Finally he talked it over with Dave Miyagawa, Dick's brother, who was a member of the 1953 team.

"Maybe you can just feather-dust him," Miyagawa said. "Use one hand."

To make matters worse, the first two Badgers lost their bouts to their Miami opponents. It was 2–0 Miami when Magestro climbed into the ring and Walsh took him aside and said, "I figured we might lose those two. But now we start." Magestro, his hand aching, wasn't sure what to think. "I fought one-handed and I fought like a southpaw," Magestro said, "which broke the cardinal John Walsh rule of not switching from your natural style. But I did because I had to and it worked out OK."

In fact, Lee Evans writing the next day in the *Miami Herald* said Magestro was the best of all the Badgers in earning a second-round technical knock out over Eddie Segall: "Magestro in this particular match appeared to have more on the ball than any of the other midwesterners."

Magestro had actually first pulled his "southpaw" switch the week before, in another crucial bout, this one in Madison, when the Badgers faced LSU. Magestro drew the Tigers' captain, Clary, and after 2 rounds of trying to punch with his aching right, Magestro flip-flopped to southpaw, causing Henry McCormick to lead off his *State Journal* column the next day with a note of astonishment: "That's something I never expected to see, one of Johnny Walsh's boxers switch from an orthodox stance to a southpaw style."

Magestro, McCormick noted, was trailing Clary after 2 rounds and "in the early part of the third" when Magestro, "an orthodox boxer—one who fights with his left hand and foot extended—rapped Clary with a smashing right, then suddenly reversed his stance so that he had his right hand and right foot extended. The maneuver caught Clary unprepared, and Magestro smashed three hard, straight lefts to Clary's head without a return." It was a fine comeback but the bout still went to the LSU boxer.

In Miami the next week, Magestro's unorthodox switch yielded a victory, and the Badgers wound up winning a tight match, 5–3. There was controversy before it ended when for the first time in Walsh's long and storied career as a college coach, a boxer was disqualified during a bout. It happened in the 178-pound fight between the Badgers' Zale and Miami's Tom Jordan. The team score was 3–3 at the time when referee, Orville Rogers, stopped the Zale-Jordan match, saying the Miami fighter was disqualified for "holding and hitting" in violation of NCAA rules. The Miami crowd—what there was of it, attendance was under two thousand—booed but the referee stuck to his decision, and said later, "I disqualified him for holding and hitting. I warned him three times."

Going into the final match of the 1953 dual season, the Badgers had a chance to stay undefeated for the first time since 1948. Minnesota came to Madison and the Badgers finished the dual season in high style with a 7–1 trouncing of the Golden Gophers. In fact, the UW boxers did not lose a match; the score was reached with 6 Badger wins and 2 draws. The crowd again topped ten thousand and the loudest roar came when Wisconsin's Meath technically knockedout Minnesota captain, Pete Lee, at 165 pounds with just over a minute left in the first round. Meath knocked Lee down twice and it was after the second one that referee, Kenneally, stopped the bout. Meath was a hard puncher—Magestro, who roomed with Meath on away trips, thought he was hardest puncher on the squad. "But Bobby was such a nice guy that he made me feel I was the 'KO kid' of the team," Magestro said. No matter: they both could hit.

The tournament that year was in a somewhat unlikely locale: Pocatello, Idaho, home of fifteen hundred-enrollment Idaho State. But as small towns often do, Pocatello rose to the occasion and made the 1953 event a great success, better, in the minds of many, than any NCAA boxing tournament not held at the Field House in Madison. The Madison events were so far and away better attended that there was no comparison. But the Idaho fans bought all the tickets for all the sessions in their four thousand-seat gymnasium and by Saturday night they were quite glad they did—Idaho State won the team championship. The Madison papers did not staff the tournament and as it developed the Badgers had a good, but not quite good enough, tournament, finishing second as a team. That second nationally was a disappointment speaks to how high Walsh had set the bar for his teams.

The Badgers had seven entries in the 1953 tourney but four went out in the first round quarterfinals. Dave Miyagawa, Meath, Morgan—the defending titleholder at 152 pounds—and Magestro all lost. Magestro lost what was described as a "wild battle" to Granger, the Syracuse fighter he beat (and injured his hand against) during the dual match season. Advancing for UW were Zale at 178 pounds, Sreenan at 147 pounds, and the irrepressible heavyweight, Hinds.

Two Badgers advanced to the semifinals—Sreenan and Zale—but the big story out of Pocatello was that Badger heavyweight Hinds had to withdraw due to illness. The Madison papers the next day said an attack of the flu had sidelined Hinds. In his 1994 book *The Six-Minute Fraternity*, Wallenfeldt said "a heavy cold" had convinced Dr. Bleckwenn, the UW professor and boxing rules official, that Hinds had to be withdrawn as a precautionary measure. Hinds himself sounded a bit confused fifty years later: "It was a cold or flu. I got sick." He was given penicillin and told not to leave his hotel room. It was a devastating blow to Hinds personally—he never would get his NCAA title—and the Badgers' chances as a team. They weren't eliminated from a chance for the team crown because both Sreenan and Zale won their semifinal matches.

In the end, the Badgers fell short, with 19 team points to 25 for Idaho State. The good news was both Sreenan and Zale won their individual national championships. Sreenan scored a unanimous decision over Emmett Gurney of South Carolina and Zale took a split verdict from Adam Kois of Penn State, who had defeated Zale earlier in a dual match. The victories for Sreenan and Zale yielded this statistic: Wisconsin now could lay claim to twenty-nine individual NCAA tournament champions. That was not only more than any other school, it was more than any two other schools combined.

Zale earned yet another distinction: He was awarded the John S. LaRowe Trophy, the Heisman of college boxing, for his mix of sportsmanship and talent in the ring. Zale credited his father and his uncle, noted middleweight Tony Zale, for getting him started in boxing as a teen. Zale grew up in Chicago and came to Madison on an athletic scholarship. Zale told author Wallenfeldt that he treasured his UW boxing experiences, the friendships with teammates such as Ranck, Morgan, Murphy, and Meath, and the glow of feeling "a little bit elite" while walking on campus after a successful night at the Field House. And Zale talked about the overall good will that existed in the college boxing fraternity, citing something that happened in the wake of Zale's 1953 victory over Kois in the NCAA finals.

"When I won the national championship and the LaRowe Trophy out at Pocatello," Zale told Wallenfeldt, "Adam Kois's father called my father. Adam Kois and I are both Polish, and somehow or other his dad found out where I lived and called my father and congratulated him on my winning the championship and talked with my dad. Obviously he was pulling for his son, but it impressed me that he would do something like that."

At the year-end banquet, held at the Loraine Hotel downtown, Hinds got some salve for his NCAA disappointment when he was given the Downer Memorial Trophy for exemplifying what's best in college boxing. Morgan and Meath, meanwhile, were named co-captains for the 1954 season.

It would prove to be a mixed year, 1954, for Wisconsin boxing, much of it very good. The Badgers ran through the dual match season with only 1 loss, on the road at LSU, and they seemed primed to make a run at another NCAA team title when the tournament was hosted by Penn State in April. The Badgers rode into Penn State having been saluted in the

March 1954 issue of *Esquire* magazine with a glowing profile of their coach and his boxing program. "A Left Hook is a Boy's Best Friend," written by Lou Sidran, was eventually reprinted in the NCAA tournament program the following month. The *Esquire* piece recounted Walsh's growing up in the Twin Cities and his love for amateur boxing. "The most successful of all American boxing coaches" the magazine dubbed Walsh, and there were few willing to dispute it.

It's worth noting that in the *Esquire* piece Walsh felt compelled to defend the sport. "He feels that any attack on boxing is a personal affront," Sidran wrote of Walsh, and then he let the coach talk about the safety measures that had been introduced into college boxing.

"In the colleges," Walsh said, "we've adopted three other practices [besides going to nine-count knockdown rule] that have made the sport as safe as any. We use a competitive headgear to eliminate cut eyes and to cushion a fall. We use honest gloves, with the added padding over the knuckles where it belongs. And finally, we insist on two inches of padding under the deck. Since then, you never hear of a college boxer being injured by boxing his head on the canvas. Yet it's the most common cause of serious injury in professional or so-called amateur boxing."

Esquire cited the remarkable record of Wisconsin boxing under Walsh: 115 dual match wins, 12 losses, and 11 draws. A string of 72 wins in a row at home.

Then the article concluded by mentioning the UW medical study of boxing that began in the late 1940s and concluded in 1952, and the positive—or at least not negative—conclusions drawn about college boxing by the conductors of that study.

"Naturally I'm pleased with the results of the study," Walsh told *Esquire*. "But for me, the most important thing has always been that my boys are working out so well after graduation. We made a follow-up survey of the Wisconsin boxers, asked them how they were doing now, and it was just what I always knew it would be. They're lawyers, doctors, engineers, teachers, farmers, Army and Navy officers, contractors—in short, they're just like the rest of us. They don't regret having boxed. Many think it helped them later on. That's all the assurance I'll need to keep on going."

It was a fine and flattering article but at the NCAA tournament that April in State College, Pennsylvania, there were storm clouds on the horizon. *Capital Times* boxing writer Harry Golden made the trip with the

Wisconsin contingent and one of his columns before the tournament proper began was headlined, "Coaches Worry of Boxing's Future."

Golden had a conversation in State College with Frank Young, the boxing coach at the University of Idaho. Young suggested the boxing program at his school was in trouble. "How serious?" Golden asked. "Very serious," Young said. The problem, the coach elaborated, was mostly economic. Travel was costly and it was getting increasingly difficult to find competing schools within a reasonable distance of the Idaho campus. Young, as it turned out, was right to be concerned. In June 1954, just two months after the NCAA tournament at State College, the president of the University of Idaho, J. E. Buchanan, made an announcement. Idaho would no longer field an intercollegiate boxing team. The sport was being dropped. It had begun to sap too much of the athletic department budget, Buchanan said. "It's the same thing that happened at Penn State."

Buchanan was referencing a shocking development from a month earlier: Just weeks before the Idaho announcement, and little more than a month after it had hosted the NCAA tournament, Penn State dropped boxing. Idaho was one thing—but Penn State? The Nittany Lions were one of college boxing's most storied teams. Thirty years earlier, in 1924, Penn State hosted the first real college tournament. The great Leo Houck, who had died in 1950, was a Penn State man. Penn State officials cited economic factors and the lack of opponents in their decision and they also pointed to a lack of fan interest. In that they were not all wrong. In the middle of tournament week the Penn State athletic director, Ernie McCoy, had admitted to Madison reporter Golden that advance ticket sales had been "lousy." Golden noted: "That's not good . . . Penn State is ranked among the pre-meet favorites."

In his 1972 master's thesis, "The Study of Boxing as an Intercollegiate Sport," UW–Madison physical education student Gerald E. Dixon noted that a 1954 *New York Times* article placed the basis for Penn State's decision on "public apathy and scheduling difficulties." The Nittany Lions, Dixon wrote, "participated in boxing for 36 years, hosted the first Eastern Collegiate Boxing Tournament in 1924, won the first national team title in 1932, and placed third in the 1954 tournament held at their campus."

Would a school with such a great boxing history really disband the program because of scheduling difficulties or the fact that fan interest was up and down? Or was something else at work?

Paul Poorman, sports editor of the *Centre Daily Times*, thought there was another underlying and more ominous reason for the Penn State decision. In a telephone conversation with author Wallenfeldt three decades later, Poorman, according to Wallenfeldt, "expressed the belief that people were beginning to realize that boxing was the only sport in which the goal was to injure the opponent and, therefore, its continuation in educational institutions was becoming increasingly more difficult to justify."

Or as one boxing coach told *Sport Illustrated* writer Martin Kane several years later: "You could blame the moms." More precisely, moms who could not differentiate between college and pro boxing: "They've seen boxing on TV," the coach told Kane, "and nothing can persuade them that the college sport is different, that their boy stands little risk of being hurt."

Wrote Kane, "What the moms feel, college administrators have acted on."

The unfortunate irony, at least for supporters of college boxing, is that the decisions by Penn State and Idaho came only a year after the final publication of the only comprehensive medical and non-medical studies ever performed on college boxers, the Wisconsin studies, begun in 1949, under pressure from Professor Morton, with progress reports issued both that year and in 1950, with the final report being dated January 5, 1953. The report exonerated boxing on every level. Dixon, in his master's thesis twenty years later, drew the following conclusions: "Collegiate boxing does not present a greater risk than other contact sports." And: "Collegiate boxing was discontinued because of social pressure." You could blame it on the moms.

Of course the actions by Penn State and Idaho were still some weeks away when the college boxing fraternity gathered in State College in April 1954. If the sport's coaches and administrators were worried, they did their best not to think about it, or at least think on the bright side, which usually meant focusing on Madison, Walsh, and his Badgers. The *Esquire* piece was a hot topic of discussion. Hazel Fall, the chief dietician at Penn State, a woman of means and a boxing fan, hosted a party during tournament week at her palatial home just outside State College. At the party was one of the tournament referees, Herb Carlson, a three-time NCAA champion from Idaho. Carlson had been knocked out by the UW's John Lendenski in one of the great bouts in college boxing history, but he bore no grudge. At the Fall home party that night Carlson suggested that Madison should host the NCAA tournament at least every other year.

"In fact why not every year?" Carlson said. "You've got the central location and it's always a success. The tournament could use a boost like that."

Ray Chisholm, a former Badger boxer, was another of the tournament officials. Chisholm had actually been on the same train as the Badgers to State College, catching on in Chicago. Chisholm's idea for pumping life into the college game was to televise some dual matches. Let the boxing fans see how fast and furious the college matches are, and let the critics see how different it is from the professionals. Chisholm had the ear of the UW's Tony Curreri, the highly regarded physician who had boxed on campus before Walsh came to Madison and who, in 1954, succeeded Bleckwenn on the NCAA boxing rules committee. Bleckwenn was also in State College and was given a parchment scroll, signed by all the coaches, thanking him for his devotion to the sport.

As for the boxers, six Badgers had made the trip, and Wisconsin was being touted as the pretournament favorite. A new Badger boxer with an interesting story was Roy Kuboyama, competing in the tournament at 119 pounds. Kuboyama was from Hawaii and had first come to the United States as a member of the University of Hawaii boxing team—Kuboyama, a 139 pounder named Francis Shom, and the Hawaii coach, Herbert Minn, had made the five thousand-mile trip to Madison for the NCAA tournament in 1952. That week in the Field House, Kuboyama made history. Fighting at 112 pounds, he became the first boxer from the University of Hawaii to win an NCAA individual championship. Kuboyama won a unanimous decision from Vic Kobe of Idaho State, a bout that included a second round knock down by the Hawaiian fighter.

That was 1952. Kuboyama was studying agriculture at Hawaii and on returning to the islands made the decision to switch his emphasis to premed. He went in to talk it over with his coach, Minn, who understood when Kuboyama said he thought he needed to transfer.

"Where are you thinking?" Minn asked.

"Wisconsin," Kuboyama said. He had enjoyed his week in Madison and the medical school had a fine reputation. Minn offered to write a letter to Bleckwenn, who of course was not only in the UW medical school but had also been involved at the national level administrating college boxing. With Bleckwenn's assistance Kuboyama was enrolled at UW–Madison and in 1954 became eligible to box for the Badgers.

Fighting most of the season at 125 pounds, Kuboyama ran up a dual match record of 5–1. He also won the contenders tournament and all-university tournament at that weight. When the Hawaiian arrived at State College as part of the Wisconsin contingent for the 1954 tournament, Golden reported in the *Capital Times* that Walsh was taking a lot of kidding for "stealing" Kuboyama from Minn at Hawaii. Only when Minn told the real story did the coaches let up on Walsh. Kuboyama, on finishing his education, would return to Honolulu as a pediatrician.

At the weigh-in Thursday, a couple of Badgers were a fraction overweight. This was a constant concern, and the fact that some boxers switched between weight classes as a season wore on did not make it any easier. Magestro told me that in one year he was switched from 132 to 139 pounds and then to 147 pounds. "There was a time I lost 28 pounds in five days," Magestro said. "Mostly water, I think. But it was for a match in Minnesota and I didn't eat or drink anything and I went up there and got knocked out."

Magestro's good friend Terry Tynan was a pound overweight for his quarterfinal bout. He had an hour to lose it. "They wrapped me up in wrestling mats and rolled me around," Tynan recalled, trying to sweat the pound off him. It worked, but when Tynan showed up at the arena for his afternoon bout, he'd lost his entry pass and couldn't get in. Walsh had to be found and the coach got his boxer inside. "I think I gave him a few gray hairs," Tynan said a half-century later. "But I sure liked him. He was kind of like my mother, keeping me in line." During that 1954 season Tynan had suffered a bruised retina in his eye, an injury that required nine days in the hospital and, once out, a patch. As it happened Tynan was taking a course in money and banking from Morton, the professor who in the early 1950s was the leading opponent of boxing on campus. The day Tynan walked in with his eye patch, Morton said: "This is why I am against boxing." Tynan did not pursue it at the time but years later he would write a letter to the editor of the Madison newspaper in which he poured out his feelings for what college boxing had given him and so many others. "You didn't have to be big to participate," Tynan said. "If you couldn't play football or other sports, you could be boxer." Through it you learned about fitness and self-reliance, about loyalty and hard work. Did Tynan think he had been well served by the sport? Only all his life.

At State College, the Badger star at 156 pounds, Meath, was a half-pound over. Golden wrote the next day: "He dried out in a hurry and was feeling fine." Another interesting note: Zale, the Badger at 178 pounds, was the only defending champion entered in the 1954 event. All told, sixty boxers from fifteen schools were at State College.

Four Badgers fought the first day—Hinds and Kuboyama, at the opposite ends of the weight classes drew byes. Zale, the defender at 178 pounds, dropped his quarterfinal bout in a split decision to Don Quarles of North Carolina A&T. Zale would later call Quarles one of the toughest

33. Bob Meath came to Madison from a small Wisconsin town and wound up winning a national championship. Fifty years later, he remembered those days fondly: "It gave me my moment of glory."

opponents of his career but Golden, writing that day, termed Zale's defeat "most peculiar." The *Cap Times* writer continued: "One judge voted for him, another against him and the third called the match even. However, it was his privilege then to decide which one he believed the winner and in this case—which is not too unusual in the case of Wisconsin, he voted for Quarles." What Golden was saying, and none too subtlety, was that ties broke against Wisconsin because of the Badgers' favorite status. Of course, other observers would say that coin had a flip side: In Madison, some said—and many events were staged there because of the sport's popularity—it was rare for a close decision to break against the Badgers.

There was no question that Tynan dropped his bout—at least the decision, which went to John Stiglets of LSU, was unanimous. Tynan tired in the third round—he'd been rolling around the floor in mats trying to sweat off extra weight an hour before the fight—and Stiglets bore in close, landing multiple blows to Tynan's midsection, and won the fight. Meath, meanwhile, won his quarterfinal bout over Penn State's Joe Humphreys. It was, according to Golden, Humphreys' first fight of the year, and as you might expect it wasn't a good one. Humphreys was a varsity wrestler and Golden suggested in his fight story that he might consider returning to the mat. "He did little to make it a good boxing contest," Golden noted, but did not ask the question begging to be raised: Why would Penn State enter such an inexperienced boxer in the NCAA tournament? Maybe there was something already in the air of the pending decision to drop boxing on the State College campus. Golden did actually address the issue again in a column a day later, saying "the rules committee should not allow such action in a national tournament." The other Badger winning on Thursday besides Meath was Magestro, who decisioned Norm Andrie of Michigan State. Andrie was not anxious to mix it up with Magestro— Magestro had beaten him earlier in the year in dual match—and so danced away at any opportunity. "Every time I got set to throw a punch, he was gone," Magestro said after the fight. Well, not quite every time. He connected with a right in the second round that staggered Andrie and may have given the decision to the Badger.

Friday, all four of the Badgers still in the tournament won matches to advance to the finals. "All in all the Badgers never looked better all season," Golden wrote. The performance virtually locked up another team championship for Wisconsin.

Kuboyama, the Hawaiian and UW's representative at 119 pounds, decisioned Linwood Chisholm of Hampton Institute 3–0. It was all the more impressive because Kuboyama was far and away the tiniest boxer in the event. You can't box when you are over the number in a weight class, but there's no rule against getting in the ring under the stated weight. Kuboyama, Golden noted, was "the tiniest boxer in the meet by a city block. Roy ducks the scales whenever possible and can't make a 115 pound mark wringing wet. In fact it is very doubtful he weighs more than 110." Nevertheless, he beat Chisholm decisively. Kuboyama began the fight with three strong lefts to the head and never eased up. Chisholm spent the six minutes of the fight back on his heels.

Magestro got off to a fast start, too, in his semifinal at 139 pounds against Vic Harris of San Jose State. The referee for the bout was Carlson, the former college great who earlier in the week had suggested holding all the NCAA tournaments in Madison. Carlson took a point away from Harris for "holding and hitting" and in the end Magestro won on a split decision.

Meath, meanwhile, advanced to the finals with a knockout of Virginia's Pete Potter. Golden called the bout the best of the tournament to that point. "A sizzler," in his words. It certainly sizzled in the third and final round when about a minute into the round Meath caught Potter with a left hook and followed quickly with a right that sent the Virginia boxer to the canvas. Potter got to his knees about the time the referee, Lou Jallos, reached the count of four. As Potter rose from one knee he began to list to the side and fell again. Jallos declared the fight over even as Potter was once again attempting to gain his feet. Jallos put his arms around the Virginia fighter in an attempt to calm him but Potter began yelling that he was not out and wanted the fight to continue. Jallos shook his head and Golden, watching at ringside, later wrote that it was smart to stop it. Potter's "eyes were glassy and he was badly shaken" by Meath's assault, Golden wrote.

Hinds won his semifinal match with a first-round technical knockout over Joel Coleman of Penn State. Golden described it as no contest: "Hinds came out full of fight and slashed at his foe's midsection. He quickly shifted to the chin and three hard lefts sent Coleman staggering about. Two more body punches and a trio of hard crashing blows to the chin sent the tall Nittany Lion southpaw onto the canvas and the referee halted hostilities in a hurry. Hinds hardly got warmed up."

So the Badgers advanced four to the Saturday night finals and were looking good for another team championship. In the end, only Meath would win an individual crown but the Badgers did capture the team title, though it was close: UW finished with 19 points to 17 for Maryland. It was a great win for Meath, who had been up and down in his early years with the Badgers but who blossomed as a senior. His father, Charlie, was in State College for the tournament and got to see his son not only win a championship—he defeated Dick Bender of San Jose State in the finals— but Meath also was awarded the John S. LaRowe Trophy for symbolizing talent and sportsmanship: the best of college boxing.

I spoke with Meath by telephone from his home in Oswego, Oregon, early in 2003. Like so many of the boxers I spoke with, he was modest, but when he began recalling specific bouts and was taken in his memory back to those days, some of the most vivid of his life, you could hear the excitement in his voice as well as the pride he took in his accomplishment.

Meath was tough. "The hardest fight I had in my career," Morgan told me, "was an exhibition against Bobby at the Dane County Fairgrounds, in a tent, on a very cold fall evening. Without warming up we really went at it even though we had agreed to take it easy. Bobby was a devastating fighter."

Meath had learned early and well, first putting on the gloves as a little boy with his dad in New Richmond, Wisconsin. When Meath was a high school freshman, he got a break any aspiring boxer would have appreciated: Rankin, the three-time NCAA champion, came to New Richmond High School to teach and coach boxing. Meath got good enough that he was pursued by Minnesota and Michigan State as well as the Badgers. "In the end I couldn't get past the fact I was a Wisconsin native," Meath said, "and so I came to Madison."

He wouldn't regret it. "It gave me my moment of glory," Meath said. "I made a number of very good, lasting friendships."

Of the 1954 tournament, Meath recalled, "For me the real fight was Pete Potter in the semi-finals. He just never quit. He kept coming and coming." Finally, in the third round, Meath recalled a move that Rankin had taught him back at New Richmond High School. "It was a hop back left hook. Potter came at me and I jumped back a little and threw the left and he went down. He beat the count but he was staggering." Meath would win that fight and the next night and, eventually, the boxing equivalent of the Heisman Memorial Trophy. Meath lived in Wisconsin for a time after graduating but eventually his job with Dunn and Bradstreet took him to the Pacific Northwest.

Golden, covering the 1954 tournament for the *Capital Times,* stated bluntly that Hinds, the Badger heavyweight, was robbed when a split decision in the final went to Mike McMurtry of Idaho State. Hinds, Golden wrote, "definitely won in the finals." McCormick in the *State Journal,* however, would only say it was "an unusually fine college heavyweight bout" and that either boxer could have earned the decision. Kuboyama also lost a split decision while Magestro lost to Granger of Syracuse. Still, the team won, in a hostile environment.

It would not get much friendlier in the 1955 tournament. The announcement was made in State College that the next year's event would return to Pocatello, Idaho. The committee's reasoning was they liked to bring it to Madison in an Olympic year like 1956. The UW contingent, not altogether happily, agreed to wait another year.

The mood was better the following Tuesday when the boxing team banquet was held at the Loraine Hotel. At the banquet Walsh decreed that no team of his had exhibited more spirit than the 1954 squad. Since this was Walsh's twentieth year as coach, longtime observers could chuckle and say this was about the twentieth time Walsh had said that about a particular team. If nothing else Walsh was a champion diplomat.

Hinds—nicknamed "Gabby" by some of his teammates—picked up on this and broke up the crowd at the Loraine with an imitation of Walsh being interviewed on radio. Walsh could never find a bad word to say about anybody. Hinds, in mimicking his coach, had the interviewer ask, "What about their fighter at 139?" "Oh, he's going to be tough," Hinds/Walsh would say. "And 145?"

"Oh, very tough. Very tough."

If Walsh could have found a critical word on occasion, he might have directed it at Hinds, whose antics, particularly on road trips, caused some grief. Tynan told me he thought he gave Walsh some gray hair—if that was the case, Hinds probably caused it to drop out. Hinds himself told the story of a road trip to East Lansing, and an important match against Michigan State. Hinds recalled that he was rooming with Joji Tomei, another Hawaiian who had found his way to Madison. "I made him laugh," Hinds said of Tomei. No kidding—Hinds made everybody laugh. When Hinds and Tomei walked into their hotel room in East Lansing, they found two young maids sitting on the bed. "They had just finished cleaning," Hinds recalled. "They jumped up and right away I said, 'Girls, girls, relax. We're boxers. We're just dropping our stuff off and in a little while we are going to a weigh-in.'"

"You are boxers?" one of the maids said.

"We sure are," Hinds said.

The other maid said, "Could you do us a favor? Could you get us four bottles of Berghoff beer?"

Was there any question? It was hardly out of her mouth before Hinds was on the phone to room service. "Four Berghoffs." A few minutes passed and the phone in the room rang. Hinds answered.

"You want Berghoff?"

"Right," Hinds said.

"No Berghoff. How about Schlitz?"

"Schlitz is fine!"

"It is not fine, Mr. Hinds. This is John Walsh."

Hinds began to stammer, "No, Coach, it's not what you think. We have a couple of women up here—"

"You what?"

Hinds could sense it going from bad to worse. And he was innocent! Relating this story a half-century later, Hinds dissolved in laughter and said, "We had a reunion of the boxing team years later, sometime in the 1970s. And they wanted to get a word from Alan Ameche, who didn't box but who was close to a bunch of us, particularly me, and to Vern Woodward. So Alan sent a note that they read at the banquet: 'Vern Woodward's greatest accomplishment, among many great accomplishments, was keeping Bobby Hinds out of jail.'"

The occasion of Ameche's note was actually a retirement party for Woodward in 1980.

At the 1954 banquet, Meath, fresh off winning his title and the LaRowe Trophy in Pennsylvania, received the Downer Memorial Trophy at the banquet. Good friends and frequent sparring partners Magestro and Tynan were named co-captains for 1955. Everyone claimed to be looking forward to the next year.

Looking around at the sea of smiling faces in the crowded Crystal Ballroom of the Loraine, who would worry? The thing is, you need to have somebody to compete against and venerable Penn State was a few short weeks away from announcing the abolition of its college boxing program. Idaho would follow suit a short time later. There were signs, for those who wanted to see. Understandably, few in Madison did.

chapter 6

TWILIGHT

Certainly the press book for the 1955 season, compiled by the UW Sports News Service, contained no sour notes. The cover showed a muscular Bucky Badger raising his arms—complete with boxing gloves—over his head while around him danced stars with the salient and impressive facts of Badger boxing inside: "Most NCAA team titles: 1939, 1942, 1943, 1947, 1948, 1954." Another: "Most NCAA individual titles: 30." And another: "Dual matches: "Won 114, lost 13, drew 11."

The schedule followed, and with that, for the close observer, there were clues that all was not rosy. Only 6 dual matches were scheduled and 2 of those were against Michigan State. Then, when the University of Virginia came to Madison in late February for the second dual match of the season, the Cavaliers' athletic director, Gus K. Tebell, told some members of the Badger boxing program as well as reporters, off the record, that it looked like Virginia was going to drop its boxing program. That spring, in the week leading up to the NCAA tournament, it happened. Earlier in the year Maryland and Army had done the same. While they were both prestigious boxing schools, Virginia—"once a leading center of the collegiate fisticuff sport," according to an AP report—was the shocker, or would have been, if the athletic director hadn't tipped the Badgers earlier in Madison.

"Virginia Gives Up Boxing" was the headline of the *Capital Times* AP story. "Athletic director Gus K. Tebell cited the difficulty in arranging a schedule inasmuch as a number of colleges have dropped boxing in recent years. He said the Cavaliers had traveled more than 5,000 miles for three of six meets this season. Tebell also pointed to waning student interest and winless records the past two seasons."

Some writers could smell blood in the water. Another AP story that moved on the wire tournament week, written by Frank Wetzel, put the question directly to the dean of college boxing coaches, Walsh.

Datelined Pocatello, Wetzel's story began: "The world series of college boxing opens today amid assurances the sport is in fine health." Interviewed

34. By the middle 1950s, college boxing was coming under attack from forces that considered the game too brutal to be sanctioned by prestigious universities. The crowds at Wisconsin dipped, but home attendance still averaged 10,000 or better.

were both Walsh and the rules committee chairman, I. F. "Crip" Toomey, athletic director of the University of California at Davis and a leading proponent of college boxing. Wetzel asked about the sport being dropped by Penn State, Maryland, Army, and Virginia (he left out Idaho). "Both Toomey and Walsh admitted college boxing would miss the four eastern schools," Wetzel wrote. "But they expressed confidence the four colleges would continue intramural programs and eventually return to intercollegiate competition." Walsh and Toomey also claimed other schools were introducing boxing for the first time.

Wetzel: "Well, what caused the four to withdraw from college boxing?" The answer from Toomey and Walsh, according to Wetzel: "Both agreed it was individual problems not maladies which afflicted the entire sport. They pointed to Idaho State, Louisiana State, Wisconsin, San Jose State and other institutions where college boxing is booming."

Walsh said: "Where they will get out and work at promoting it, they won't have any trouble."

Walsh then said the financial problems caused by travel weren't unique to boxing, adding that a deal was in the works to televise college matches in the future, which he thought would help. "There's always criticism of contact sports," Walsh said. "They just pick on boxing more because it isn't as well established as football." Boxing, Walsh said, more than any other sport, gave the small man a chance to compete.

Toomey was more ready than Walsh to concede the sport was in trouble. "But I'm not too alarmed," Toomey said. "Many sports are going down right now. It's just a passing phase. I think boxing will come right back up. It's gone through these declines before."

Well, it hadn't. Not like this. If there was a bright side for Walsh and the Badgers, it was that the 1955 team, after beginning the dual match season with a bad loss to Michigan State at East Lansing, had come roaring back with 4 wins and 1 draw, with one of the victories in the last dual event of the season, a rematch with the Spartans on March 26 at the Field House. Earlier that week, just five days before, the Badgers had hosted LSU and fought the unbeaten Tigers to a 4–4 tie.

More than eleven thousand fans crowded the Field House for the Michigan State match. The Badgers won it 5–3 and one of the team's seniors, Magestro, scored a particularly impressive victory over his previously unbeaten Spartan opponent, John Butler. Magestro later became emotional reflecting with reporters that this would be his last bout in the Field House.

Walsh took five boxers to the 1955 NCAA tournament in Idaho. There were the three stalwarts—Hinds, Magestro, and Tynan—along with a pair of relative newcomers, Jim Schneider, a sophomore from Toledo, Ohio, at 156 pounds (Schneider had won the campus Contenders tournament earlier in the year) and Everett Chambers at 165 pounds. Chambers was a junior, and a graduate of Tomah High School in Wisconsin. He had gone unbeaten during the 1955 dual match season and would be involved in what most observers felt was the bout of the tournament, if not one of the best ever.

There was a dinner for the fighters in Pocatello Wednesday night—though presumably none of them would overdo it at the table, since weigh-in was Thursday morning—sponsored by the chamber of commerce, and naturally the talk centered around who might do well in the event starting the next day. The consensus: of the seventeen teams entering a total of sixty-two boxers, Michigan State and LSU were rated the teams to beat, while Wisconsin and Idaho State were viewed as possible dark horses. In the end it would not prove a great tournament for the Badgers.

The start, however, was all right. The first Badger to fight in the quarterfinals was Magestro, and he drew an old rival, Gil Inaba of Washington State. Magestro had fought Inaba in the semifinals two years prior—that tournament was also in Pocatello—and Magestro would recall that first fight as an "hallucinating experience."

Magestro explained: "This was my first experience in a high altitude athletic contest. I came back to the corner at the end of the first round—which I felt I won, and got hit little or not at all—and said to John Walsh, 'What round is it?'"

Walsh replied, "Are you OK?"

Magestro later theorized it was thin oxygen making him groggy. But he finished the fight, and wasn't alone in thinking the decision, which went to Inaba, could have gone to him. Magestro said even the opposing coach, Deeter, felt the decision was wrong. Yet Magestro would lose twice more to Inaba prior to the 1955 tournament. Now, two years later, Magestro would get a final shot, at altitude, with Inaba—this time in the quarterfinals. Magestro emerged victorious in a split decision—finally the judges' call fell his way.

Hinds advanced to the semifinals with a bye while Schneider and Chambers, the two newcomers to NCAA competition, won decisions—Schneider over Mike McKiernan of Washington State and Chambers over LSU's Gary Bowden. The only Badger to lose Thursday was Tynan, who dropped a close decision to Ted Contri of Nevada.

The semifinals were Friday and the report by AP writer Wetzel led with the inspired performances by three of the four Badgers still in the tournament: "A burly Wisconsin slugger, Bob Hinds, furnished the only major upset of the NCAA boxing tournament last night by stopping heavyweight defending champion Mike McMurtry of Idaho State college. Hinds joins teammates Ev Chambers and Charlie Magestro in the title bouts tonight."

The Hinds victory was regarded as an upset, particularly among the hometown fans in Pocatello. McMurtry had defeated Hinds in the finals a year earlier—though Badger fans could note that Hinds had won when the two fought dual meet bouts in 1954 and 1955. At the tournament, Hinds accomplished something no other college fighter had against McMurtry—a technical knockout. A vicious right hand by Hinds put McMurtry to the canvas in round two and although the Idaho State boxer got up, he was groggy enough that Hinds caught him with another series of blows and the referee stopped it.

Earlier, Magestro had won to advance to the finals but Schneider had lost. A Chambers victory would give the Badgers three in the Saturday night finals and a chance at a successful defense of the team championship. Chambers fought the bout of his life. But then, so might have his opponent, L. G. Neal, of the host school, Idaho State. Their athletic director, Wally Garets, observed later, "Never before in the history of collegiate boxing in Pocatello had the fans seen as exciting a bout." Both threw punches until they could scarcely lift their arms. At the end of the third and final round, Woodward, in Chambers's corner, wondered why the fighters suddenly stopped. They stopped because the fight was over. The crowd noise had been such that Woodward couldn't hear the bell. The decision, split 2–1, went to Chambers. Woodward told his exhausted fighter, "I didn't even hear the bell." Chambers replied, "There were two of us in the ring listening pretty hard."

Saturday, though, proved enormously disappointing for the Badgers. The day began well with the announcement, in the papers, that Wisconsin had asked to host the 1956 tournament and all indications were that the event would be coming again to Madison the following April. On Sunday, in fact, the NCAA announced that the tournament would go to Wisconsin. The Badgers, however, would not be trying for a record third straight national team championship. All of the Badgers to make it to Saturday in the '55 event got dusted in the finals.

Magestro was first, losing at 139 pounds to his old nemesis, Granger of Syracuse. The judges' cards later showed Magestro had a slim lead starting the third round but Granger came out strong, landed a couple of rights, and took a close decision. It was the same thing with Chambers, who dropped a close decision to Max Voshall of San Jose State. Chambers, too, had a lead going into the last round, but perhaps feeling the effects of his bruising semifinal, Chambers wore out in the third and the decision went to Voshall. That left Hinds, who would be fighting his last college fight, with his last chance to get the elusive individual title. A Hinds victory would also have earned the Badgers a tie for the team title with Michigan State. It was not to be.

Crowe Peele of LSU had a surprisingly easy time with Hinds. The issue was never in doubt and the judges' decision was unanimous—Hinds had lost. The Badgers as a team took fifth.

The year-end banquet was held the following week at the Elks Club. Chambers was elected captain. "We have the national tournament here next year," Chambers said. "No team ever has walked out of the Field House with the championship except Wisconsin, and it isn't going to happen next year, either."

Schneider won the Downer Memorial Trophy. Athletic director Guy Sundt spoke at the banquet and if there was any uneasiness about the overall health of college boxing, you couldn't tell it from Sundt. "We have five home matches next year along with the national tournament," Sundt said. "The tournament should have six individuals defending titles. It should be great."

Sundt wasn't wrong. About the tournament or about the Badgers themselves. "Hey, we were the best team ever assembled," Dick Bartmann told me early in 2003, regarding the 1956 Badgers. It was a contention that could be argued but not dismissed out of hand. The '56 Badgers were better than good, and they benefited, to a great extent, from a rules change brought about expressly for the 1955–56 college boxing season.

35. UW coach John J. Walsh accepting the championship trophy after one of the Badgers' eight national titles. Eventually the trophy was named in Walsh's honor.

In Pocatello, at the same time the NCAA Boxing Rules Committee recommended the 1956 tournament be held in Madison, the committee decided to loosen the eligibility requirements for boxing varsity in college. The two major changes were allowing freshmen to box in both dual matches and the tournament, and waiving a rule that stated no college boxer could participate in other amateur bouts after high school graduation. The NCAA may have changed the rules to help the sagging fortunes of college boxing, but their stated reason was that since 1956 was an Olympic year, patriotism required allowing as many young American men as possible a chance to show their stuff in the ring. Both of the rule changes were hugely important for the 1956 Badgers, as they had a strong freshman class and, as one of the freshmen, Bartmann, said: "I don't think any of our guys had less than 25 fights before coming to the university."

Bartmann—young, but tough and experienced—was not atypical of that freshman class. He grew up in a bad neighborhood in the Milwaukee inner city. When we spoke by phone in February 2003 Bartmann was in his winter home in Bradenton, Florida, having just finished jogging and with an hour or so before his golf tee time. He summers in Wisconsin.

"Did your family have much money when you were a kid?"

"None," he said.

His inner city grade school pals included a kid named Orville Pitts, who would eventually join Bartmann on the Badger team in 1956. Bartmann was one of two white kids in a grade school where most of the kids were tough and nobody had any money.

How tough was it? Bartmann was shot in the head when he was ten years old. He was playing marbles outside with a couple of other kids and caught part of a shotgun blast. "Some guy in the neighborhood was having a fight with his wife," Bartmann recalled. "So he shoots off the shotgun. Probably to scare her, I don't know. But the shot goes out the window and hits me. I go to the hospital and they tell me an inch either way and I would be dead. But you know, everybody wasn't lawsuit crazy back then and not a whole lot came of it. The guy apologized."

Bartmann began boxing when he was twelve. He fought in Milwaukee Urban League sanctioned bouts and when he turned sixteen, in 1953, he fought in the Golden Gloves and won the statewide title at 126 pounds. He won again in 1954—that year he was named outstanding boxer for the whole tournament—and by that time Bartmann had come to the attention of Walsh and Woodward in Madison. Woodward came to watch one of his Golden Gloves matches and afterward invited Bartmann to Madison. "Both Woodward and John Walsh knew how to handle people," Bartmann said. "They introduced me to Bobby Hinds and, in fact, Alan Ameche was the guy who showed me around the campus."

Did Bartmann have any qualms about boxing for the UW as a freshman? "Walsh and Woodward convinced me I could do it," he said. So he did. Nearly fifty years later, his Field House memories are vivid. "You'd come out of the locker room and the crowd is roaring and you follow a drum majorette down the aisle and, I mean, it was a great thrill. You'd be embarrassed to lose." As it turned out, Bartmann was so good that he only boxed one year for the Badgers. Despite the best efforts of Walsh and Woodward to talk him out of it, Bartmann turned pro after the 1956 college season and moved to New York City, where he promptly got his nose broken. "I was young and the guys out there were telling me I could make it as a pro," Bartmann recalled. He brought his busted beak back to Milwaukee and eventually had a number of pro fights in the Midwest. Bartmann would wind up as vice president of a mortgage corporation and never really regretted turning pro. Why would he? He could have stayed in college but there was no topping his experiences with the 1956 Badgers.

Bartmann's fellow freshman on that squad, Vince Ferguson, was from New York originally. Other than geography, Ferguson's background was similar to Bartmann's, and after meeting in Madison the two would stay in touch for the next five decades.

"Did you have a lot growing up?" I asked Ferguson in 2003.

"Of course not," he said, his city accent thick and his voice gruff. "My father had a job and I had a nice mother. But a lot? No."

One thing Ferguson's father did was manage prizefighters, so he (Vinnie)—"don't call me Vince"—was boxing by the time he was ten years old. By the time he was fifteen he had traveled to Europe for matches. He attended Peter Stuyvesant High School in Manhattan. "I licked everybody in New York as a kid," Ferguson said. "I was undefeated. I don't like to say it, you know, blowing my own horn. But that's how it was."

By his junior year in high school Ferguson was getting letters from prominent boxing colleges—he heard from Virginia (before they dropped the sport) as well as LSU. And from Wisconsin, both Walsh and Woodward had written and called. In his senior year Ferguson sat down with his dad and asked him, "What do you think?"

"What do you think?" his dad said.

"I think I'll take a shot at Wisconsin. I've never been there."

He was eighteen years old. "I was five days in Madison," Ferguson said, "and they had me fighting in the all-university tournament." His opponent at 156 pounds was a seasoned veteran, Jim Schneider, who would be named captain the following year. But the teenager from New York could really box. "I put him on the deck," Ferguson said. In that regard Schneider may have been first but he was far from last. Ferguson wound up running the table—he was unbeaten over the course of the 1956 season. Maybe because he had a father in the business, Ferguson was not as impressed as others with Walsh's coaching ability—"I'd say he was shrewd but did he really know boxing? I don't think so"—but respected the program Walsh had built. And he liked Madison. "The people in Madison are the nicest in the world," Ferguson said. "They were so kind to me."

Like Bartmann, Ferguson was the beneficiary of the NCAA rule changes that allowed freshmen to box in 1956 and allowed them to have had amateur fights after their high school graduation date. Ferguson had dozens— he'd fought professionals, not as a pro himself, but because of his and his dad's connections in New York. Ferguson was about as experienced a boxer as it was possible for an eighteen-year-old to be.

That was one reason why, also like Bartmann, he left Madison after one year. He'd gone undefeated. What was left to accomplish? "I thought, 'Do I want to do the same thing three more years?'" Ferguson said. "That didn't make any sense."

He called his dad. "I want to be a professional prizefighter."

His father said, "You are sure?"

"Yeah."

"Then come back from Madison. You can turn pro. But the day you turn pro you also enroll at Manhattan College. And if the day comes when you drop out of Manhattan College will be your last day as a prizefighter."

Ferguson recalled, "He wanted me to be a college educated guy. Probably because he was not."

Ferguson got his degree. His pro career, meanwhile, started with a bang. "My first pro fight was in Madison Square Garden. I wound up winning

11 straight and then I fought Doug Jones, who later fought Muhammad Ali. I lost and my dad tore up my pro contract."

Ferguson took his physical education degree and landed a good job teaching at his old high school in Manhattan. In February 2003 when we spoke at length by phone, he in New York and me in Madison, Ferguson said at one point: "I am a New York guy. Right now I am sitting one block from the hospital where I was born. One block, you know?"

For all the talent on the 1956 squad, and its eventual performance in the NCAA tournament in Madison, their dual meet record was not exceptional. The season had begun with disturbing news for all close to the program. In February, it was learned that Crocker had undergone major cancer surgery. It seemed unthinkable. Of all the Badger boxers over all the years, Crocker seemed the most invincible. To his fans he was the "Haymaker" or the "Assassin." His record was marred by only 1 loss, and that came on a scorekeeping error when an official had meant to mark Crocker the winner and only learned too late of his mistake. So fierce was Crocker in the ring that years later, in a 1976 interview with the Wisconsin Oral History Project, assistant athletic director Bill Aspinwall said he actually feared for the opponents who got in the ring with Crocker—as Tom Butler said, his punches made a different sound.

Out of boxing Crocker became a war hero, decorated for his service in the South Pacific. His record included being wounded in the Papua campaign. He married Carol Jean Nelson, daughter of a State Street jeweler, in 1951, and they operated a mink farm near Verona, Wisconsin.

Everyone around the program was shocked to learn of Crocker's illness. The updates after surgery were not encouraging. And on October 26, 1956, Crocker died in a Madison hospital. It was front page news the next day in the *Wisconsin State Journal.* Henry McCormick was away covering a Badger football game at Ohio State but when he returned he devoted a column to Crocker, with this eloquent lead: "He never backed away from a fight, and he did very well in every engagement until the last one."

McCormick continued: "Crocker was a friend of mine of long standing, but I never saw him after he went to the hospital for his final stay there. It isn't the way I wanted it, but it's the way Omar wanted it, and his wishes were respected. Friends and admirers of Omar must remember that. He didn't want to see anybody except members of his immediate family while he was going through the toughest battle of all." The editor concluded:

"Crocker will always be remembered hereabouts as the greatest intercollegiate fighting man ever to represent the school with the greatest record in intercollegiate boxing."

Columnist Roundy Coughlin, the great philistine of the prairie, also weighed in on Crocker with his singularly fractured prose: "Well it's hard to believe but Omar Crocker has passed on when I told some the news they seem to freeze and weep. Omar was great man he had war record that was full of honors on battlefields. In crowd he stood out with his smile and kindness. He was one of finest men to ever stride down the street. Had so much respect for others and was an idol of the younger generation. And was the best college boxer and fighter in Wisconsin history he could hit like world champion, was quick and could take a punch. Was nifty in ring was good boxer and his punches seemed to paralyze other college boxers when he hit them. He could have fought world champions and runner-ups and been great in his weight. Yes folks Omar Crocker was that great."

Crocker died on a Friday and the funeral service the following Monday was at Bethel Lutheran Church in Madison. He was buried in Forest Hills Cemetery. The pallbearers were all former Badger boxers, including two of Crocker's teammates—Jollymore, who flew in from San Francisco, and Swancutt, who came from Maine where he was stationed in the air force. The others were Truman Torgerson, Gene Rankin, Vito Schiro, Bobby Fadner, and Ray Chisholm. There was one pallbearer who was not a Badger boxer: head coach Walsh.

The dual meet season that began with the news of Crocker's illness was not Wisconsin's best, but they started strong, with 4 straight wins. Then on March 17 they went to Pocatello and were beaten 3½–2½ by Idaho State. The Badgers finished the dual meet season with 5 wins and 3 losses—Ferguson and the Badgers mainstay at 178 pounds, Pitts, finished the regular season undefeated. Pitts's win in Baton Rouge in the last dual match was a forfeit. Did the fact that Pitts is African American play into the LSU decision not to put up a fighter against him in their home arena?

If so, it would hardly be the last time Pitts came face to face with racism. He was a fine boxer, from the same inner city Milwaukee grade school as Bartmann. Pitts went to Lincoln High in Milwaukee where he ran track and then, out of high school, he joined the air force, where he picked up considerable boxing experience. Pitts was another with vast boxing experience by the time he got to Madison, having won a middleweight gold medal in the Pan American Games of 1955. Pitts eventually went to law school and moved back to Milwaukee, where he ran successfully for alderman. He was both an attorney and a mortician and would occasionally be introduced as someone qualified "to defend you or bury you."

Pitts was less successful in 1969 when he applied for membership in the Milwaukee branch of the Eagles Club. Pitts was one of four applicants rejected out of 193 and he had no question about why he wasn't accepted. It was skin color, plain and simple, "consistent with the bigotry that is rampant in this sick society," Pitts said. "You would not have needed a crystal ball to forecast what was going to happen at that meeting." Racism was something Pitts continued to battle against and he had a younger brother, Terrance Pitts, who was also an elected official in Milwaukee, serving as a county board supervisor from 1972 to 1973.

If Pitts got the forfeit in Baton Rouge in early April 1956 because of his race, there was some irony in the fact that a week later, at the NCAA tournament in Madison, Pitts wound up facing LSU's Malcolm Buhler in the quarterfinals.

For one of the few times when the tournament was in Madison, Wisconsin was not made the pretourney favorite. That role was reserved for Idaho State, which had nine boxers in the field, as did the Badgers. Fans and administrators had to be pleased with the field—a total of ninety-one boxers sought to enter the tournament. Based on their records the tournament committee accepted a more manageable seventy-one; even so, it was the largest field ever for an NCAA tournament, beating the previous record of seventy in 1952, the last time the event was held in Madison. It promised to be one of the best tournaments yet. A group of Madison boxing fans had been working for months and came up with quite a gift package for the boxers. At the welcoming luncheon at Maple Bluff Country Club each would receive a warmup jacket, courtesy of Madison-based Oscar Mayer foods, a pen and pencil set from Parker Pen—based in nearby Janesville—and a box of cheese from Swiss Colony in Monroe. At weigh-in it was announced that all individual champions would receive a watch, courtesy of Goodman Jewelers in Madison, and the runners-up would get a gold identification bracelet.

The week before the tournament Wisconsin officials put out word that all ringside seats for the event had been sold out. Aspinwall, who handled sales for the athletic department, announced that many orders for the seats—on the floor of the Field House—had been returned unfilled with a note saying that first level bleacher seats and second level balcony seats remained. In Madison college boxing was still a tough ticket.

When the pairings for the first round bouts were announced early in the week, Golden noted in the *Capital Times* that "many Wisconsin fans were getting a good laugh over the final Badger bout of the first day. That bout pits hard-hitting Orv Pitts against Malcolm Buhler of Louisiana State. Last week LSU forfeited the bout to the Badgers at the 178 pound weight and in the opinion of many the southern boy was apparently ducking the fine Wisconsin Negro scrapper. The luck of the draw pairs them tomorrow night."

In the *State Journal*, meanwhile, McCormick previewed the 1956 tournament in a Wednesday column that said of Pitts: "He's a picture boxer who can hit hard and with stunning quickness."

Columnist Coughlin weighed in, in his inimitable way, first observing that most of the tournament visitors were ensconced at the Edgewater Hotel and then noting that the manager of the Edgewater, Augie Faulker— a good friend of Walsh—was telling people not to come into the hotel this week without a tuxedo. Coughlin sniffed: "Augie says he has got one on. I seen him in a tux once I wouldn't want to see him twice." As for tickets to the tournament, Coughlin said, they "were going like hotcakes." Coughlin let his readers know that, incredibly, he now had his own TV program, on WMTV in Madison. He said he'd come on at 9:00 p.m. Friday and talk about the boxing tournament. Or as Coughlin put it: "They must think I am OK on the KO."

Coughlin's first TV appearance began with some unintended hilarity. The columnist smiled broadly at the camera but viewers were looking a little lower: His fly was wide open.

All told in 1956, five Badgers were scheduled for first round bouts. Dean Plemmons at 112 pounds, Ferguson at 156 pounds, and Chambers at 165 pounds drew byes. Plemmons was an interesting study. Like Ferguson and Bartmann, Plemmons was just a freshman, fighting under the relaxed rules put in place for the Olympic year. But unlike the other two who grew up poor in the inner city, Plemmons came from the south, Winston-Salem, North Carolina, and only began boxing in high school after breaking his arm playing football. At 112 pounds he was probably too small for football but as Tynan said, boxing gave you a chance no matter your size. Plemmons was five feet five inches and had fought at several different weights during the 1956 season, up to 132 pounds—for the tournament he was all the way down to 112 pounds. He returned to Winston-Salem after college and ran a successful chemical company while remaining active at the top levels of amateur boxing, as a volunteer, into the 1980s. He spoke often of his devotion to the sport. Plemmons gave a thoughtful answer in November 1984 when author Wallenfeldt asked him what it was about boxing that seemed to build such character into boxers and such camaraderie among them.

"I think anyone going into the ring has a fear," Plemmons said, "he has a feeling. As a boxer you call it nervousness. It happens every time you go into the ring, so you respect people [who go through the same experience]. Even after umpteen bouts when you start up those stairs, you say to yourself, 'Hey! Do I really want to go through with this?'"

I read Plemmons's quote in Wallenfeldt's book only a day or two after talking myself with Ferguson, and reading the quote I felt a shock of recognition. Ferguson had alluded to the same thing. It spoke to the simple courage it took to get into the ring to box. The courage it took could and did get lost in the fanfare of spotlights and thousands of fans in the Field House, or, more often, in the endless intellectual debates over whether or not boxing was a "proper" activity, especially as it pertained to whether it should be sanctioned by good universities. The idea of the courage it took could get lost in all of that but in the end it didn't matter, because the boxers themselves knew. What they knew was as simple as this: It took guts to get in the ring.

Ferguson, speaking to me by phone from New York City, had said, "Have you ever boxed?"

"Never," I said.

"What you have to realize," he said next, "is that this is a sport not like any other. You do not have teammates to help you once you are in the ring. Well, I suppose on the tennis team you don't either, but you know how that's different?"

"How?"

"You don't get hit."

It was interesting that the boxers didn't talk about it much, but it was always there. You hit and get hit. It was the glory and curse of their sport.

What was it Hinds told me about the first time you get knocked dizzy in the ring? It stayed with you like a scar.

Of the five Badgers who fought Thursday, four came away with wins. Only Schneider, at 147 pounds, lost in the quarterfinals, a tough and close split decision. Tomei won for the Badgers at 132 pounds—a unanimous decision over Jack Fair of Houston. Bartmann also won an undisputed decision, over John Dusenberry of Louisiana State. The Pitts-Buhler match at 178 pounds, with the racial overtones stemming from Buhler's forfeit in Baton Rouge the week before, proved to be both a terrific exhibition of boxing and something more than that. Pitts was on fire in the first 2 rounds and almost had Buhler put away, but the LSU fighter hung on gamely, refusing to quit, never going to the canvas despite being staggered more than once by ferocious blows from Pitts. The decision gave every round to Pitts but it was afterward that the fighters truly distinguished themselves, black and white, wrapping arms around one another "in a gesture of sincere respect," as McCormick put it.

Had race been an issue when Wisconsin traveled to Baton Rouge a week earlier, and Pitts received his point by forfeit? Pitts's teammate Bartmann told me it was absolutely racism. "Orville didn't even make the trip," Bartmann said, and when I checked it turned out he was right. On Tuesday of that week LSU announced it would not suit a boxer at 178 pounds. Pitts then said he wouldn't make the trip to Louisiana but instead would remain in Madison and spar with the recently graduated Hinds. It would have been nice if the administrators down in Baton Rouge could have seen Buhler and Pitts arm and arm in the ring after their bout at the Field House.

In another quarterfinal, Wisconsin heavyweight Truman Sturdevant fought an interesting bout with Jerry Dooling of Detroit. Afterward, Sturdevant, who got the decision, said that he felt he had a chance to knock out Dooling after the first round but that in his corner, Walsh suggested it might help Sturdevant to go all 3 rounds in this opening bout. "So from that point I just kept jabbing and moving," Sturdevant said.

All told Wisconsin sent seven fighters into the semifinals. By the time Friday's action was done, the Badgers had virtually wrapped up another championship. The night ended with Wisconsin ahead in the team score with 22 points while favored Idaho State was next with 15. Of the seven Badgers to box in the semis only Chambers got beat. The Field House crowd of 10,319 had plenty of chances to roar. The two-day attendance of just over twenty-four thousand was some three hundred more than the 1952 event in Madison drew over the same time.

Was the crowd well behaved? Not if you asked one Idaho State boxer. Idaho State's McMurtry, who had fought some epic battles over the years with Field House favorite Hinds of the Badgers, was not beloved in Madison. Actually nobody from Idaho State was likely to get a warm reception, but McMurtry was the least liked among equals. And on Friday, McMurtry boxed what proved to be a very controversial semifinal fight with George Pelonis of California. Of the three judges, one gave all three rounds to Pelonis, but the other two gave a thin 2–1 edge to McMurtry so the Idaho State fighter advanced to the finals.

The Madison reporters were aghast, especially Coughlin, who lead off his Saturday "Roundy Says" column by ridiculing the decision. Coughlin was so upset that he wrote in nearly complete sentences: "That boxing decision at Field House where they voted Mike McMurtry winner over George Pelonis was the rankest boxing decision ever announced in the Field House. That decision smelled like nine cesspools that covers were left off of. What a stinko to announce. The booing was heard out to Middleton and Sun Prairie. After that decision they should shut off the lights and said bouts are over. I don't think McMurtry won a round at all." Coughlin continued on to say that if McMurtry won the bout, "I am going to win that spelling bee in Washington next month." The referee that scored it for Pelonis, Coughlin noted, "should be given badge of honor for such perfect call." And finally, Coughlin said, "the judging of boxing bouts is on nutty side. It's ruining boxing. I will get into that next week and how."

Somewhat less emotional and far more grammatical was the assessment of Monte McCormick, Henry's younger brother, who capsulized all the semifinal bouts in the same paper. Of the McMurtry fight, McCormick wrote that the split decision for the Idaho State fighter produced a "spontaneous, prolonged booing that nearly raised the rafters of the Field House. Pelonis apparently, to us and many others, had built up an early lead and certainly landed the better punches. He often landed a right lead flush on the jaw and followed with a rocking left hook."

McMurtry heard the boos, and worse. As the fighter stepped out of the ring and turned, waiting on the steps for his corner man, McMurtry felt a pain below his waist and looked with astonishment upon a rabid female Wisconsin fan who was yelling and hammering at him with her purse. Apparently this woman had not read the NCAA's suggestions on proper fan decorum. Years later McMurtry recalled the episode in a letter to author Wallenfeldt: "I was rather upset to say the least," McMurtry noted. "I was really wondering how and in what direction I was supposed to go in order to get back to my dressing room. Then, all of a sudden and much to my delight, two of my teammates, Roger Rouse and Dave Abeyta, came to my rescue."

McMurtry also noted: "I did get an apology from Mr. Walsh many years later."

The Badgers' semifinal bouts were less controversial—probably because six of the seven UW fighters scored victories. First up was Plemmons at 112 pounds who according to McCormick "gave T. C. Chung of San Jose State a neat boxing lesson" in winning a unanimous decision. Tomei at 132 pounds was fighting a boxer, Harold Hebert of LSU, who had defeated him during the dual meet season. Indeed, Hebert's record for the year was 7 wins and 1 draw, but in the tournament semifinal, the unanimous decision went to Tomei. Bartmann at 139 pounds was next and it was another unanimous verdict for the Badger, though Bartmann couldn't quite put Pete Godinez of Cal Poly on the canvas. Ferguson's win at 156 pounds was the New York native's ninth straight of the season. The bout, fairly even for the first 2 rounds, went to Ferguson in the last after a hard punch to Gus Fiacco of Syracuse's right cheek raised a nasty welt. The bout at 165 pounds was the Badgers' only loss of the night—Wisconsin captain Chambers suffered a technical knockout at the hands of Idaho State's Rouse. There was no disgrace in losing to Rouse, who later turned pro. Rouse's college record was a most impressive 31–1 and he would be the U.S. representative at 165 pounds in the 1956 Olympics.

The Badgers' Pitts—who would himself almost make the Olympic team, losing the tryout finals after sustaining a cut and a subsequent technical knockout—moved into the NCAA finals with a quick and fierce win over Jack Shaw of Cal Poly. It was the shortest fight on Friday. Pitts dropped Shaw with the second right he threw and though Shaw got up he was shaken, and Pitts put him to the floor twice more before the fight was stopped after a little more than a minute of the first round. In the heavyweight division, the Badgers' Sturdevant whipped Hal Espy of Idaho

State with a unanimous decision that moved six Wisconsin fighters into Saturday night's finals.

Saturday, April 14, 1956, was a date to remember in the storied annals of Wisconsin boxing. A frenzied crowd of 13,879—attendance at the Field House would never again be so high—saw the Badgers smash the team point total record as five of Wisconsin's six finalists won individual championships. That meant that fully half the weight classes went to the Badgers. UW had 47 team points to runner-up Idaho State's 27 and their third national championship in five years. No one could have predicted it would also be their last.

It's interesting how memory works or doesn't. I had a chance early in 2003 to ask two of the Badgers' 1956 champions about their final bouts. Bartmann, who won a close split decision (one of two split decisions that night) over Dan Axtman of Idaho State, could remember very little. "The newspapers say you landed a lot of rights in the third round," I told Bartmann. "I guess I did," he said.

His friend Ferguson, on the other hand, said, "I remember everything. Are you kidding me? It was my life." Ferguson had the other split decision win that night. "I was an 18 year old kid fighting a seasoned fighter," Ferguson said. "He'd had 92 amateur fights by the time I got him." Ferguson was talking about his opponent in the finals, Dick Wall of Oklahoma. Wall had been the national Golden Gloves champion in 1953 and 1955 and his bout with Ferguson, in the estimation of Henry McCormick writing that night, was "savage."

McCormick noted: "Ferguson won the first round, and shook Wall badly about mid-way through the second. But the Wisconsin boy got a trifle careless going for the kill, and the Oklahoma representative shook him with a couple of savage wallops." In the end two judges had it for Ferguson, one for Wall, and it was that bout that mathematically gave the Badgers their eighth NCAA team championship.

The 178-pound final was still of high interest in that it matched Wisconsin's Pitts with McMurtry of Idaho State, the boxer whose controversial semifinal win had brought a wave of boos, not to mention a purse-wielding attacker, from the Field House audience. Pitts moved to settle the issue early and knocked McMurtry down in the first round. McMurtry rose in time to keep the fight going but never really challenged and the unanimous decision went to Pitts. Then, in the last bout of the tournament,

Sturdevant won the heavyweight crown with a unanimous decision over Billy Ray Smith of Arkansas. Monte McCormick called it "the dullest bout of the night" but it gave Wisconsin five individual champions.

It was an impressive performance by any measure but perhaps more so when you consider that Frank Gilmer, one of the tournament's three judges and a veteran boxing administrator from Chicago, later said the overall caliber of the field was as good as any college event he'd ever seen, on par with the 1952 crop which yielded five Olympic champions in the games later that year. In a column a few days after the event McCormick heaped yet more praise on Walsh, whose squad had come in as an underdog to Idaho State and then not only won but did so in record fashion.

"When it comes to getting a team ready for a tournament," McCormick wrote, "and handling that team during the tournament competition, there is no college boxing coach who can match Wisconsin's Johnny Walsh. That was a magnificent job he did of getting Wisconsin ready for the NCAA meet which closed here Saturday night and he was as sharp as a horse trader at handling his boys during the action."

The Elks Club was once again the site of the year-end banquet. Sturdevant got the Downer Memorial Trophy and Schneider was named captain of the next year's team. There was a particularly nice moment when Walsh presented a watch to graduating captain Chambers. All individual champions were given a special watch, designed by Madison jewelers Bob and Irv Goodman, and the Goodmans made an extra watch especially for Chambers, who didn't win a title himself but whose leadership, the Goodmans said, had produced the best showing by any team in the history of the tournament. New UW athletic director Williamson spoke for many when he said: "The test of a team is to put on a peak performance when it is needed." The Badgers had done that as if by blueprint.

A good thing, too, since the outlook for the 1957 season was not the best. Even the official program for the preseason all-university tournament included a feature on the inside cover titled, "Wisconsin Boxing Prospects For 1957 Season" and the story began with a glum note: "The outlook for the University of Wisconsin's boxing team, after a sensational 1956 season, appears slim, indeed." The previous year's team was decimated. Bartmann and Ferguson had decided to turn pro. Pitts was in school but "undecided," according to the program, if he would continue as an amateur. Sturdevant, Chambers, and Tomei had graduated. Schneider, the captain-elect for 1957, was ruled scholastically ineligible. Slim was right.

"John Walsh was occasionally fit to be tied over grades," Terry Monson said. Monson was a member of the 1957 team, a Madison kid who graduated from West High and had never boxed at all before enrolling at UW–Madison. Monson had been too small for football in high school and never told his parents when he began boxing. "They found out when they saw my picture in the newspaper," he said.

Monson had been encouraged to start boxing by two UW boxers, John Hughes and Charlie Mohr. Hughes was also a Madison townie who grew up near Monson, and in an agriculture class he introduced Monson to Mohr, who in 1957 was a freshman just arrived from New York City.

Ferguson—the 1956 champion, also from New York—told me he was responsible for Mohr's coming to Madison. "I was the first New York kid to come to Madison to box," Ferguson said. "I knew Charlie, he was a year younger than me, and at one point he called up and said, 'Do you think I could get a scholarship?' I said I would talk to Walsh. And I did. I went to his law office and I told Walsh, 'Look, there's a kid out in New York who is not only a hundred times nicer than me, but he's a good student and a good boxer.' They gave him a scholarship."

Mohr arrived in September 1956 and later that fall he encouraged Monson to try out. Monson recalled: "He said it was a sport that takes the edge off things, studying and what have you." Monson, who at that point didn't know a speed bag from a shopping bag, began stopping by practice and found he liked it, although he didn't know about it taking the edge off studying. There were times after practice, at the library, when he found himself cracking a book with his ears still ringing. But Monson did enjoy the camaraderie of the boxing team.

"We did everything together," he recalled. "Study, go to movies, go to dinner at Paisan's." Three weeks after Monson had begun practicing he found himself entered in the all-university tournament, which preceded the start of the 1957 varsity tournament by one week, and his opponent was Pete Spanakos, who had come out from New York City with Mohr and had a vast amount of experience in the ring. Pete would say later, everyone would, that the one thing Mohr lacked as a boxer was the killer instinct. He was too nice a guy to finish his opponent off. That was not a problem for Spanakos, but Monson would remember that the day of his all-university bout with Spanakos at 139 pounds was February 15, the day before there arrived by messenger a Valentine's Day card for Monson— signed by Spanakos!

Monson would remember their fight when I spoke to him in February 2003, forty-six years to the month later. "I nailed him early with a good left hook," Monson said, "and that was one of two times I heard the crowd really roar. I was from Madison, after all. The other time was when I first walked out into the Field House and the roar scared the daylights out of me." Monson's good early punch was not enough to derail the much more experienced Spanakos, and in the second round he put the fight away. "He was shorter than I was and got inside me a lot," Monson said. The fight was stopped in the second—a technical knockout for Spanakos.

Spanakos roomed in Madison with Mohr. The Olympic year rule of freshman being eligible was not in place for 1957 so while they could work out with the varsity team they didn't box in the matches. The team could have used them. The year 1957 was a forgettable one for Badger boxing, and Spanakos said he made it even less enjoyable for Walsh by suggesting at one point that the college fighters should be paid. "He went nuts," Spanakos said. "He said I was ungrateful." Spanakos replied, "We should have a union." Spanakos eventually transferred to the College of Idaho and would make a triumphant return to Madison in late April of 1959, when the Pan American Boxing Trials—a kind of off year Olympics— were held at the Field House. Those games were most remarkable for the appearance in Madison of a young boxer from Kentucky named Cassius Clay—later Muhammad Ali.

The 1957 Badgers fought 6 dual matches, winning only 2. The largest crowd they boxed in front of was just over five thousand for a match with Washington State at the Field House that the Badgers won 4½–3½. Probably the most interesting note on the 1957 schedule was the appearance of San Jose State, whom the Badgers had not faced in dual competition since 1939. San Jose would become a regular foe over the next few years and as the Badgers' squads remained mediocre—certainly by UW's high standards—San Jose State made strides in establishing itself as the premiere collegiate boxing program in the country. They hammered the Badgers in the first dual meet of 1957, 6–2 on February 22 in Madison.

The 1957 NCAA tournament was another return to Pocatello, Idaho. The decline in the Badgers' fortunes can be seen in the decision by both daily Madison papers to not send a reporter to cover the event. The Badgers had been to Pocatello just the week before the tournament and were handed a 6–2 defeat by Idaho State, which along with hosting the 1957 finals was also established as a heavy favorite to win the team title.

The Badgers had five fighters entered in the tournament. Two fought on Thursday in the quarterfinals and both went down. At 156 pounds San Jose's Stu Rubine won a third round technical knockout over the Badgers' Ron Marshall while at 132 pounds Dick Rall of Washington State decisioned UW's Rollie Nesbitt.

By Saturday, the Badgers had only one boxer left in the tournament— Ron Freeman at 178 pounds. In the semifinals the Badgers' Bobby "Tex" Wilhelm lost at 147 pounds to Billy Haynes of Idaho State and at 119 pounds another Idaho State fighter, Abeyta, out-pointed UW's Armando Zeledon. Freeman kept the Badgers from being shut out of the finals with a close decision over Don Adams of Cal Poly.

Freeman almost won the title. He fought a valiant final bout against Dale Leatham of Idaho State. According to the non-bylined *Wisconsin State Journal* report, Freeman and Leatham put on an old-fashioned slugfest with several toe-to-toe exchanges that had Freeman ahead on points as the third round wound down. With a little less than twenty seconds left in the fight Leatham backed Freeman up against the ropes and with a withering right hand cross the Idaho State fighter caused Freeman's knees to buckle. As Freeman struggled for his feet the bout referee, Joey August, stepped in and stopped it. It was a technical knockout win for Leatham.

It should be noted that while the Badgers were shut out—no individual champions—Idaho State ran up an incredible total of seven individual championships in the 1957 tournament. Giving the team trophy named for him to the Bengals' coach, Dubby Holt, Walsh graciously said the Bengals were one of the best college teams ever assembled. Perhaps only the Badger squads of 1939 and 1956 could compare.

Back in Madison the next week, UW boxing fans distinguished themselves again by coming out in force for the team banquet even though it had been, by Badger standards, a disastrous year, UW's poorest ever. The banquet was held at a new West Side restaurant, the Cuba Club, on University Avenue, and Walsh was touched by the overflow crowd. "I simply can't tell you how much this means to all of us," the coach said. "With this kind of support, all I can say is, 'Idaho State, look out next year.'"

Athletic board chairman Marvin Schaars said, "You did not have the same experience this year as many of our previous boxing teams had, but

you did the best you could. Nobody expects more than that." Athletic
director Ivy Williamson spoke and said about the same thing: "You were
in there punching all the time." Awards were handed out, as always, and
the "best freshman" award went to Mohr, identified in the *State Journal* by
writer Roger Cantwell as "a talented New York southpaw." The Downer
Memorial Trophy went to Freeman, the Badger light heavyweight who
had come so close to a championship in Pocatello.

"This wasn't the end of a glorious boxing tradition," Freeman said. "It's
just the beginning."

Noble sentiments, but Freeman couldn't have been more wrong. Within
a year, the biggest name in all of college boxing, a living legend in the sport
and a breathing symbol of Wisconsin's supremacy, would be gone from
the scene. Nobody knew it yet, but the next season would be Walsh's last
as head coach.

It would have been nice if he could have gone out a winner, but that
wasn't going to happen. In fact, the 1958 season was even less successful
than the disaster of 1957. Again the largest crowd of the year barely topped
five thousand. The Badgers had 6 matches but could only find four opponents, and met Idaho State and Michigan State twice. Their dual match
record was 1 win, 3 losses, and 2 ties.

Yet the sport in Madison continued to attract some interesting personalities. Two of them fought in the finals of the Contender's tournament in
January 1958. Along with the annual all-university tournament, the Contender's was one of two major preseason events for boxers on campus.
Given the depth of talent in Madison, some years it may have been as hard
to win the campus title as a national championship.

One of the heavyweight finalists in the January 1959 Contender's was
Tom Wiesner, who came to UW–Madison from Neenah, Wisconsin, to
play football, which he did, serving as co-captain for the football Badgers
in the 1959 season that saw UW go to the Rose Bowl. The Badgers lost
that game to Washington, 44–8, but Wiesner, a running back, scored the
only touchdown, and in fact the first touchdown ever by a Wisconsin
player in the grandest of all the bowl games. UW had made it to the game
once before, in 1953, but had been shut out 7–0 by University of Southern California.

Wiesner would eventually box in the 1959 NCAA tournament as a
heavyweight, and as one might expect of an athlete who excelled at two

sports, Wiesner had the drive to become a successful businessman after graduating. Wiesner moved to Las Vegas and after starting in the tire business, he eventually operated a bar and restaurant that quickly became several bars and restaurants. Big Dog's Hospitality Group was the name of Wiesner's company and because he maintained his Wisconsin contacts, Wiesner's places were must-stops for Badger fans or any Wisconsinite visiting Vegas. Wiesner hosted a big fund-raiser for UW athletics in Las Vegas every summer and was the moving force in getting a football series started between the UW and the University of Nevada–Las Vegas (UNLV). Wiesner served on the board of regents for UNLV and was elected a supervisor of Clark County. Yet part of him always bled Badger red. Any tourist from Wisconsin could call him for an insider's guide to his adopted hometown. I did once, in the middle 1980s, at the suggestion of a mutual friend, and Wiesner was so friendly and so helpful that by the end of our fifteen-minute talk I felt like we must have gone to high school together. But, no, that was how he was with everyone.

Late in 2001 Wiesner came down with leukemia. He went to Seattle for treatment and we spoke once by phone while he was there. He asked me not to write about his illness in my newspaper column and of course I agreed. "I'm going to beat this," he said, "and then we'll talk." He died the following July and the memorial service in Las Vegas included a large group of Madison movers and shakers, among them UW athletic director Pat Richter and head football coach Barry Alvarez. "His spirit symbolized the toughness that football coaches try to achieve," Alvarez said.

Nevada Governor Kenny Guinn and former U.S. Senator Paul Laxalt were also there, as was former congressman and presidential candidate Jack Kemp. Kemp spoke and mentioned that he had first met Wiesner in 1961. At the time Kemp was quarterbacking the San Diego Chargers of the new American Football League and Wiesner had just been cut by the National Football League's Los Angeles Rams. At the service Kemp said that it was a full decade before he heard from Wiesner again. Kemp was in Congress, representing a New York district and Wiesner was becoming active in Republican politics around Las Vegas.

After a pleasantry or two, Wiesner said, "Kemp, do you believe in free speech?"

"Well, Tom," Kemp said, "I worship at the shrine of the First Amendment. How can you ask me if I believe in free speech?"

Wiesner replied, "How would you like to give one in Nevada for the Republican Party?"

Of course, Kemp gave the speech. I remember talking to Richter in July 2002 just after he had returned from the service in Las Vegas, and the athletic director was particularly impressed with the breadth of the impact Wiesner had in Nevada. "Of 10 speakers," Richter said, "all knew him well and yet all were from a different area of his life. We didn't know all the many things he did."

Boxing was one. And while Wiesner would capture the 1959 Contenders' Tournament heavyweight title, he lost in the January 1958 finals to a young agriculture student named Bill Urban.

Urban, who would eventually also win an NCAA tournament bout, though not a championship, was from Mosinee, Wisconsin, in the north central part of the state between Stevens Point and Wausau. Urban boxed Golden Gloves in high school and when he first came to Madison in the fall of 1955—to take a short course in agriculture—he found his way to the training room at the Field House, where he met Walsh and Woodward and worked out with members of the boxing team. Walsh urged Urban to enroll as a full-time freshman, which he did the following fall.

Though the teams he boxed on were not among the best in Badger boxing history, far from it, Urban's experience in the ring in Madison was extremely positive. "It was a great sport," he said when we spoke in February 2003. "It taught you self-discipline and it taught you never to quit. Some of the things you learned might be cliches, but you learned that they were true. When the going gets tough, the tough get going." Urban, who became a high school guidance counselor and administrator in the Madison area, said: "I'm still that way. I don't back away from anything." Of college boxing, he concluded: "It made you a man."

More than forty-five years later, Urban recalled that walking into the Field House to box "gave me chills." He remembered the crowds as bigger than they were—by Urban's era, attendance had dropped from the thirteen thousand-plus that once packed the house. But if there were only five or six thousand, it was still a bigger crowd than could be produced at any other school, and they were loud.

Urban was a member of the 1958 team that received stunning news from Walsh one day in the locker room. The coaching legend told his fighters that the '58 season would be his last. "It was a shock," Urban said. "It was a blow to us." Longtime observers had noticed that Walsh had been a little less hands-on in the past few years. Monson, during the 1957 season, had noticed that Walsh was leaving more and more of the coaching duties to Woodward.

Walsh announced his intentions during the 1958 season in a letter to athletic director Williamson:

"My connection with Wisconsin," Walsh wrote in part, "the boys who reported each year for boxing, the athletic department staff, and athletic fans and friends has been an experience for which I am extremely grateful. I hope in the future to lend every effort and be active as a Wisconsin alumnus, and to keep the University of Wisconsin out in front, both as an outstanding educational institution and athletic power in all sports." Walsh recommended in the letter that Woodward be promoted as his replacement.

Williamson issued a statement: "In the past 25 years, John Walsh has been the outstanding figure in intercollegiate boxing. During his brilliantly successful career he not only influenced thousands of boys as coach, but as a friend and advisor as well. His loss will be deeply felt, not only by the athletic department, but by the entire university."

Why did Walsh decide to retire? The most popular theory is that his law practice was growing ever more complex and taking increasing chunks of his time.

"I think he was burned out," his wife, Audrey Walsh, told me in 2001.

Walsh discussed his decision in a 1998 interview for *Ring Sports* magazine with longtime Wisconsin-based boxing writer Pete Ehrmann.

"It was starting to get to me," Walsh said. "At 4:20 I'd leave my law office, and I'd blow the whistle [for practice] at 4:45. I started to shake at 45 years of age and I said, 'This is it!' Coaching was my avocation and law was my vocation. I went full time with my vocation, and I haven't shaken since."

Others speculate that Walsh also had begun to feel that his longtime assistant, Woodward, who had been with the program since 1937, deserved a shot as head coach. The theory least charitable to Walsh is that with college boxing in general and the Wisconsin program in particular in decline, getting out was a good idea if the goal was to preserve his legendary status. Conceding that it is much more fun to win than not, and that rebuilding a college sports program is a young man's job, most observers reject that theory. Walsh quit as a head coach but stayed close to the program. In 1959 he was even president of the program's booster club, the Downtown Seconds. He spoke that year at the season-end banquet and the following year, when the NCAA tournament was held in Madison, Walsh served as a referee. He had coached for twenty-five years. By the late 1950s it was someone else's turn.

Sad to say, Walsh's last campaign was not a good one. With only 1 win in the dual meet season the Badgers didn't have a lot of hope for a good NCAA tournament showing when the event was held in Sacramento in late March 1958. That California should host the tournament was not surprising—college boxing over the past several seasons had become a western sport. Of the twelve teams with entries, itself a disappointing number, only Wisconsin and Michigan State were from east of the Mississippi River. There was also one Virginia boxer, William Hartz, though his school no longer had a varsity program.

Walsh brought four fighters with him to Sacramento for his last tournament as coach: heavyweight Freeman, Mohr at 156 pounds, Bob Christopherson at 165 pounds, and John Drye at 139 pounds. Drye went out the first night, losing a decision to Ray Almeida of Hawaii, but the other three Badgers won their preliminary bouts and wound up in the finals. Saturday in Sacramento was not a good night for the Badgers. The AP report that ran in the next day's *State Journal* began: "It was a sad end to the coaching career of the man who once raised college boxing to the status of a major college sport."

All three Badgers lost, and the team point total of ten put the Badgers fourth—San Jose won the team title with 33 points and four individual champions. Walsh was uncharacteristically bitter about one of the bouts, feeling that Christopherson had won his fight with Jim Flood of Sacramento State but that the Badger had been "homered" out of the decision. Walsh called it the worst decision he had seen in a quarter-century of coaching. Later, at a party for everyone involved in the tournament at the Newman Club on the Sacramento campus, the coach cooled down and found himself joking with Michigan State athletic director, Biggie Munn, about the 1932 Olympics, for which they had both tried out without success: Walsh as a boxer and Munn in track and field. Walsh must have also been pleased at the award ceremonies to receive a desk set recognizing his extraordinary twenty-five years in the game. It was inscribed: "To Johnny from the National Intercollegiate Boxing Coaches Association for 25 years of service."

Of course, that was just the beginning of the honors and awards. Back in Madison the following week, the annual year-end banquet turned into a love fest for Walsh. It was held in the Crystal Ballroom of the Loraine Hotel on West Washington Avenue and more than five hundred people turned up. Maybe the only one of consequence who couldn't make it was Walsh's longtime Boswell, *State Journal* sports editor Henry McCormick, who had left that day on a Caribbean cruise. In a column that ran that morning, McCormick saluted his friend: "Johnny Walsh has been a good friend of mine for most of the 25 years he has been here. I have always had the highest respect for him as a teacher and have respected him for the way he has conducted his sport. They'll be giving Walsh a fitting present tonight, and that's fine, but his real reward for 25 years of working with young men at Wisconsin is the respect and affection with which these young men regard him."

36. John Walsh (left) retired in 1958. The gala dinner in his honor was not an altogether serious affair.

JOHN WALSH

HEAD BOXING COACH

1934 - 1958

• COMPILED AN OVERALL 116-22-1 RECORD FOR 23 YEARS AS WISCONSIN'S BOXING COACH.

• NINE OF HIS TEAMS WERE UNBEATEN.

• COACHED WISCONSIN TO EIGHT NCAA TEAM TITLES.

• COACHED 31 INDIVIDUALS WHO WON A TOTAL OF 38 NCAA CHAMPIONSHIPS.

• CO-COACH OF THE 1948 U.S. OLYMPIC TEAM.

• MEMBER MADISON PEN AND MIKE CLUB-BOWMAN SPORTS FOUNDATION HALL OF FAME.

CHARTER MEMBER
INDUCTED APRIL 26, 1991

37. Figures don't lie. With the exception of UCLA basketball coach John Wooden, Walsh may have been the most successful coach of any college team in any sport.

That was well said, and true, and the twenty-six former boxers who made their way back to Madison, some from considerable distance, to honor their coach was proof, if any was needed. That evening in the *Capital Times* Bonnie Ryan did a column that was headlined, "Ex-Badger Boxing Stars Successful In Many Fields."

One of them, former national champion Warren Jollymore, had come over from Detroit, where he had become a top public relations executive with General Motors. Jollymore was to act as master of ceremonies at the banquet and he brought with him a 1958 Chevrolet Impala convertible, which was the gift for Walsh that McCormick had alluded to in his column that morning.

Jollymore started out the evening recalling that when he first laid eyes on Walsh, he hated his guts. That was because that first sighting came in an amateur boxing match in Minneapolis in which Jollymore's older brother, Jock, went up against a tough Twin Cities fighter named—Walsh. Walsh did not lose too many amateur bouts and he knocked Jock Jollymore out in the Twin Cities Amateur. Warren Jollymore, of course, conquered that first impression and not only came to Wisconsin to box for Walsh but came to revere him. Another champion, Truman Torgerson, spoke at the banquet as representative of all the former boxers, an honor he said might never be topped.

"This is the proudest moment of my life," Torgerson said that night at the Loraine. "To express for all former Wisconsin boxers their appreciation to John Walsh, not only as the greatest boxing coach but the greatest coach."

Torgerson spoke about Walsh's gifts as an instructor: How he over and over again emphasized fundamentals and not settling for less than one's best; how he demanded his athletes be in the best possible physical condition; how he insisted on good sportsmanship and how, time and again, a word of advice from Walsh in the corner had made the difference in a Badger fighter winning in the following round.

"Anybody was welcome to try out for the boxing team," Torgerson said. "He never cut anybody. Coach Walsh would say, 'That's what college boxing is for—to build men.'"

Torgerson concluded by reading a poem, "Throne In My Heart for My Boys," that he dedicated to Walsh. "I think Coach Walsh's greatest attribute was his humanness," Torgerson said. "He is kind, keen, patient and understanding."

Years later, Hinds, the great heavyweight from the broken home in Kenosha, could be moved quite easily to tears when recalling Walsh's kindnesses. "John was like a father, a *good* father," Hinds said. "He was tough, but you knew he cared about you, cared about how you were doing in school. We knew he loved us, really loved us, like we were his own kids."

It was a theme that repeated itself. In another interview, Morgan, a champion in 1952, said, "I didn't have a father. John became my father. A surrogate father, anyway."

Other speakers included George Barton, who when Walsh was making his great run as an amateur boxer in the Twin Cities was sports editor of the *Minneapolis Tribune*. Barton recalled other Twin Cities amateur boxing greats in saluting Walsh.

"John was a product of the Mike Gibbons style of fighting," Barton said. "I saw him work out and get tips from Jock Malone and Sammy Mandell. He became the nearest amateur boxer to Gibbons that I ever saw.

"I am as proud of John as if he were my own son," Barton concluded. "He strove for perfection and got it, and that was a beautiful thing to watch. He's the greatest college boxing coach of all time."

Governor Vernon Thomson had been scheduled to speak but a complication getting back from out of town kept him away. In his place, Wisconsin Attorney General Stewart Honeck spoke glowingly of Walsh, with whom he enjoyed a good friendship: "John's teaching was typical of himself," Honeck said. "By his quiet confidence and teaching of ethics, he was merely imparting to his boys the things he has practiced all his life. His sportsmanship in the ring reflects in his business. The boys he coached are a silent testimonial to his teaching. You, John Walsh, over the years have honored us."

It was all a little overwhelming. But then a series of gag gifts lightened the mood—a toupee, false teeth, and a plastic nose—and then in conclusion Walsh was made the gift of the new Chevrolet. Finally, it was the outgoing coach's turn to speak.

"These have been very happy years," Walsh said, his voice cracking just a bit. "I get a great satisfaction out of seeing all of the boxers back, but I get a greater satisfaction out of knowing what they have accomplished and feeling I may have had a little something to do with their success.

"I am not retiring," the coach concluded. "I will be around and maybe I can help Vern, who has helped me so much."

Earlier, Woodward had handed out the boxing awards at the banquet. Mohr was the big winner, receiving both the Downer Memorial Trophy and the co-captaincy for the 1959 season, an honor he would share with Christopherson.

The hope expressed at the banquet was that the 1959 season would be better and it was, if barely. It marked the arrival on campus of a tall, tough Minneapolis native who at twenty-six had boxed professionally, and so could not box on the varsity team, but who would serve as a student assistant coach (and frequent sparring partner to the varsity fighters) and become one of the most astute observers of the Wisconsin boxing program in its final years.

Bob Lynch had grown up in Duluth-Superior, Minnesota, and actually attended the same high school as Morgan, the Badgers' national champion from 1952. But where Morgan graduated high school and got on the bus for Madison, Lynch was invited not to return to high school for his senior year and wound up joining the U.S. Army, which he would serve with distinction in Korea, taking both shrapnel in his neck from a land mine and, two months later, a rifle bullet to the left chest. Lynch was tough, all right.

The last six months of his service duty he was in Fort Ord, California, where he served as head coach of the Army Twentieth Infantry boxing team. Out of the service he entered Superior State College where he won the school's heavyweight boxing crown, at which point he turned professional, with bouts in Minneapolis, Duluth, Los Angeles, and Las Vegas. He finally decided to go back to school, and still without a high school degree Lynch had enough small college credits to get into UW. There he would earn an undergraduate degree, he would work full time as a lifeguard supervisor and security guard, and he would spend whatever hours were left in his week sparring and soaking up the atmosphere at the varsity boxing practices.

"I had seen quite a few boxing gyms," Lynch told me when I asked his impressions on arriving in Madison in October 1958, "amateur gyms, half a dozen Army gyms, professional gyms, but I had never seen anything like the operation at UW–Madison. It was the most organized and sensible approach to how to handle boxing I had ever seen, and I had seen quite a bit. It was the best operation I was ever around."

Lynch recalled, "I wasn't eligible but Vern really utilized me as a sparring partner."

It was Woodward's show now, though Lynch would recall that Walsh dropped around every once in a while. Dale Lang, a team manager also from Superior, had introduced Lynch to both Walsh and Woodward. Both impressed him immediately, though he had more contact with Woodward.

"He was kind of fatherly and a nice guy," Lynch said. "But let me tell you, he knew boxing. He picked up something I was doing the first day. I complained to him, when I was working on the heavy bag, that my right hand punch just didn't have the zing that it had once had, and I couldn't understand why. Vern caught a flaw right away. He watched for a minute and he said, 'Bobby, you are not pushing off your right foot correctly.' He got me back on track in a matter of minutes."

Lynch over the next forty-five years would go on to become one of the most respected voices in Wisconsin boxing, promoting professional shows, serving as a boxing inspector for the state of Wisconsin, and managing the careers of professional fighters, most notably Eric Morel of Madison, a world champion.

In 1987 and 1988, Lynch was invited by the United States Information Agency to travel overseas as part of a program to help Third World countries learn sports and fitness. Lynch would teach boxing and the program accorded him a lasting memory of just how far-reaching the UW boxing program was. In 1987 Lynch spent a month in the Sudan, and then the following year he spent seven weeks in Indonesia, traveling from island to island.

"In Indonesia," Lynch recalled, "we'd have the coaches come in in the morning, and we'd spend 2 hours teaching them how to coach boxing. Some times we'd have 15 coaches, sometimes 50. Then in the afternoon they would come back for two more hours, only this time they would have their boxers with them, and they would teach them the techniques we had worked on in the morning."

On one of those days in Indonesia, Lynch found himself drawn to a coach who was clearly superior to any of the others. "His boxers were just outstanding," Lynch recalled. "Far better than any I had seen on the trip. So I complimented the coach. 'You've done a very good job on fundamentals. Where did you learn?'"

The man, who had pretty good English, said, "When I was a little boy, in the 1960s, a gentleman named Vernon Woodward came from the United

States and put on a clinic for our coaches here in Indonesia. I was a little boy watching. That's where I learned everything I know about boxing."

Lynch could get a little misty-eyed recalling that when he had that experience, in 1988, Woodward was no longer alive and Lynch couldn't tell Woodward that his teaching had so influenced a young man half way around the world.

Woodward was still very much alive, and in his first season as head coach, as the calendar turned into 1959 and the Badgers approached an ambitious 8 match dual season.

But again, the 8-match schedule was somewhat deceptive. The Badgers would face two teams twice and there was bad news out of East Lansing: Michigan State, with a boxing tradition nearly as storied as the one in Madison, had dropped the sport. The Spartans had produced the great Chuck Davey and won two NCAA team championships, but the lack of schools nearby which still had boxing and a decline in attendance at the home matches in East Lansing had convinced the administration to abandon it. Then, too, there was the less tangible but always whispered sentiment on campus: Boxing does not belong at an institution of higher learning. Well, it was no longer at Michigan State.

The Badgers had a rough 1959 schedule, facing always-tough Idaho State and San Jose State twice. In early 2003 I asked Lynch, who worked out daily with the 1959 team, which of the Badgers he thought were the best boxers. No surprise, he mentioned the co-captains, Christopherson and Mohr, with Christopherson first among equals. "He was so accurate," Lynch said. "If Christopherson wanted to hit on the left cheekbone, as opposed to the right cheekbone, he'd get it on target. I couldn't slip or pick off his punches because he was so damn accurate." Of Mohr, Lynch said: "He was left-handed and his hands came fast as machine guns, but he was a light puncher." That would always be the rap on Mohr from ring purists: He lacked the knockout punch.

The Badgers dual match record in their first season under Woodward was 2 wins, 3 losses, and 3 ties. The NCAA tournament that year was in Reno, Nevada, and Woodward took six boxers with him for the event. All told, the tournament drew fifty-five fighters from twelve schools—according to the AP pretournament story—though *Sports Illustrated* claimed twenty schools had entries. Either way, both the largest wire service and the national sports weekly of record took the occasion to question the future of college. The AP pretournament story that ran in Madison's *Wisconsin State Journal* began: "College boxers, a species battling to avoid extinction . . ."

The *Sports Illustrated* piece was one that has been alluded to before in these pages, a four-page essay by a writer sympathetic to college boxing, Martin Kane, titled, "You could blame it on the moms."

Kane quoted a blunt Ray Chisholm, who boxed for UW one year in 1938 prior to transferring to Minnesota and who in 1959 was secretary-treasurer of the boxing coaches' association.

"The underlying reason for the decline of interscholastic boxing," Chisholm said, "is the unfounded and unsubstantiated criticisms of boxing in education by the physical educators who mistakenly identify college boxing with the most sordid aspects of the pro game."

Kane observed that most college coaches traced the troubles of the sport to a paper that I have also referenced earlier in this book, a work of dubious scholarship published in *Research Quarterly* in 1940 by three University of Illinois professors and titled, "The Evaluation of Boxing as a College Activity." Kane also quoted at length Arthur Steinhaus, dean at George Williams College in Chicago, a man who published frequently on the subject of college boxing and tended to view it as the dominion of the anti-Christ.

Kane was a journalist and not a scholar, but his bullshit detector was sensitive enough to at least raise red flags about the scholarship in both the Illinois "study" and Steinhaus articles. Too bad for Kane he couldn't have had access to the 1972 master's thesis written at UW–Madison (thirteen years after Kane's *Sports Illustrated* article) by Dixon, which did delve into the methodology of both studies and found it woefully biased. I found the Dixon thesis on microfilm at the UW–Madison Memorial Library and recommend it to anyone with more of an interest than what I will pass along here, which is one example each of Dixon debunking the negative studies. Of the 1940 University of Illinois study, Dixon observed: "With the appearance of the questionnaire study on the medical as well as non-medical aspects of boxing by Kenney, Thacker, and Gebhart, outspoke criticism of boxing in education really began. They concluded, after a careful study of data collected, that boxing should not be included in the sports program of an educational institution." But a paragraph later, Dixon lets the air out of their sails: "This study was evaluating boxing as a college activity by dealing with facts that were gathered about professional boxers." And anecdotal facts, at that, about pro boxers who don't wear headgear and go ten or twelve or fifteen rounds and whose gloves are less inflated than the college gloves and—why go on? The Illinois professors weren't even in the right ballpark.

Neither was Steinhaus. A little later in his thesis Dixon notes: "The Kenney, Thacker, and Gebhart study was followed by several boxing articles by Dr. Arthur H. Steinhaus, noted physiologist, teacher and Dean of George Williams College in Chicago until his retirement in 1963. His articles on high school boxing (1944), on brain injuries that could result from boxing (1950), and on trading of brains for medals through boxing (1951), had a major impact because of the reputation of Dr. Steinhaus in the physical education field." Yet Dixon shows that Steinhaus, like the three blind mice from Illinois, base their conclusions on data (largely anecdotal) from professional boxing. Dixon writes: "Steinhaus produced no facts on high school boxing but condemned it by inference. At the time this article was written boxing had been carried on as an intercollegiate sport by the University of Wisconsin for 11 years and [others] for over 20 years. Yet, Steinhaus was content to draw his conclusions from professional boxing instead of boxing in an educational institution." As Dixon then notes, the only scientific study ever done on college boxing, the UW–Madison study from 1949–52, supported none of the conclusions drawn in the other studies and concluded boxing was no more or less dangerous than other college sports involving contact between participants.

Kane's article in *Sports Illustrated* made the rounds of the 1959 NCAA tournament in Reno. No doubt the vast majority in Nevada would have concurred with the last person Kane quoted, at the conclusion of his piece. Eddie LaFond, who chaired the rules committee and had been associated with college boxing going back to 1924, told Kane: "College boxing keeps alive an ideal of rugged fitness on which our country was founded."

Of the six Badgers who fought quarterfinal bouts Thursday night, three carried on to the semifinals. Mohr at 165 pounds carded the most impressive win, over John Daugherty of Virginia, and Drye (132 pounds) and Urban (178 pounds) also were victorious. Woodward singled out his losing heavyweight, Wiesner, for a valiant effort against the fierce former NCAA champion from Idaho State, Hal Espy.

Only Mohr made it to Saturday's finals, which meant the Badgers would not take the team trophy in 1959. Drye and Urban both dropped decisions while Mohr won a unanimous nod over a tough foe, Bob Epperson of Michigan State, who had entered individually even though his school was no longer participating.

Mohr would face a tough opponent in the finals, Jesse Klinkenberg of Washington State, who won an NCAA championship the year before at 156 pounds (over Mohr, actually) and had moved up one weight class. In the semifinals Klinkenberg defeated the 1958 defender at 165 pounds, Flood of Sacramento State.

Also that Friday, it was announced that the 1960 NCAA championships would be returning to Madison. Woodward, who assumed the presidency of the Collegiate Boxing Coaches Association the same day, told reporters, "We would like to get our tournament on TV and let the nation see how college boxing is conducted."

Saturday night, Mohr became the fifth UW boxer to win the coveted John S. LaRowe Trophy as the best college fighter in the country and he did it on the strength of a relatively easy decision over Klinkenberg in the finals. All three judges had Mohr on top in each round and his performance led Rankin, who as an assistant coach had traveled with the team to Reno, to say, "Charlie Mohr is the best college southpaw I've ever seen. He hits harder than Chuck Davey did, and boxes just as well." Henry McCormick had not been in Nevada but in the *Wisconsin State Journal* the next week McCormick noted: "As for Mohr, he ranks with the finest college boxers I have ever seen. He belongs with such boxing masters as Teddy Kara of Idaho and Chuck Davey of Michigan State, and Mohr has one year of competition remaining."

The AP report out of Reno found Mohr to be an unlikely, or at least unusual, champion, referring to the Badger boxer as "bashful . . . looks more like a choirboy . . . a quiet 21-year-old who worries before each bout [and] plans to stick with amateur boxing. He ranks as a top prospect for Uncle Sam's Olympic team next year."

Mohr was at the peak of amateur boxing, and as fate would have it, there was a big event slated for Madison just a few weeks after the NCAA tournament in 1959. The Third Pan American Boxing Trials would be held at the Field House the last week in April. First came the annual year-end boxing banquet where to no one's surprise Mohr was awarded the George

Downer Memorial Trophy, for epitomizing the best of college boxing, and for the second year running Mohr was named co-captain for the following year, 1960, with Bill Sensiba, a 156 pounder from Green Bay.

McCormick called the Pan American Games "the greatest collection of amateur talent ever seen in Madison." Spanakos was back—he'd lasted a year at UW in 1957—and he had with him his twin brother, Nick. Spanakos would eventually win a bronze medal in the Pan American Games in Chicago. But if the 1959 Pan American Games are really remembered today it is for the appearance in Madison at the Field House of a tall and talented seventeen-year-old fighter from Louisville named Cassius Clay. "Clay is a fine-looking youngster," McCormick wrote, "rangy, long-muscled and pleasant-faced." McCormick was ringside in the Field House for Clay's semifinal bout at 178 pounds with Leroy Bogar of Minneapolis, described by McCormick as "rough, aggressive and fearless."

Bogar took the first round and was on the attack in the second round. Many in the Field House may have wondered what all the fuss over Clay was about. "This changed with shocking speed," McCormick wrote. "There was a quick spouting of brown gloves and Bogar was on the canvas. He climbed to his feet to resume the fight but another flashing combination by Clay almost put Bogar through the ropes. The fight was stopped there, as it should have been."

Clay made almost as big an impression in Madison outside the ropes. Lynch was working at the UW lifesaving station on the shore of Lake Mendota on campus when a few young African Americans stopped by one day during the Pan American Trials. Lynch, who had been in attendance the night before, recognized one of them as Clay. He got in a rowboat and couldn't seem to coordinate the oars so pretty soon he was rowing in a circle. "I never done this before," Clay said with a big grin. Said Lynch, "He was a real outgoing kid."

My friend John Roach Sr., a lifelong Madisonian and former minor league baseball player, was working at Badger Sporting Goods on State Street in April 1959 when Clay came in to buy a piece of equipment and quickly charmed everyone in the store and left them with what would one day be his verbal calling card: "I'm going to be the greatest!" Clay said.

One observer who wasn't totally taken with Clay was Walsh. The retired Badger coach was helping officiate the Pan American Games at the Field House and later told writer Bob Gard, "I don't like cockiness in a boxer,"

Walsh said. "I always discouraged it in my boys. I wouldn't have any showy robes or anything like that. Cassius Clay was one of my unfavorite people. The only match he ever lost was here at the University of Wisconsin in the American tournament. I refereed a couple of his bouts. He got beat by a Marine, and even his coach said the beating would do him good because he was too cocky."

Clay's loss in the Pan American finals was his last until, as Muhammad Ali, he was stopped more than a decade later by Joe Frazier. But Walsh's view of the young Clay as cocky was at odds with what Wilbert "Skeeter" McClure told author Thomas Hauser for Hauser's book, *Muhammad Ali: His Life and Times.* McClure was a fighter in the amateur ranks at that time, friendly with Clay, and in Madison in April 1959.

38. In 1959, young Cassius Clay (left) fought an amateur bout at the Field House during try-outs for the Pan American Games. Clay lost the decision. He wouldn't lose again until he faced Joe Frazier.

"We were together again for the Pan American trials at the University of Wisconsin," McClure said, "where he lost to Amos Johnson. Johnson was a grown man, a Marine, and a southpaw. I think that was the last fight Ali lost until Joe Frazier beat him twelve years later. And what I remember most about that time was, my dad had driven over [to Madison] from Toledo and a bunch of us went out to dinner afterward. We were in this restaurant, and Cassius was philosophical. All he said was, 'I just couldn't figure him out.' And if you think about it, when you're 17 years old and you meet a man who's 25 or 26, in the service, who fights left-handed, that's a big disadvantage. But he didn't grumble or moan or complain. He just said like a champion, 'I couldn't figure him out.'"

Watching at ringside, McCormick noted that Clay appeared "weary" and that the decision for Johnson, Clay's first loss in 37 bouts, was just. The Badgers' Christopherson made the finals but was knocked out there by the air force's Bobby Foster. The most notable Badger name, however, was conspicuous by his absence: Mohr. The UW NCAA champion and LaRowe Trophy winner did not enter. The official program of the games had devoted a page to Mohr and Clay and though the page remained, a line was added to say Mohr had passed up the Pan American Trials "to concentrate on his studies." The program continued: "[Mohr] promises to be ready next year to defend his collegiate title and make a serious bid for the 1960 Olympic team."

Lynch doubts Mohr had any intention of trying out for the Olympics: "Charlie had no intention of turning pro," Lynch told me. "Boxing for him was a way to get an education. The Pan Am Games or the Olympics would hold no interest."

For Spanakos, who ran into his old friend that week in April 1959, it was something more than that. Forty years later Spanakos told writer Jim Doherty that he, Spanakos, had said to Mohr in Madison that week: "Charlie, this is what you and I always wanted." Why hadn't Mohr entered?

And that Mohr had replied, "Pete, my heart just isn't in it any more."

That seems odd, at the very least, considering three weeks before Mohr had won a national championship and the college boxing equivalent of the Heisman Trophy. In February of 2003 I asked Spanakos about it.

"Is that what Charlie said? 'My heart just isn't in it?'"

"It was to that effect," Spanakos said. "I'm not sure those were the exact words."

Given what lay ahead, less than a year away, everything Mohr said and did in the twelve months between April 1959 and April 1960, every gesture and nuance, would be analyzed, and even agonized over, for decades to come. The end was near. The boxing program that had known so much triumph in the past quarter century was headed inexorably for tragedy.

chapter 7

KNOCKED OUT

Of all the young men who came to Madison to go to school and box for Walsh and Woodward, nobody was more universally well liked than Mohr. Of the dozens and dozens of people I spoke with who knew Mohr and were close to the boxing program at Wisconsin, not one had a bad word to say about him. "I was his traveling roommate," former UW boxer Bill Urban told me early in 2003. "He was just so very, very kind. I always enjoyed being with him. Everybody did."

In 1958, a year before Mohr's national championship win in Reno, *Capital Times* sports columnist Bonnie Ryan profiled the boxer who was just making a name for himself around Madison.

"It was 10 years ago that Charlie started his boxing career, at the tender age of 10," Ryan wrote. "Frank Ahearne, a man who dedicates his life to working with boys, started him off at a neighborhood boys club in Long Island, New York.

"All during his formative years," Ryan continued, "his parents, Charles and Rita, always gave encouragement to the younger Mohr. Around home, Charles was known as 'Joe' to differentiate him from his dad.

"His dad, a meat cutter by trade, always saw to it that Charlie had a big [and undoubtedly the best] steak every day that he was in training. Charlie, on completing his prep schooling at Bishop DuBois High School in the Bronx, was searching for a college to further his education, but he wanted one which sponsored boxing.

"Finally," Ryan continued, "on a recommendation by Pete Mello, Olympic coach in 1952, Coach Walsh contacted Mohr and this was to continue another bright page in Wisconsin boxing history. A shy lad, and a perfectionist . . . Mohr is working his way through school with a meal job at Paisan's restaurant and by janitorial work at Newman Commons. . . . With Johnny Walsh closing out a brilliant career coaching at Wisconsin this year, it is fitting that a lad of the high type of Mohr should be on the scene to highlight his valedictory.

"Charlie Mohr stands for everything that Walsh wanted in a boxer."

That was 1958. Over the next two years, Mohr's reputation in Madison would only grow more sterling. Later, the same columnist, Ryan, would note: "During that time his bewitching charm and personality touched not hundreds, but thousands. Handsome, gentle and soft spoken, Charlie had a way about him that when he talked to you he made you feel that you were the best friend he had in the world. It wouldn't be amiss to say that Charlie had more genuine friends in Madison than anybody else. Highly sensitive was Charlie and he always worried about doing wrong. Never, never would he ever think of saying a bad word against anyone.

"Despite the many honors he won, he still retained that shyness and he always put himself secondary to other people. He was the first to open the door. He was the first to apologize, but there never was any need for him to apologize. A devout Catholic, on many Sundays he would travel to nearby Oregon with his close friend father Phillip Keyes of St. Paul's university chapel to assist in Mass at the girls school there."

It was all too good to be true, and, of course, it was. The first real indication that all was not perfect in Mohr's world came the week after the 1960 NCAA tournament in Madison when the *Capital Times* ran a page-one story saying that Mohr had been a patient in the psychiatric department at University Hospital sometime either late in 1959 or early in 1960 and that he had also been a patient in the psychiatric unit "at least once" at another Madison hospital, St. Mary's.

The article was written by Elliott Maraniss, a rising reporting star on the newspaper who would later become its editor.

"I got a couple of tips from people in the medical school," Maraniss told me when we spoke early in 2003. I had asked how Maraniss found out about the psychiatric visits. "I didn't really like the idea of having to go into his medical condition, but we were looking for the truth."

The truth. Someone once said that the pure and simple truth is rarely pure and never simple. Mohr was a wonderful young guy, who, it turned out, had problems and doubts and anxieties and like a lot of twenty-two-year-olds occasionally felt the weight of the world on his shoulders.

Just how heavy a load Mohr carried was not known until a former UW student named Doherty saw an article in the *New York Times* that triggered some memories and eventually led Doherty on a prolonged search for the soul of Charlie Mohr.

Doherty was a respected journalist who had worked at *Newsweek* and was, in 1996, an editor at the *Smithsonian* magazine in Washington, D.C., when he picked up his *New York Times* on September 16 and saw in the Metro section an article on Spanakos and his twin brother, Nick. The

39. Charlie Mohr (second row, third from right), highly respected by his teammates, was loved like a son by his coach, Vern Woodward (standing at left).

article recalled their hardscrabble youths in New York City, their embrace-
ment of boxing, and Pete told the writer about seeing Cassius Clay at the
Pan American Games in Madison in 1959.

"My first memory of him," Pete told the *New York Times*, "is sitting at
a weigh-in in Madison, where everybody is nervous and quiet and he's
dancing around, punching the bag and already he's yelling he's going to
be the greatest. And I thought to myself, 'This guy is whistling past the
grave. He's scared. I bet he can't even fight.'"

Spanakos paused and then said, "He could fight."

Doherty, reading this in the *New York Times* nearly forty years later,
picked up the telephone and called Spanakos. Doherty reminded Spanakos that they had met in 1957, the year Spanakos boxed for Walsh and
Doherty, also on campus, worked out with the boxing team. "He pre-
tended to remember me when I called," Doherty wrote of Spanakos. "We
arranged to have dinner in New York and ended up talking about Charlie
all night."

So began three years of off and on research for Doherty. "It didn't take
me long to find out there was a lot more going on with Charlie than many
of us realized," Doherty wrote. "The legend was true, as far as it went. He
was a hero, for sure—but not the one we all thought we knew. Concealed
behind the jaunty facade he beamed at the world was a tormented young
man who had the misfortune to end up in a place where he didn't want to
be, but who never quit fighting and always tried to do the right thing."

What Doherty unearthed, or perhaps expanded upon is better, given
Maraniss's *Capital Times* story forty years earlier, was that Mohr was
feeling ambivalent about boxing his senior year. This was not altogether
unusual among the UW boxers. Vito Parisi was in and out of the program
several times. He told me he lacked the desire to keep in shape and, of
course, if you are not in shape, you should not be in the boxing ring.
Another, Tynan, said that by his last year, he had "more skill but less heart"
when it came to boxing. He was married and a father by that time. "Boxing became something I had to do to keep my scholarship," Tynan told me.

Mohr's road roommate on the team, Urban, told me he didn't see that
in Mohr. Of the last year, Urban said, "He was into it. He loved it. I never
knew him not to love boxing."

But others weren't so sure. Lynch said he did think that Mohr's desire
for boxing had slipped in his last year. "It's painful as hell to say this,"

Lynch said, "but the truth is Charlie was pulling away, emotionally and commitment-wise, from boxing."

Spanakos mentioned a college fighter who had boxed against Mohr earlier in Mohr's college career and then again in 1960. "He told me he was hitting Charlie with punches that would have missed before," Spanakos said.

Mohr's friend and teammate Wally DeRose e-mailed me this: "Charlie Mohr had no business in the ring by virtue of the fact he was not emotionally or mentally fit and the coaches should have recognized it. . . . I had noticed gradual changes in Charlie for some time. Once he asked me if I thought he was a coward because some punks had made remarks to him when he was walking with his sister and he did not confront them. That was prior to his treatment for depression. After he was hospitalized he asked me if I thought he should continue fighting the last days of his senior year. I said no because he had a career in social work ahead of him. It was not worth taking a chance if he felt in the least way hesitant—which he did."

It seems certain that Mohr's ambivalence hinged on more than just his feelings about boxing. Lynch points out that he was going to graduate and was looking toward life beyond the sport. Then there were upheavals in his personal life. After a strict Catholic upbringing, Mohr had in the past year dated an older, divorced woman. "She seduced him," somebody told me. But after that he had dated a girl closer to his age, and some said that by April 1960 Mohr was prepared to give her an engagement ring. That should have meant happiness, but other friends saw Mohr slipping under the weight of it all. "He was obsessing about everything," Doherty wrote. "Girls, his studies, his sisters [who had joined him at UW–Madison], his fights, his future." It led him to a shrink on at least a couple of occasions. Doherty indicates that Mohr underwent electroshock therapy, a crude but not infrequent treatment in the 1950s. "When Charlie got out of the hospital," Doherty wrote, "his friends were dismayed. He was not the same. He was more plagued by memory loss and seemed more obsessive, preoccupied and on edge than ever."

I talked to Mohr's friend and boxing teammate, Drye, today a physician in Montana, and he said that the shock treatments definitely made Mohr more sluggish. "He didn't have the same vim and vigor," Drye said. "Nor the same enthusiasm."

With all that it would seem he couldn't have been as focused on his boxing, or have the same desire he had once had to climb into the ring. Lynch told me, "Once the real desire falls off, it can get damn dangerous." And yet, on a brilliantly clear and brutally cold February morning in 2003, I sat with Lynch in his living room in Madison and watched a VHS tape made from a Mohr bout in the 1960 tournament, and Lynch could not determine that Mohr looked less skillful or more uncertain in the ring.

"He doesn't look apprehensive," Lynch said. "His hands look just about as fast as they ever did."

The simple truth is never simple.

The 1960 dual meet season was the best one in years for the Badgers. UW fought 8 matches and won 6, tying 1, and losing another. The crowd at the last dual match, April 2 in the Field House against San Jose State, was just shy of ten thousand—the largest attendance since 1956.

The early buzz during tournament week in Madison was that the team championship would likely go to either the host Badgers or the defending champion San Jose State Spartans. The two teams had met twice during the season in dual matches, with each getting 1 win.

Heading into the finals, April 9, 1960, Wisconsin appeared to have the edge. The Badgers had six boxers still in the competition and a total of 24 team points. As predicted, San Jose State was next, but the Spartans had just five fighters in the finals and their team score going into Saturday was 18. The tournament was the Badgers' to lose.

The first Badger to fight that night was Jim Mack, at 112 pounds. Mack was a decided underdog as he stepped into the ring for his bout with Heiji Shimabukuro of the College of Idaho. Shimabukuro was from Hawaii and was the defending champ at 112 pounds, though there was less to that than it might seem at first blush. In Reno the year before, Shimabukuro had won his NCAA title without throwing a punch—there had been no other entrants in his weight class. But he could fight. Later that month in 1959 the Hawaiian came to Madison for the Pan American trials and captured the title, this time against actual competitors.

Mack was a likable, somewhat self-deprecating scrapper with a lion's heart. He was a Madison native, the son of an amateur boxer, and Jim had begun boxing with Woodward's Little Badger Boxers when he was only eight years old. "I fought John Walsh's son," he recalled. "He beat me." He went into the army after graduating from Madison Central High School in 1957 and came to the UW eighteen months later in the fall of 1958. In between, Mack had been in a serious car accident and suffered some compressed vertebrae in his back. He felt his overall good physical conditioning from boxing both kept the injury from being worse and also speeded his recovery.

More than forty years later, the 1960 NCAA tournament remained vivid in his memory. Mack beat Bob Bruner of Cal Poly in the semifinals. "I think he was over-confident," Mack said.

The final was Saturday. "It was the biggest night of my life," Mack told me. "The biggest thing that ever happened to me." He paused. "Until I saw my son born, I suppose."

Mack had seen Shimabukuro fight in Madison at the Pan American Games the year before and knew he was good, better than good. But Mack was determined that in front of a home crowd in the city he grew up in he would not dishonor himself. "I had it in my mind that he was not going to embarrass me," Mack said. "He wasn't going to knock me down."

Mack recalled his flush of excitement as the national anthem was played at the Field House. The blessing and curse of being 112 pounds was that his bout would be first. The fact that he was a small man seemed to increase Mack's love of his sport. "For little guys," he told me, and paused. "How can I say this? Boxing helped me build up my confidence." He became a successful attorney practicing in Beaver Dam, Wisconsin. Mack liked the purity of boxing: "There was no trash talking. Afterward, you and the guy you fought were like best friends."

Mack didn't beat Shimabukuro, but he gave the Idaho fighter all he wanted. While the decision went to Shimabukuro, Mack said: "You know, if it had gone another round. . . . He was tired. I don't know if he could have gone another round."

Henry McCormick, in the *State Journal:* "Game little Jimmy Mack of Wisconsin didn't have enough to match Shimabukuro, but the slim Badger gave it a full try."

Still, it was a defeat, and when two of the next three Badgers also lost—Howard McCaffery at 139 pounds and Gary Wilhelm at 147 pounds—the team title was in jeopardy. Brown McGhee won a title and 5 points for UW at 132 pounds but by the time the Badgers' Jerry Turner stepped into the ring for the 156 pound final, three San Jose boxers had also won. It was going to go down to the wire between the Badgers and Spartans.

McGhee's win had moved the Badgers' team total to 29 points. He would be the second to last national champion ever at Wisconsin and, later in life, a successful physician. McGhee was a native of Memphis, Tennessee, and started boxing when he was nine-years-old. He won the Chicago Golden Gloves title in 1957 and was probably the only classical music lover on the 1960 Badger team.

After McGhee's win—over Joe Bliss of Nevada—a victory by San Jose's Steve Kubas over Badger McCaffery brought the team score to 33–29 San Jose. When the Badgers' Wilhelm lost to Mills Lane of Nevada at 147 pounds, much was riding on the 156 bout, where Jerry Turner would fight for the Badgers against Terry Smith of Sacramento State.

Turner was, in the estimation of Lynch, "a pit bull brawler." He grew up on the north side of Chicago, not far from Wrigley Field. "Rough and tumble," Turner told me early in 2003. "A lot of street fights." He started boxing early, trained under the great Tony Zale and went south to San Antonio Junior College for two years. By 1959 Turner had pretty much decided to turn pro. Someone in Texas, though, knew about the UW boxing program and said, "Why don't you try to get a scholarship to Madison?" Turner asked around a bit more, and learned that the coach was Woodward. "I wrote Vern a letter telling him how wonderful I was," Turner said with a chuckle. He got the scholarship and thought about becoming a social worker. Instead, Turner wound up at Marquette Law School and when we spoke, in February 2003, he was in his law office in Milwaukee. He talked in gruff, quick, jab-like sentences. There was not a lot of nonsense about Turner, then or now.

Arriving in Madison in January 1960, Turner, like virtually everyone else, was impressed by the UW's training facilities. He liked the fact that the workout room was usually bustling. "There was always somebody to beat up on," he said. He ran through the dual meet season undefeated— "I didn't want word getting back to San Antonio that I had lost"—and in the semifinals of the tournament in Madison he met Norm Ygnatowicz of Idaho State. The two had boxed 2 tough dual meet matches earlier in the year, both won by Turner.

Speaking of the Idaho State coach, Turner said, "Dubby Holt called the first one the best collegiate fight he had ever seen."

Turner beat Ygnatowicz for a third time and on Saturday night faced Smith of Sacramento State in the finals. Smith was tall and rugged and

Turner recalled that on the day of the fight a former Badger boxer, Dick Miyagawa, had come up to him and said, "Go after his body."

As Turner remembered the championship fight that night, they came out after the opening bell and Turner did not follow Miyagawa's advice. "I threw a long overhand right and it didn't quite get to his chin." Smith, he felt, was acting a little cocky. "He thought he was hot shit," Turner said.

As the fight wore on Turner began to take the advice to lower his punches, and he began to connect. To watch a tape of the fight is to see Turner relentlessly closing in on Smith, not allowing the taller fighter to use his reach advantage. Lynch, watching the bout on tape forty years later, thought it was a classic. "Just a helluva lot of action for an amateur fight," he said. In the end it was a split decision, but it went to Turner. The Badgers now led San Jose State in the team competition 34–33 and the next fight would match a Badger against a Spartan. It could not have been more close or exciting.

The 165-pound bout was announced: Wisconsin's Mohr against San Jose State's Stu Bartell.

They had split their 2 dual match bouts earlier in the year, with Mohr having won just the week before. Mohr was the favorite, but Dave Nelson, Bartell's 125-pound teammate who won a title in Madison that night, remembered seeing Mohr earlier in the day and thinking Mohr seemed frightened.

Bartell was capable of producing fear in an opponent. He was a tough Jewish Italian kid who had grown up in the Canarsie neighborhood of Brooklyn. Originally he had gone to LSU on a football scholarship but when that hadn't worked out, he joined the navy, where he learned to box.

Mills Lane, the Nevada fighter who won a championship in Madison in 1960, said of Bartell: "Stu wasn't fancy, just a tough guy who was a walk-in puncher." In his book, *Let's Get It On*, Lane called Bartell "a real banger."

It certainly made an interesting contrast with Mohr. Lynch described Mohr's boxing style: "He countered beautifully. He didn't lead that much himself. His hands were quicker than most other guys and he had incredible head quickness. He used his feet intelligently."

Lane on Mohr, again from his book: "He stood about six feet one and was not particularly well built, but damned if he wasn't a great boxer. He was a southpaw who knew how to operate in the ring. He was able to keep orthodox fighters off-balance, and he had a good right jab. Although I don't believe he won many fights by knock out, he sure could box your ears off."

The writer Doherty would remember encountering Mohr in the Wisconsin training room: "I could tell right away there were two kinds of boxers—Charlie, and everyone else. With everyone else, it was hit and be hit. With Charlie, it was just hit. Nobody, as the saying goes, could touch him. He sparred with the best fighters. They chased him, tried to corner him, muscled him against the ropes. It didn't matter what they did. He slipped away or ducked inside or spun them around."

Doherty did not have a chance to see the tape of the second round before he wrote his *Smithsonian* piece in April 2000. Later, he saw the critical twenty seconds or so, when Mohr was caught with a hard right by Bartell. In February 2002 Doherty wrote me his reaction to the clip: "Bartell looked every bit as menacing as I remember [you should see him now, a mellow old man] but Charlie looked much, much more vulnerable. That's the striking thing. He was a sitting duck for that thunderous shot."

I watched the tape of the Mohr-Bartell fight with Lynch. It is an eerie experience. Watching the first round, Lynch said he could not detect a drop-off from Mohr's earlier form. But seeing him in the second round, Lynch said, "Charlie looks a little sluggish."

Lynch recalled that he had been sitting in the Field House that night, in a rear seat near an exit. "I had to leave at 9:30 to go work as a security guard." Mohr's back was to him when Mohr took the punch that sent him to the canvas. Now in his living room Lynch silently replayed the moment over and over. It was just a few seconds of tape, repeated again and again. Finally Lynch said, quietly, "It was a classic right hand."

There is little disagreement over what happened next. Lane, the Nevada boxer, recalled: "I remember the Madison Field House being a gigantic place, and I was standing in back near my dressing room because I had already completed my fight. I saw Charlie walk back to his corner and sit down on his stool, and I saw him talking to his coach, Vern Woodward. I later found out that Charlie was apologizing for having lost the fight. Charlie felt as if he had let the school down because his defeat enabled San Jose State to win the team trophy.

"After about a minute or so Charlie got up off his stool, slipped through the ropes, and started walking back to the dressing room. Under any circumstances, that is a long walk. It's even longer when you have been defeated. But it didn't seem to bother Charlie, because he signed autographs all the way back to the locker room.

"I remember how bad I felt for Charlie," Lane wrote. "I also remember thinking that I hoped I would never have to make a walk like that under those circumstances. I watched Charlie step toward the Wisconsin dressing room, then turned away, lost in my own thoughts. Within minutes, however, the word spread throughout the Field House that Charlie had collapsed."

Turner, Mohr's victorious teammate, remembered Mohr walking into the locker room. "He was completely coherent," Turner told me. "I put my arm around him and tried to console him." Mohr sat down on a bench and Turner turned away. "Just about the next thing I knew," Turner said, "John Flinn was yelling at me to get a tongue depressor."

Flinn was the director of student health at UW–Madison and as Mohr convulsed on the floor Flinn was worried the stricken boxer would swallow his tongue. Eventually he got the tongue depressor into Mohr's mouth and as a frantic Woodward, who had been alerted, burst into the locker room, Flinn told the coach it didn't look good and that an ambulance had been called.

Mack, who had fought the first bout of the night, was back in his street clothes and standing outside the locker room when the emergency team arrived. He would remember a night not long before standing outside the Kollege Klub, a popular campus-meeting place on State Street, with Mohr when somebody had tried to pick a fight with the boxer. Mohr could have creamed him but of course he didn't. "He was a Christian," Mack said, and so turned the other cheek. Now in the Field House Mack watched helplessly as the emergency team wheeled Mohr out of the locker room on a gurney. "You know what I remember?" Mack said. "I remember one of his arms dropping off that gurney. Dropping off and just hanging there."

At University Hospital, Dr. Manucher Javid, an associate professor of neurosurgery at the University of Wisconsin Hospital, operated for several hours on Mohr. More than forty years later, we sat across a lunch table from each other at the Blackhawk Country Club in Madison with some diagrams of the brain spread out between plates. Javid spent a long time patiently trying to show me, a layman, the exact extent of the injury he found when he first operated on Mohr. "A massive subdural hemotoma," was the medical term. Profuse bleeding in the brain, and most significantly, a tearing of a major vein that could only have been caused by some sort of powerful blow to the head. This became important later, when it was suggested, and came to be believed by many, that Mohr had some kind of brain abnormality, like an aneurysm, that could have burst at any time, perhaps while he was doing something as mundane as blowing his nose into a handkerchief. "Aneurysm had nothing to do with this," Dr. Javid told me. The doctor said an aneurysm is generally found at the base of the brain, which is not where Mohr was incurring such massive bleeding.

"It was such a massive blow that it completely sheared off the vein from the sinus," Dr. Javid said. "It caused a tear in the sinus itself. That is extremely rare."

I asked Dr. Javid if it was unusual that Mohr had been able to walk back to the locker room under his own power. He said it was not. "Not at all unusual," Dr. Javid said. "It is called a lucid interval."

Only one paper in Madison published the day after the fight, Sunday, April 10. The *Wisconsin State Journal* went to press while Mohr was still in surgery. The top line head of the sports page concerned San Jose State winning the 1960 NCAA championship but a smaller story also appeared under the headline: "Mohr Undergoes Brain Operation." The story, which appeared without a byline, quoted Flinn saying Mohr's condition was "generally good." That was either a misquote or Flinn just not yet wanting to discuss the situation.

Dr. Javid told me they knew right away the situation was gravely serious. "Dr. Flinn told me the first thing he noticed was that [Mohr's] right pupil became dilated. That is an ominous sign, and it is why I [began operating] on the right side." Mohr had been hit on the left side but Dr. Javid said that there is a French term, "contrecoup," that explains that phenomenon: "You are hit on one side but it is the opposite side that has the maximum damage."

Near the end of the brief *State Journal* story Sunday was this description of Bartell's second round punch: "A tremendous right to the head as Mohr attempted to throw a left. The punch lifted Mohr off his feet and dropped him flat on his back."

The Monday newspapers had more. The front page *Wisconsin State Journal* top line, "UW BOXER MOHR BATTLES FOR LIFE."

The subhead on the *Capital Times* front-page story read, "Intercollegiate Boxing Future May Be Affected."

Mohr's mother and father had flown in Sunday from New York. His sisters, Carole and Joan, were already in Madison and were at the hospital with his girlfriend, Darlene Dobeck, a UW student from Schofield, Wisconsin.

The UW President, Conrad Elvehjem, made a statement: "The serious injury suffered by Charles Mohr has shocked and saddened us all. We hope that the immediate and skillful medical attention given by members of our medical faculty will be successful. Mrs. Elvehjem joins me in extending to his mother and father our hopes for his recovery. Charles has made a real place for himself on our campus—a good student, a game athlete and a fine person."

So began a long vigil, one without much hope. A priest had given Mohr the last rites Saturday night. He survived the operation and the night but he was still in a coma. And while as the days passed everyone's main concern continued to be Mohr, the fate of his sport, college boxing, also began to be debated. Somehow word began to circulate that Mohr had a pre-existing condition that contributed to his injury. In the *Capital Times'* report on Monday, their first day of publishing since Mohr was hospitalized, the paper had this: "Dr. John H. Flinn, director of the student health center, said the operating doctors suspected that a condition existed which made Mohr's blood vessels 'more than normally susceptible to injury.'"

The head surgeon, Dr. Javid, sure didn't suspect that. He knew the opposite was true. One physician who was at the hospital at the time was Tony Curreri, the all-university champion in the 1920s who had stayed close to the sport ever since. UW boxers remembered him sparring in the workout room into the 1950s. Curreri, of course, was a world-renowned cancer specialist.

Dr. Javid, the head surgeon: "When I was operating, Curreri was outside the room. He didn't come inside. When he asked me, I told him. 'This is a massive brain injury. One of the major veins had completely sheared off from the sinus.'"

So Curreri knew the truth. Yet anyone who loved college boxing and believed in the many positive aspects of the sport had to be sick with worry that Mohr's injury, on top of all the other knocks the sport had taken in

the last decade, might finish it for good. Could Curreri have looked at that
bleak future and, looking again, seen an aneurysm? Could it have come
up in conversation with Walsh, a man who had given his life to college
boxing, who knew its virtues and was devastated by even the thought it
might be ending? Such speculation does not take one very far. The story
spread and was believed by many. Mohr had an aneurysm. He never really
got hit by Stu Bartell. When something gets told enough maybe even the
people who made it up begin to believe it.

In 1995 I was the editor of *Madison Magazine* and I asked a good writer,
Dan Knapp, to do a story about UW boxing. He did a fine job and the
article paid appropriate homage to the greatness of the program. Walsh,
then eighty-two, was among those interviewed. When the subject turned
to Mohr, Walsh told Knapp this: "Dr. Tony Curreri, a former UW boxer
and NCAA boxing rules committee chairman, who watched the operation, said, 'Don't blame this on boxing. This was an aneurysm. It could
have exploded at any time. It could have happened while he was blowing
his nose.'"

About that same time, in the mid-1990s, Lynch gave a newspaper interview about some fight or fighter he was promoting, and somewhere far
down in the story Mohr's name came up and Lynch told the reporter he
had been in the Field House the night Mohr got knocked down by Bartell.

A few days later, Lynch's phone rang. It was Walsh, and Lynch, a true
admirer of Walsh's, was glad to hear from him. Walsh began by compli-
menting Lynch on his boxing successes in recent years. Then he said,
"Bob, Charlie Mohr was never down in that fight."

Lynch was surprised. One thing was certain: He was not about to argue
with Walsh. "Well, Mr. Walsh, that's my memory. Of course I was sitting
pretty far back and maybe it was a knee or—"

Walsh cut in. "Charlie did not go off his feet."

"Okay, Mr. Walsh. Do you think I should call the writer?"

"No, no," Walsh said. "That won't be necessary."

Today many of those close to the boxing program still think Mohr had
an aneurysm.

If he had lived, there is a chance that story might have influenced
events. Sunday, the day after the injury, athletic director Williamson had
declined to address the issue of whether boxing would remain on the
Madison campus.

"Right now we are thinking only of Charlie's condition," Williamson said. "We are praying that he gets well."

He didn't. By mid-week Dr. Javid was telling reporters that Mohr had "irreversible damage to his mid-brain." The annual boxing banquet, scheduled for Wednesday night, was cancelled. Only Mohr's parents and sisters were allowed in his room but friends and teammates and hundreds of well-wishers came and went in the hospital lobby, where his condition was posted. A reporter reached Bartell, who was home in New York for spring break. The San Jose boxer was grief-stricken. "We were good friends," Bartell said, adding that he and Mohr had been chatting just moments before they got in the ring to box. "We always talked before our fights. And then this had to happen." Mohr's dad, Charles Mohr, wrote a letter to Bartell urging the Spartan boxer not to blame himself. Charles Mohr also told a reporter in Madison on Wednesday, "Don't blame the sport." He said boxing had always been his son's main interest, and that both he and his wife approved of their son's participation.

On April 17, Easter Sunday, at 8:40 a.m., Mohr was pronounced dead. Lloyd Hughes, superintendent of University Hospital, said, "The immediate cause of death was failure of vital centers to respond. Those are the centers deep in the brain that control the heart rate, blood pressure, and respiration. He had no blood pressure or pulse one hour before his death, despite all our treatment."

A *State Journal* story on Monday said: "There will be no post-mortem performed on the body because of Mrs. Mohr's objections."

The Mohr family, accompanied by Charlie's girlfriend, Darlene Dobeck, left Madison Sunday afternoon for New York, where the funeral was scheduled for Thursday.

On the day Mohr died, Easter Sunday, the propriety of college boxing was being hotly debated in the pages of the Wisconsin's largest newspaper, the *Milwaukee Journal.* Two long interviews appeared side by side in the paper. In one, Curreri said that college boxing deserved to continue, though he wasn't overly optimistic about its future: "Those who are upset about college boxing are those who haven't seen it. The hue and cry will come for an end of college boxing and it may well end it, too."

In an interview with the *Milwaukee Journal* sports editor Oliver Kuechle, Fred Saddy, secretary of the Wisconsin state athletic commission, was asked if he would support abolishing varsity boxing at UW.

"Yes," Saddy replied.

Kuechle: "Do you see boxing as brutal?"

Saddy: "I hate to admit it, but yes. It's a throwback to barbaric days. Its roots lie there. Before people had clubs or swords or guns they fought with their hands."

Back in Madison, a political science professor named David Fellman was having lunch in Tripp Commons—"where the faculty used to eat in those days," Fellman said—and the subject of Mohr, who had died a few days earlier, came up. Fellman would later say that Mohr "was a good friend of my daughter, who was then a student at the university. She felt very badly about it and I felt very badly about it."

There were a number of other professors at the lunch table that day. Fellman recalled: "I'm not a crusader and I'm certainly not a crusader against athletics. I'm not opposed to the athletic department but I always thought boxing was an improper sport." At the one boxing match Fellman attended, he had been appalled when a fan had yelled, "kill him" to a Badger fighter in the ring.

40. David Fellman, the UW political science professor who led the movement on campus to ban boxing.

"I might add that the University of Wisconsin [by 1960] was the only quality university in the country that still had a college boxing team," Fellman said. "We kept it alive because of the sheer influence of our reputation. But we had to go all the way to the east coast or west coast to find a team to box against."

At lunch that day, Fellman said, "That's just a shame about Charlie Mohr."

Another professor at the table said, "Why do you just sit there and talk? Why don't you do something about it?"

In an interview years later for the Wisconsin Oral History Project, Fellman said: "Since I am an activist by nature, that's something no one must say to me because I can't resist the temptation to rise to the challenge."

At the table that day in April 1960, Fellman said, "Well, I will." He recalled taking his place mat, turning it over, and writing a motion addressed to the secretary of the faculty at the University of Wisconsin–Madison. "At the University of Wisconsin," Fellman said, "the faculty has complete control over athletic policy. Even the Regents can't overrule us. That's a requirement of membership in the Big Ten."

Fellman asked the other professors at the table to sign it, and they did. "Then I spotted a few other graybeards around the room and I got about 20 signatures. I sent it to Alden White, who was the secretary of the faculty, and it went on the agenda of the next meeting."

That meeting wasn't until May 9, which would be a month to the day after Mohr sustained his injury. Meanwhile, the newspapers continued to weigh in on the issue.

Henry McCormick, the *State Journal* sports editor who had been writing about college boxing for thirty years, was a lonely voice in support of the sport. "Nothing can be made absolutely safe," McCormick wrote in a column while Mohr lay in a coma. "Youth itself is hazard." In another column a few days later, after Mohr had died, McCormick wrote, "Inevitably, Mohr's death recalls that of another gallant young Wisconsin athlete 16 years earlier. I say inevitably because Allen Shafer Jr. was a young man who had the same exemplary qualities as Mohr, because young Shafer died of an athletic injury, because the parents in each case exhibited the same courage and charity."

Shafer was a Madison kid, a West High graduate. The difference was his sport was football, not boxing. And one November day in 1944 he sustained an injury on the football field at Camp Randall in Madison that killed him. It was a terrible tragedy. The difference was that no serious discussion ensued following Shafer's death as to whether college football should be abolished. There was another difference. Football hadn't been under fire for a decade prior to Shafer's death. College boxing, in some circles anyway, most certainly had.

Elliott Maraniss broke his story about Mohr twice visiting psychiatrists in the *Capital Times* while Mohr was still in a coma.

In the story Maraniss posed a tough question: Did UW athletic and medical authorities in charge of the boxing program know that Mohr had been undergoing the psychiatric treatment?

In early 2003 I asked Maraniss if the UW ever answered that question. "They never did," he said.

Doherty, the *Smithsonian* writer, in an e-mail: "The UW wriggled out of this thing by misrepresenting what had happened and basically by not being upfront with the public or Charlie's family about it."

Even before Mohr died, the *Capital Times* editorialized for an end to the sport on campus. On the Saturday before Easter, an unsigned editorial in the paper read: "If the primary purpose of a boxer is not to inflict physical injury, we'd like to know what it is. Surely, the two opponents do not enter the ring for a lesson in the waltz. If they do, then perhaps Arthur Murray should be brought in to coach boxing."

It was a hard point to argue with Mohr lying comatose in University Hospital. There were valid arguments to be made. UW grad student Dixon would lay them out in his 1972 master's thesis on college boxing. To a man, the boxers I interviewed felt that the rewards they brought away from participating in their sport outweighed the risks. I remember bringing up the name of Shafer, the football player who died at Camp Randall, in a conversation with Lynch.

He thought for a moment and said, "If I am going to be put in a wheelchair, or maybe even die, I want it to be in a sport where I am looking my opponent in the eye. Not in what I call the blind-side sports, where you can get hit and knocked out and not even see it coming."

Over the years Lynch would recall several conversations with people who would say, "Boxing is the only sport in which the intent is to hurt someone."

Lynch would always reply, "You mean, when you stepped between the ropes, you were thinking—"

The person would say hastily, "Oh, no, I never boxed."

"Then how can you know what's going through my mind when I walk up those steps?" Lynch said. "I'll tell you what I'm thinking. I walk up those steps hoping to hell to have a good performance, and above all, to try not to have the crap kicked out of me. I go up there with the idea of survival. I'd throw a lot of punches, trying to survive. But I never disliked an opponent I was in there with."

The faculty meeting was scheduled for Music Hall on May 9. But before that, on April 29, the athletic board had scheduled a meeting to make a recommendation to the full faculty. The board had not wanted reporters present but the papers went to court and Wisconsin Attorney General John Reynolds ruled that athletic board sessions fell within the scope of the state's (relatively new) anti-secrecy law and had to be open to the public.

There were three hours of discussion at the meeting. In hindsight, it's easy to see that for anyone hoping to see boxing remain a varsity sport at UW–Madison, the meeting was futile. The train had left the station and boxing was doomed, as doomed as Charlie Mohr. The athletic board chairman, Schaars, who had stood at year-boxing banquets and praised the courage and talent of the young Wisconsin boxers, got into an argument at the meeting with Woodward, who was pleading for the board to at least let the dust settle and not make any decision in haste.

"Many schools across the country will be guided by the decision you make here," Woodward said. "I hope it isn't made because of the anti-boxing or anti-athletic faction that went into play after that tragic accident."

Woodward then brought up football, and said more deaths could be linked to football than boxing on campuses. "It is the roughest of sports," he said.

Schaars, the chairman, dismissed his boxing coach. "Football attracts more participants. And the injuries sustained in football are something far different from the head and brain injuries sustained in boxing."

Try selling that to the people at Camp Randall in November 1944 who watched Shafer die on the field.

Woodward changed tactics. The coach said college boxing administrators were now looking at ways to modify the gloves so that the "sting" would be taken out of it.

Which was, of course, impossible. Take the sting out of boxing? It just goes to show how desperate Woodward, a kind and decent man, had become. Maybe he had been naive enough to think that boxing's opponents wouldn't try to capitalize on a tragedy. It was there for anyone who wanted to look. Check the report of the athletic board's meeting the next day, April 30, in the *Capital Times,* a non-bylined story. It talks about Woodward's pledge at the meeting to "*clean up the sport* and take the sting out of it." Clean it up? The young boxers and the coaches were pillars of the community. They knew it because governors and athletic directors and Athletic Board Chairman Marvin Schaars—now helping lead the fight against them—had told them so at many year-end banquets. On top of what Schaars said, and it's clear he wetted a finger to the wind of public sentiment before uttering a word, college boxers really were, in the great majority, outstanding citizens.

Clean it up? It's clear that Mohr's death, a terrible tragedy by any measure, came at the worst possible time and at the worst possible place for college boxing. The decade of the 1950s had seen screaming newspaper headlines announcing an endless series of investigations into corruption in professional boxing. One, from the *New York Post* about mobster Paul Carbo, known as Frankie, should give the appropriate flavor. The headline: "Boxing and the Mobs: Who is Frankie Carbo?" And the story began: "Paul John Carbo had a constant companion as a youth. It was a gun. Today, some 30 years later, Carbo is still the man behind the firearms in the shotgun marriage of underworld mobs and the prize ring."

Walsh spent thirty years urging his boxers not to turn pro, pleading with them at every opportunity, and denouncing the pro game at every turn. His reward was a newspaper story in a Madison paper saying Woodward must prove he could "clean up" college boxing. Maybe it's no wonder the aneurysm story started being spread among the boxers. It's like what Norman Mailer once said of the conspiracy theories about the John F. Kennedy assassination, which sprang up in the aftermath of the whitewash of the Warren Commission report. In a review of an Oliver Stone movie, Mailer said that when confronted with bullshit perhaps one needed to counter with superior bullshit.

At the athletic board meeting in Madison April 29, board member and UW Engineering Professor George Washa introduced a motion to have the board recommend to the faculty that boxing be dropped as a varsity sport at the University of Wisconsin. The measured passed. But then, before adjournment, a young board member and law school professor, Frank Remington, who would serve with distinction for years as the UW's faculty representative to the Big Ten athletic conference, proposed compromise. Remington suggested the board "defer action" until the changes that Woodward had talked about could be implemented and examined. The wording of Remington's proposal said the board would wait pending "changes in the rules . . . that would have significant affect on the individual safety of participants in the sport."

Remington's compromise motion carried 6–2. Schaars and Washa voted against it. Schaars said there wasn't enough time before the next boxing season to effectively test any rule or equipment changes that might be offered. As for Washa, he said that maybe none of this mattered, anyway. The faculty would be meeting in less than two weeks and they could act without regard to the board's recommendation. "The decision could still be made there," Washa said. And the current mood of the faculty, Washa said, favored revocation of boxing.

In this, Washa was right. On May 9, the turnout at Music Hall was enormous. "I spoke with a professor years later," Lynch told me, "who said the only crowd that could compare to it was a meeting they had during the Vietnam War protest era."

Fellman recalled: "We met in Music Hall because we needed a large room. We had a huge turnout for a faculty meeting. There must have been five or six hundred people there. Since I had filed the motion, I had to get up and say something."

Years later, Mack, the Badgers 1960 NCAA tournament finalist at 112 pounds, would remember that he had dated Fellman's daughter around this time. "I went to pick her up once," Mack said, "and the professor was watching the Friday night fights on TV. I thought that was strange."

Fellman read his resolution: "Resolved that it is the sense of the faculty that boxing is not an appropriate intercollegiate sport, and that it should be discontinued at the University of Wisconsin."

This was followed by polite applause.

Schaars offered the athletic board's proposal, which called for waiting and further study.

Fellman said, "Acting now could hardly be called precipitate. We've been debating the subject for years. Ten years ago we were given a report that said that boxing should continue because it is a safe sport. Now we are asked to defer action in order to make it safe."

Fellman told the faculty that boxing is by nature brutal, its main intent a knockout of the opponent.

"Boxing is inappropriate for a university for other reasons as well, but that is reason enough."

Remington spoke, and urged deliberation. "Leadership can be exercised by study," Remington said. Wisconsin could take the lead in making the sport safer. In any case, all avenues should at least be explored. "Even," Remington said, "if it is your judgment that the sport should be abolished."

Two voice votes were taken. The first was to accept Fellman's motion as a substitute for the athletic board's motion. It passed, Maraniss wrote in the *Capital Times,* "by a huge majority."

The second vote was on the substance of Fellman's motion. Fellman himself recalled that it carried "by an overwhelming margin. My resolution was adopted by an overwhelming majority."

That was it. On May 9, 1960, varsity boxing at UW was discontinued.

In other action at the meeting, the faculty voted to allow men and women over twenty-one years of age to live together in apartments and hold unchaperoned parties.

After the meeting, Woodward was asked for comment. "I'm terribly disappointed," he said. Rankin, the three time national champion who had been assisting Woodward, was very bitter. "Any group of people off the street would have given us more consideration."

Athletic director Williamson said, "Apparently they felt their action was in the best interests of the University."

Editorializing the next day, the *Capital Times* was gleeful. "*The Capital Times* for years has taken the position that any sport that has for its main purpose the inflicting of injuries is not a fit one to be carried on in an educational institution. We have been mystified that Wisconsin should cling to the activity after other schools dropped it long ago."

Not everyone in Madison was pleased. Fellman said he had "a bad week" after the resolution passed.

"There were stories about the action of our faculty in Europe, Asia and Australia," he said. "I got letters from all over the world. The farther away the letter came from, the more favorable it was to me. There's a worldwide movement against boxing. I got a lot of nasty letters, near at hand, from local people, especially from people who had boxed on our team. I also had some nasty phone calls, for about a week. I had a bad week. But if a letter came from Paris, or Hong Kong, I knew it would be favorable."

Four days after the vote, on May 13, UW President Elvehjem spoke to the UW Board of Regents about the decision, and the criticism by some that there had been a rush to judgment.

"It is not true that this was railroaded through the faculty," Elvehjem said.

Woodward had been quoted in a local paper complaining that he had not been allowed to speak at the faculty meeting. Not that it would have done any good.

"Woodward says he was not given the opportunity to speak but he never called for the floor," Elvehjem said. "He sat in the third row and I watched him and he never made an attempt to speak."

There had been some confusion over whether the campus all-university and Contender's tournaments would be allowed to continue, and Elvehjem took the opportunity to clear it up: they were done. "No public boxing matches will be held," Elvehjem said. He allowed that physical education teachers would still be allowed to have boxing as part of the their courses if they wanted. "If a student wants to take boxing as part of physical education courses I think he should be permitted to."

Fellman was pleased that the UW's action appeared to have a ripple effect. "Our abolishing boxing resulted in the collapse of boxing as a college sport in the United States," Fellman said. "That was the end of it. We had kept it alive because of the sheer prestige of the institution. When we abolished boxing as a competitive intercollegiate sport we pulled the rug out from under that so-called sport, and there was no more college boxing as a sport."

Fellman concluded, "I've never regretted it. It's a brutal sport that brutalizes the audience as well."

Fellman was right: the rug was pulled out. After the vote by the UW faculty, three other prominent college boxing schools, Sacramento State, San Jose State, and Washington State voted to discontinue their varsity boxing programs. The executive committee of the NCAA met on January 7, 1961. It was pretty easy to see that holding a boxing tournament didn't make much sense if few schools had teams. The committee voted to discontinue boxing as an NCAA sport and four days later, the NCAA board endorsed that vote.

From the National Collegiate Athletic Association 1961–1962 Yearbook:

"Because of the limited number of institutions conducting an inter-collegiate program, the NCAA Executive Committee at its January, 1961 meeting voted to discontinue boxing as one of the National Collegiate Championship events conducted by the Association. This action was endorsed by the 55th Annual Convention in Pittsburgh."

chapter 8

BROTHERS

Virtually to a man, the boxers, past and present, were angered and dismayed over the decision to end their sport.

Jackie Gibson, who had grown up near the Field House and been adopted as the Badgers' mascot way back in the 1930s, met me for lunch in the first year of the new millennium and had no problem recalling his reaction. He was upset. Gibson himself had boxed on the team in the early 1940s.

"My dad was an accounting professor at the UW and he was at that faculty meeting," Gibson said. "He apologized to me afterward. He said maybe he should have stood up and defended the sport."

Charlie Magestro was bitter. "If you were a professor who could get publicity by knocking something that was cherished by others, well, that's what some of them decided to do. They had never boxed. What did they know?"

Tynan remembered writing letters to the editor after the faculty vote, in which he listed the sport's many virtues for himself and countless others, and criticizing the professors for their emotional and hasty action. "One of Charlie Mohr's sisters came up to me later," Tynan said, "and told me that's just what Charlie would have said."

Bob Ranck, the national heavyweight champion, went to law school and became a judge. Forty years after the faculty votes he told me his reaction: "I think they were way off base. I was really quite angry. I don't think they understood what it meant to this school. The people it touched. It didn't just touch one guy for the six minutes he was in the ring. It touched everybody."

Ranck's great friend, Dick Murphy, himself a national champion, said, "I think it was absolutely horrible that they discontinued the program. At the time I was living in Ohio and I wrote a letter to the Board of Regents. 'What are you going to do if a football player, God forbid, gets killed?' When you participate in a contact sport there is an element of risk."

Turner had concerns that transcended being angry, or just not being able to box. The 159-pound national champion in 1960 had a meeting with athletic director Williamson in which he was told that since boxing had been dropped as a sport, Turner no longer had an athletic scholarship to UW.

"That upset me," Turner said. "I told them they were not taking my scholarship away."

Williamson, Turner told me, suggested maybe he could go out for the track team. No thank you, Turner said. How about wrestling, Williamson

41. Walsh was saddened by the sport's demise but his record spoke for itself. He had come a long way since coming to Madison as a young man in the early 1930s.

said. "I am not a wrestler," Turner replied. "Look, I helped fill that Field House. I am a boxer. I came here because you offered me a scholarship."

In the end, Turner got to keep his scholarship. He graduated, went to law school at Marquette University and has had a fine career as an attorney.

As the years passed, an interesting thing happened. For some reason, maybe because of the nature of the sport, or perhaps because of how abruptly it ended, mired in controversy, the UW boxing alumni kept in touch more than athletes from any other Badger sport. The men who had been in the ring for Walsh and Woodward in Madison seemed to sense they shared something that was not divisible. Many of them, anyway. Some left the university and never revisited their boxing days again. But more often, they stayed close, close as brothers.

Murphy told me: "As big for football as Elroy Hirsch always was, he once said that of all the athletes at the University of Wisconsin, the ones with the best camaraderie, hands down, were the boxers."

42. Two-time national champion Bob Ranck returned to Madison often from Wyoming after he graduated, often to visit teammates.

Bob Morgan said, "Of all my classmates, the only ones I've stayed in touch with are the boxers. The best stories, the best memories, the best men I've ever known are all part of that time when I was privileged to walk down the aisle and stand in the ring in that darkened Field House and experience the singing of the national anthem as the flag was lowered from the ceiling. I get chills thinking about it.

"Terry Tynan called the other day," Morgan continued. This was 2003. "I hadn't talked to Terry since our last visit at a reunion of the boxers in Madison. He made me guess who it was. In moments we were back as old friends sharing something few people share. We really didn't talk about boxing this time. We didn't have to. The bond was there and it would never be broken."

43. Former NFL star and UW athletic director Elroy Hirsch said no athletes stayed closer over the years than the Badger boxers. Here, a reunion of the 1952 team, from left to right: Dick Murphy, Gene Rankin, Tom Butler, Vito Schiro, Dick Miyagawa, Bob Hammel, Glen Nording, Jackie Gibson, Coach John Walsh.

In 1973, on the fortieth anniversary of the start of the varsity-boxing program at Wisconsin, a reunion was held in Madison and the organizers were stunned when 675 people turned up. Madison businessman George Holmes hired *Capital Times* sports columnist Bonnie Ryan to put together a printed homage to the legacy of college boxing in Madison and Ryan, with the help of Monte McCormick and some others, published a thirty-two-page magazine titled *Badger Boxing Legend*. No doubt Henry McCormick, Monte's brother and the true bard of UW boxing, would have participated, but he died not long after Mohr. Cancer got him in August 1961. Henry McCormick was fifty-seven.

When Mohr died, Murphy said he had written a letter to some university administrators asking what would happen if a football player got killed on the field. Of course, when Murphy wrote that letter, it had already happened once—in 1944, when Madison native Allen Shafer Jr. died at Camp Randall in a game against Iowa.

In 1979, it happened again.

The parallels of Jay Seiler's death to the death of Mohr are chilling.

Seiler was a nineteen-year-old freshman defensive back from Schofield, Wisconsin, friendly and well liked. Like Mohr, he had two sisters. It was around Easter, March 31, 1979, on the second day of UW spring football practice that Seiler came up from his safety position during a scrimmage and made the tackle on a running back.

"It was a form tackle, a good solid tackle," Dr. James Keene, a team physician who was there, said. "His head was forced to a lateral position as it struck his shoulder pads. Jay and the player he tackled went to the ground. He [Seiler] got up and went back to the huddle but it was time for him to get relieved. He came to the sidelines and after about two or three minutes complained of dizziness."

Seiler was eventually taken by ambulance to University Hospital and then to Madison General, which had a CAT scanner. Neurosurgeon Dr. James Tibbitts, after consulting with Dr. Javid at University of Wisconsin Hospital, did the operation on Seiler at Madison General. Tibbitts, in an interview two days after the surgery, said there had been massive bleeding after a vein had sheared off where it enters the sinus. "I'm afraid the injury is very severe and there's a question whether he ever will be able to survive it," Tibbitts said.

Tibbitts said the blow Seiler received produced "a shearing force just in the wrong way to pull the vein out of the sinus."

Dr. Javid had told me, referring to Mohr: "It was such a hard blow one of the veins had sheared off from the sinus."

Seiler was in a coma for a week, and then he died. Eerily similar. In fact there was only one thing dissimilar about the Seiler tragedy. As far as I can tell, not only was football not abolished on the Madison campus, there was never even any preliminary discussion or remotest hint of suggestion that the propriety of football should be examined.

In his 1972 master's thesis at UW–Madison, Dixon quoted a 1951 statistical survey of fatal injuries in sports:

"In recent years opponents of boxing have expressed the opinion that the sport should be abolished, that it is potentially dangerous and not necessary to the development of those attributes which are most desirable in young men. Thirty-two years of boxing competitions, however, have produced fewer deaths, in proportion to the number of participants, than occur in baseball or football and far fewer deaths than result from daily accidents. It seems that the moral and physical benefits derived from boxing far outweigh the dangers inherent in it or any of he other competitive sports."

When Mohr died, one of those most affected had been Woodward. "It nearly killed Vern, too," Audrey Walsh told me. "He so liked Charlie and he was so excited about being head boxing coach."

The UW had kept Woodward on in an administrative capacity, which was nice, but they didn't give him much to do and his office was more of a closet, which wasn't so nice. Tom Butler would go and visit him and recalled: "It was kind of pitiful. It was a little like going to Stillman's Gym—he had a little cubby hole, it was hot, but at least they had kept him on. Vern always hoped boxing would be resurrected."

He did some traveling—there was that great story Lynch told of being in Indonesia and meeting an earnest young boxing coach who said a visit by an American named "Vern-on Wood-ward" had made a huge impact on the quality of the teaching of the sport in that part of the world.

And in 1980, when Woodward retired, there was a very nice "recognition night" for him at the Park Motor Inn in Madison. Butler wrote about it and about Woodward himself in glowing terms, though the columnist jabbed the UW a bit for putting Woodward "out to pasture prematurely."

A lot of Badger boxers came back for that and even more came to town three years later when the fiftieth anniversary reunion of the start of varsity boxing at the UW was observed with a two-day party in Madison. There was a dinner Friday night, August 26, 1983, at Union South on campus and then tire executive George Holmes hosted a barbecue at his ranch outside of town the next night.

Both Madison dailies used the occasion to run long interviews with Walsh, who at seventy was continuing to work as an attorney in Madison.

"We had some very good kids," Walsh told the *Capital Times*. "They were good, hard workers. You had a different type of boy at the time. You didn't have to force them to go out and do road work. Half the time you had to tell them to knock it off because they would train too hard. We had great crowds and we had boys who wanted to do well."

44. Coach John Walsh toasts the good memories.

Then, as always, understated and with class: "I guess I didn't do too bad a job of coaching."

Butler's piece in the *Wisconsin State Journal* was more comprehensive and Butler got Walsh to reminisce all the way back to his days as a kid in south Minneapolis when he idolized Tommy and Mike Gibbons. Tommy had lost a heavyweight title fight to Jack Dempsey and later, when Tommy refereed one of young Walsh's Golden Gloves matches in the Twin Cities, Tommy said after that Walsh reminded him more of his brother Mike than any boxer he'd ever seen.

"That was the best compliment I ever received in my life," Walsh told Butler.

The coach remembered the classic fights: Truman Torgerson over Syracuse's Americo Wojiejas in the 1939 NCAA finals; Don Miller's decision over Washington State's Mike Nelson in the 1943 NCAA finals; Vito Parisi's famous decision over Art Seay of Miami in the 1948 NCAA final; and, finally, the classic 1947 dual meet bout between John Lendenski and Idaho's Herb Carlson, a technical knockout victory for Lendenski.

Inevitably, Charlie Mohr came up, and as he always did in later interviews, the coach made it clear that in his view Mohr had some preexisting condition that made him vulnerable. "Ironically," Walsh said, "he wasn't even hit a hard blow."

In 1986 Woodward died at his home in Madison. He was seventy-seven.

Increasingly, it was deaths and funerals that brought the fraternity together. Like Woodward, Woodrow Swancutt was seventy-seven when he died. The great national champion from 1939 and 1940 suffered a heart attack while walking near his home in San Antonio, Texas. His *New York Times* obituary concentrated on his record during World War II: "In the war, Gen. Swancutt flew 49 combat missions in the China-Burma-India theater. He was among the pilots in the first daylight attack on Japan and was also chosen to fly Lord Mountbatten, the Allied Supreme Commander of Southeast Asia, to a conference in Washington. . . . Later he was a wing commander at Lockbourne Air Force Base, deputy director of operations and plans at the Strategic Air Command headquarters, division commander at Turner Air Force Base and director of operations at Air Force headquarters."

The New York *Times* noted that Swancutt retired from the military in 1968 and became an executive with Executive Jet Aviation in Ohio. And the paper did not forget his college boxing, mentioning his back-to-back national championships.

The year after Swancutt's death, 1994, Wallenfeldt's homage to college boxing, *The Six-Minute Fraternity*, was published. It was read eagerly by the grateful brothers in that fraternity but not widely outside it, which was too bad, for it is a prodigiously researched book, a labor of love written by someone who fell under the magic of intercollegiate boxing while still a boy growing up in Madison, and later while enrolled at UW. "As a university student I became acquainted with some varsity boxers and came to regard them as being different from other athletes," Wallenfeldt wrote in his preface.

By the time the reader reaches the epilogue, Wallenfeldt has introduced us to hundreds of men, former college boxers, coaches, and administrators, most of whom he regards with high admiration. In that epilogue, he notes that in the 1970s another organization, the National Collegiate Boxing Association, or NCBA, was formed, based in Nevada, and it exists as this book is being written, as a club rather than a varsity sport.

"Since the revival of intercollegiate boxing was undertaken in the 1970s," Wallenfeldt wrote, "emphasis among its sponsors has been on the involvement of persons with no prior experience whatsoever in the sport. Anyone with any previous experience has been denied the opportunity to participate. While such an approach clearly avoids the taint of professional boxing that has concerned college boxing officials throughout the history of the sport regardless of the level at which it has been conducted, it has not fostered an activity that might be of interest to the general public in the way that college football and basketball have been."

Lynch told me that in the early 1970s, he took three UW boxers to the NCBA tournament in Cincinnati, Ohio. "It grew out of a defensive boxing class Vern Woodward was teaching on campus," Lynch said. When he got back from Ohio, a UW administrator talked to Lynch and said any more trips of that kind would be frowned upon on Bascom Hill. That was the end of the NCBA in Madison.

In December 1997, UW prepared to move its men's basketball program out of the Field House into the brand new Kohl Center a mile or so away. Although the Field House would still be used on occasion for minor sports, the symbolism of basketball leaving was large and the occasion elicited a number of newspaper and broadcast media stories about the glory days of the old barn. Boxing figured large in many of them.

The afternoon of December 20, official tribute was paid to the boxers when close to two dozen of them were formally introduced at halftime of one of the last Badger basketball games played at the Field House. A cheerleader escorted each of the former boxers to center court as the crowd roared. The last man introduced was Walsh, a bit feeble but smiling broadly at eighty-five. Walsh's escort included not only a cheerleader but also UW athletic director Pat Richter, himself a three-sport Badger hero. The Field House crowd, which had been warmly appreciative as the boxers were introduced, rose to their feet to salute Walsh. Dick Callaway, a Dane County judge who had been the manager of the boxing team in 1955, told me the next week that "every one of the boxers had tears in his eyes" when Walsh was introduced. After the game, Dick and Janet Murphy hosted a party at their home west of Madison.

That evening, everyone got a scare when Walsh, perhaps overcome by the excitement and emotion of the day's events, was hospitalized and placed in intensive care. He had been fighting high blood pressure for some time. But the old warrior was still pretty tough. He went home a few days later.

In August 2001, a writer for the *San Jose Mercury News,* Mark Emmons, spent some time with Bartell, the boxer who had been in the ring with Mohr that last night in Madison, in April 1960. Forty-one years had passed. The Bartell who emerged in Emmons's profile was a thoughtful man of great dignity who had lived through much.

In the dressing room in Madison after the fight, Bartell had been celebrating—San Jose State took the team title, after all—with his teammates, including Dave Nelson, when word arrived that Mohr had been taken to the hospital. "Stu just got kind of quiet," Nelson told Emmons. "We all told him that Charlie would be all right. But everyone thought: 'Glad it wasn't me.' You want to knock a guy out. But you don't want to maim a guy."

Eight days later, Easter Sunday, Mohr died.

In 2001 Bartell said, "All I could think of was 'Why? Why was I picked to land that lethal blow?' People told me that it wasn't my fault, but they weren't in my shoes."

A couple of weeks after Mohr died, Nelson and Bartell were walking down a hall at San Jose State when somebody said in Bartell's direction: "Hey, killer, how you doing?"

Nelson recalled: "Stu just wilted. We sat down and he said, 'I'm not a killer. I didn't mean to hurt the guy.'"

Bartell did keep boxing for a time. He lost in the 1960 Olympic trials and then turned pro, where he worked under Rocky Marciano's old trainer, Charlie Goldman. In one of his first pro bouts Bartell had a fighter on the ropes. He told Emmons: "Only I hit the guy hard and I couldn't finish him off. It brought back too many things. I kept seeing Charlie. So I hung it up."

Bartell went back to San Jose State and got his degree. He taught school in San Jose, married, and had a son and daughter. And then, in June 1979, unspeakable tragedy visited Bartell again: His eleven-year-old daughter was riding her bike when she was struck by a car. She was in a coma for a week and then died.

"I did wonder if it was payback," Bartell said. "You wonder if it is an eye for an eye. You just wonder why."

Two decades later, Emmons asked how he could possibly have coped.

"What you're really asking me is how do you not become an alcoholic or decide to go out and kill yourself," Bartell said. "I'm a realist and these things do happen. There's nothing you can do about it. Sure, I could have put a gun to my head, but that wouldn't help anything."

Instead, he raised his son, and he began to talk to groups about grieving. Talking helped. He said that when he was done there was never a dry eye in the room.

He hadn't moved completely away from boxing. He helped with the club team at Santa Clara University and in April 2001 Bartell attended the collegiate club championship in Nevada, where he was given a VHS tape of the final night of the 1960 NCAA tournament in Madison.

When Emmons visited Bartell at home to write his piece for the *Mercury News,* Bartell slid the tape into his VCR. Emmons wrote: "Charley Mohr deftly jabs and moves. Relentlessly stalking him is a younger version of Bartell, a muscular fighter who keeps missing—just barely—with his lunging right hand."

Then something strange happens. The first round of the Mohr-Bartell fight ends, and so does the tape. There was, of course, a second round— the most publicized round in the history of college boxing—but there was no second round on the tape.

"There's no more," Bartell told Emmons. "I don't know if tape of the other round exists."

In the late 1990s, when Doherty had been researching his article on Mohr for the *Smithsonian* magazine, naturally he hoped to see a tape of the fight.

"One of Walsh's many innovations as a coach," Doherty wrote, "was to have every dual match and tournament in Madison filmed by a university photographer, so he and his boxers could critique the fights afterward. A copy of each film was routinely sent to the NCAA for safekeeping in its archives. The original negative and the other copy were stored with a growing collection of sports films and photographs on the fourth floor of Camp Randall Stadium."

Doherty spent several hours going through all the material in the collection. But try as he might he could not locate the film from the 1960 NCAA tournament in Madison.

"My one last hope," Doherty wrote, "rested with the NCAA. For more than a year, I badgered the organization for a duplicate of its copy of the 1960 film which, I was informed, was in an underground storage facility in Kansas. Finally one day a Federal Express man showed up at my front door and handed me the long-sought prize."

Doherty put the tape into his VCR.

"The first round went pretty much as I remembered it," he wrote. "Then came the moment of truth: the second round. But there was no second round. I played the tape over and over again and each time it was the same. The second round had been edited out."

Doherty sent the tape to the photo lab in New York City that had made it. They couldn't tell him how the deletion had been made. Nobody at UW whom he spoke with had a clue. "The most important round ever fought in the history of college boxing," Doherty wrote, "was gone, gone, gone."

Well, it wasn't. It was gone from the film sent to the NCAA in Kansas City, Missouri, but it was not gone from the film in Madison that, while Doherty was searching for it in Camp Randall, was in the possession of a producer at Wisconsin Public Television who was preparing a documentary history of UW athletics. Parts of that second round, including the crucial seconds of the fight when Mohr takes the hard right from Bartell and staggers and falls to the canvas, were included in an eight-minute segment on UW boxing that aired in February 2002 on an episode of Wisconsin Public Television's *Wisconsin Stories* program.

To see Mohr fall to the canvas is chilling. In minutes he will be in an ambulance heading for University Hospital. The Wisconsin Public Television segment mentioned that speculation centered on Mohr's having had an aneurysm. Word got back to Dr. Javid, the surgeon, now retired and still in Madison. He called and asked that in future broadcasts such speculation be removed, and the producers agreed.

Old wounds and old controversies, perhaps resolved at last. Much of that eight-minute report was wonderful. I have a tape and play it still. A young Dick Murphy, just a kid, strong and handsome as a movie star, working on the heavy bag with John Walsh at his side. Bob Morgan is interviewed. He says Walsh was like a father to him.

In November 2002, Morgan came back to Madison from Colorado for the fiftieth anniversary of the 1952 championship team. Morgan spoke to an overflow crowd at the Downtown Rotary and at a front table were boxers Murphy and Tom Zamzow. Lynch was there, too, and Audrey Walsh, and Audrey and John's son, David Walsh, a prominent Madison attorney who was a few months from being named to the UW Board of Regents by the new Wisconsin governor, Jim Doyle.

Just a few weeks after that team reunion and Morgan's talk at the Downtown Rotary, Chuck Davey died. He had been paralyzed since 1998 and the body surfing accident off Costa Rica. Somehow the death of the only four-time NCAA boxing champion wasn't news anywhere but in the Detroit papers. "Boxing was barely out of the bare-knuckle, barroom brawling stage when Davey came along in the early 1940s," the *Detroit News* wrote. "Several colleges—including Michigan State, Army, Navy, even Penn State—pulled together teams and convinced the NCAA to sanction their competition in the early '40s."

It was in the early 1930s, of course, that the NCAA began having their tournaments, and to mention prominent teams and not mention Wisconsin is—well, I guess it's not totally unexpected, since the whole remarkable era seems to have passed in a blink from the country's collective memory.

When I heard that Davey had died I called Audrey Walsh, the lovely and gracious woman who had been spotted in line waiting to register at the UW–Madison by a young boxer named Walsh down from Minneapolis for law school. And, oh yes, he said when she finally agreed to a date, he was also going to coach boxing.

"Thank you so much for calling," Audrey said, when I told her about Davey. "I hadn't heard." She paused. "I don't know who's left for me to tell."

John Walsh was gone by then. In the last few years he had been ill, his memory fading, but his boys, as he called his boxers, loyally visited and on good days he remembered them.

On November 1, 2001, at age eighty-nine, Walsh died in Madison. Both Madison dailies carried long stories and the *Capital Times,* which had not always been a great friend to boxing, put his picture above the fold on page one with this headline, "Boxing legend John Walsh dies." It was news on ESPN and in the *Los Angeles Times* and Pete Ehrmann, a Wisconsin-based boxing historian, contributed a nice tribute to *Ring Sports* magazine, the bible of boxing, in which he said of Walsh: "Nobody brought more integrity, decency and know-how to the game than the mild-mannered lawyer who passed away November 1."

Butler wrote a fine tribute in the *Wisconsin State Journal.* The *Milwaukee Journal Sentinel* found some of Walsh's "boys" for comment. "He talked about boxing like a painter talks about paintings," Bobby Hinds said. Dick Bartmann said: "He was a great recruiter and a great administrator and he knew how to get 100 percent out of everybody." Bartmann also talked to Ehrmann for the *Ring Sports* magazine piece. There Bartmann said: "They should put up a statue for this guy."

Paul Konnor, who boxed for Walsh in the late 1940s, told the *Journal Sentinel* that Walsh made such an impression on him he changed his plans to be a history professor and instead became a lawyer like Walsh. "I loved him," Konnor said. A lot of his boys did, and a lot of them became lawyers. Most of them, whatever they did, they did pretty well.

Many came back for the memorial reception that was held at Maple Bluff Country Club in Madison. Walsh had touched people in all walks of life in the city, so the reception was crowded but still, the boxers stood out. His boys.

A little over a year after that reception, I was driving on Madison's near west side, near my old high school, Madison West, a mile or so up Regent Street from the Field House and adjacent to Forest Hill Cemetery.

I did something I had been thinking about doing for some time. I drove into the cemetery and sought out a gravestone.

In 1973, at the first big reunion of the Badgers boxers, a survey had been taken of all the people around the program, the boxers and managers and assistants, to see who was regarded as the best Badger boxer ever. Nearly seven hundred people attended that first reunion but the boxer who was the overwhelming choice as the best couldn't make it. Omar Crocker had died in 1956, at only forty, of cancer.

What a fighter. He thrilled the crowd and worried the administrators because he hit so hard. A country boy from Michigan's Upper Peninsula. I found the grave. There was a large standing stone bearing his last name under two beautiful pines and then a smaller stone that lay in the ground. "Omar Steele," that small marker said, "1916–1956." I hadn't known his middle name and I remember smiling. Steele was right. The Haymaker, they called him.

Omar Steele Crocker. The fiercest of all the Badger boxers and yet, like any human, all too fragile. In the end you could say the same of college boxing.

ACKNOWLEDGMENTS

This book would not have been possible without the support of David Walsh, a prominent Madison attorney, UW Regent, and perhaps most significantly for these purposes, John Walsh's son.

David's early enthusiasm for the project got it off the ground. He never tried to influence the content or direction of the book. He may well have been too busy to bother, but I prefer to think he trusted me to tell the tale.

Two writers deserve mention and thanks, and both are noted in the text itself. E. C. Wallenfeldt's seminal book on NCAA tournament boxing, *The Six Minute Fraternity*, was a wonderful map for me. In addition, Professor Wallenfeldt kindly made available correspondence and taped interviews with UW boxers that he hadn't included in his own book.

Jim Doherty wrote a lengthy piece in the April 2000 *Smithsonian* magazine on Charlie Mohr and the Badger boxers. While I did not agree with all his conclusions, I respect him highly as a journalist. Jim shared addresses and phone numbers of former boxers, along with his opinions, over a lunch in Madison during my research.

Audrey Walsh, John's widow and David's mother, deserves special mention. Audrey invited me into her home for an interview, and shared photos and memorabilia that help the book immeasurably.

Naturally I want to thank the former boxers who agreed to be interviewed, and whose recollections form the heart of this book.

Two deserve special mention. Bob Lynch, who was not a Badger boxer but helped train them, and Bob Morgan each read and commented on a draft of the manuscript. Morgan's memoir *Goodbye, Geraldine* is a moving story beyond the boxing passages that helped me. Lynch also spent considerable time with me viewing videotape of UW boxing matches, particularly the 1960 NCAA tournament in Madison.

My friends Bill Dixon, Jeff Scott Olson, and Joe Hart also read and commented on the manuscript in draft.

The other Badger boxers interviewed include: Bobby Hinds, Bob Meath, Jackie Gibson, Jim Mack, Cal Vernon, Pete Spanakos, Vince Ferguson, Vito Parisi, Dave Miyagawa, Bob Ranck, Tom Zamzow, Dick Murphy, Charlie Magestro, Terry Tynan, Dick Bartmann, Terry Monson, John Drye, Bill Urban, Wally DeRose, and Jerry Turner.

I did many other interviews as well, none more important than the one with Dr. Manucher Javid, who operated on Charlie Mohr in April 1960. Also retired sportswriter Tom Butler; John Hickman, who shared memories from some 60 years ago; Tom Moen, who as a boy was befriended by Charlie Mohr; Elliott Maraniss, who died in 2004, the *Capital Times* journalist who tried to tell the story of Charlie Mohr's life out of the ring. Wisconsin boxing historian Pete Ehrmann helped me with many elusive dates and facts.

Invaluable, too, were interviews on record with the Wisconsin Oral History Project in Madison: John Walsh (most importantly); David Fellman; and Walter Morton.

The microfilm archives of the *Wisconsin State Journal* and *The Capital Times* were likewise invaluable to me. A posthumous thanks to those who covered the matches when they happened: Henry McCormick (the true bard of Badger boxing); Hank Casserly; and the inimitable Joseph "Roundy" Coughlin. Current *Capital Times* librarian Dennis McCormick showed great patience helping me through my many battles with the microfilm machine.

Various periodicals were of assistance, as well, notably *Esquire* and *Sports Illustrated,* and the specific articles are noted in the text. Books are referenced in the text also, as is Gerald Dixon's UW masters thesis, "The Study of Boxing as an Intercollegiate Sport."

Photo credits can be found elsewhere, but thanks to the Wisconsin Archives, the Wisconsin State Historical Society, and UW Sports Information, especially Steve Malchow, for providing the images from long ago that so enhance the finished book.

Speaking of which, it would not have been finished without the help of many at the University of Wisconsin Press, particularly Steve Salemson, who, in the boxing parlance, always answered the bell.

PHOTO CREDITS

University of Wisconsin Archives: 2, 4, 7, 8, 10, 12, 15, 16, 17, 18, 19, 20, 21, 22, 24, 34, 36

University of Wisconsin Sports Information: 3, 13, 14, 23, 25, 28, 30, 31, 33, 39, 41

Wisconsin Historical Society: 38

Contributed: 5, 11, 26, 27, 40

Audrey Walsh: 1, 6, 9, 35, 37,

Jeff Scott Olson: 29

Charles Magestro: 32

Dick Murphy: 42, 43, 44